国内外经典教材辅导系列·英语类

刘润清《新编语言学教程》笔记和课后习题（含考研真题）详解

（修订版）

主编：圣才考研网
www.100xuexi.com

中国石化出版社

内 容 提 要

本书是语言学经典教材《新编语言学教程》(刘润清、文旭主编)的学习辅导书。全书完全遵循该教材的章目编排，共分12章，每章由三部分组成：第一部分为复习笔记(中英文对照)，总结本章的重点难点；第二部分是课后习题详解，对该书的课后思考题进行了详细解答；第三部分是考研真题与典型题详解，精选名校经典考研真题及相关习题，并提供了详细的参考答案。

圣才考研网(www.100xuexi.com)提供刘润清《新编简明英语语言学教程》辅导方案【视频课程、电子书、题库】。购书即可享受大礼包增值服务【本书电子书(电脑版、手机版)+全国名校真题详解电子书】。手机扫码(本书封面右上角)领取本书大礼包。

图书在版编目(CIP)数据

刘润清《新编语言学教程》笔记和课后习题(含考研真题)详解/圣才考研网主编.—2版(修订本).—北京:中国石化出版社,2019.7(2021.6重印)
国内外经典教材辅导系列·英语类
ISBN 978-7-5114-5429-4

Ⅰ.①刘… Ⅱ.①圣… Ⅲ.①语言学-研究生-入学考试-自学参考资料 Ⅳ.①H0

中国版本图书馆CIP数据核字(2019)第144586号

中国石化出版社出版发行

地址:北京市东城区安定门外大街58号
邮编:100011 电话:(010)57512500
发行部电话:(010)57512575
http://www.sinopec-press.com
E-mail:press@sinopec.com
武汉市盛宏源印务有限公司印刷
全国各地新华书店经销

*

787×1092毫米 16开本 12.5印张 310千字
2019年11月第2版 2021年6月第2次印刷
定价:62.00元

序　言

我国各大院校一般都把国内外通用的权威教科书作为本科生和研究生学习专业课程的参考教材，这些教材甚至被很多考试(特别是硕士和博士入学考试)和培训项目作为指定参考书。为了帮助读者更好地学习专业课，我们有针对性地编著了一套与国内外教材配套的复习资料，并提供配套的名师讲堂和题库。

《新编语言学教程》(刘润清、文旭主编)一直被用作高等院校英语专业语言学教材，被部分院校指定为英语专业考研必读书和学术研究参考书。作为该教材的学习辅导书，本书具有以下几个方面的特点：

1. 梳理章节脉络，浓缩内容精华。每章的复习笔记以该教材为主并结合其他教材对本章的重难点知识进行了整理，并参考了国内名校名师讲授该教材的课堂笔记，因此，本书的内容几乎浓缩了经典教材的知识精华。

2. 中英双语对照，凸显难点要点。本书章节笔记采用了中英文对照的形式，强化对重要难点知识的理解和运用。

3. 解析课后习题，提供详尽答案。本书对刘润清、文旭主编的《新编语言学教程》每章的课后思考题均进行了详细的分析和解答，并对相关重要知识点进行了延伸和归纳。

4. 精选考研真题，补充难点习题。本书精选名校近年考研真题及相关习题，并提供答案和详解。所选真题和习题基本体现了各个章节的考点和难点，但又不完全局限于教材内容，是对教材内容极好的补充。这些知识点参考了其他权威语言学教材整理归纳而成，以帮助读者，尤其是参加考研的学生，扩展知识、加深对教材的理解。

与本书相配套，圣才考研网提供刘润清《新编语言学教程》网授精讲班、电子书、题库。

购书即可享受大礼包增值服务【本书电子书(电脑版、手机版)+全国名校真题详解电子书】。手机扫码(本书封面右上角)领取本书大礼包。

圣才考研网(www. 100 xuexi. com)是圣才学习网旗下的考研考博专业网站，提供考研公共课和全国500所院校考研考博专业课辅导【一对一辅导、网授精讲班等】、电子书、题库、全套资料(历年真题及答案、笔记讲义等)、国内外经典教材名师讲堂、考研教辅图书等。

考研辅导：kaoyan. 100xuexi. com(圣才考研网)
资格考试：www. 100xuexi. com(圣才学习网)

圣才考研网编辑部

目　录

第1章　导言

1.1　复习笔记

本章要点：

1. The definition and main branches of linguistics study
   语言学的定义和研究的范围
2. The definition and the origins of language
   语言的定义与起源
3. The design feature and the function of language
   语言的特征和功能
4. Some major concepts in linguistics
   语言学中重要的概念

本章考点：

1. 有关语言学的常考考点

(1) 语言学的定义，现代语言学与传统语法学研究的区别。
(2) 语言学中几组重要概念，每组两个概念的含义、区分及其意义。
(3) 普通语言学的主要分支学科及各自的研究范畴。
(4) 宏观语言学及应用语言学的主要分支及各自的研究范畴。

2. 有关语言的常考考点

(1) 语言的定义；语言的基本特征(任意性、二重性、能产性、移位性、互换性、专门性和文化传递性)；
(2) 语言的功能(寒暄、指示、信息、疑问、表达、劝说和施为)；
(3) 语言的起源(本能论、唱歌说、模仿说、摹声说、感叹说、劳动喊声说等。)

本章内容索引：

6. Bow-Wow Theory

Ⅵ. Design features of language

1. Arbitrariness
2. Duality
3. Productivity
4. Interchangeability
5. Displacement
6. Specialization
7. Cultural transmission

Ⅶ. Functions of language

1. Phatic function/communion
2. Directive function
3. Informative function
4. Interrogative function
5. Expressive function
6. Evocative function
7. Performative function

Ⅷ. Some major concepts in linguistics

1. Descriptive and prescriptive grammar
2. Synchronic and diachronic linguistics
3. Langue and parole
4. Competence and performance
5. Syntagmatic and paradigmatic relations
6. Functionalism and formalism

Ⅰ. Definition of linguistics 【考点：名词解释】 The scientific study of language which is led by the three scientific canons: exhaustiveness, consistency and economy. **Ⅱ. Linguistics vs. traditional grammar** Linguistics differs from traditional grammar at least in three basic ways. 1. Linguistics describes, while traditional grammar prescribes. 2. Linguistics believes that speech is prior to writing. 3. Linguistics describes each language on its own merits, while traditional grammar analyzes language based on a Latin-based frame-work. **Ⅲ. Scope of linguistics** **1. Microlinguistics** Phonetics	**Ⅰ. 语言学的定义** 语言学是对语言的科学或系统的研究。语言学研究的科学性可以归纳为：穷尽性、一致性以及简洁性。 **Ⅱ. 语言学与传统语法** 语言学在以下三方面不同于传统语法。 1. 语言学描述语言，传统语法设定规则。 2. 语言学认为口语是基础而非文字。 3. 语言学根据语言本身的优点来描述每种语言，而传统语法则基于拉丁语的框架来分析语言。 **Ⅲ. 语言学的研究范畴** **1. 微观语言学** 语音学

Phonology
Morphology
Syntax
Semantics
Pragmatics

2. Macrolinguistics

Sociolinguistics
Psycholinguistics
Neurolinguistics
Stylistics
Discourse analysis
Computational linguistics
Cognitive linguistics
Applied linguistics

Ⅳ. Definition of language

【考点：名词解释】

1. Language is a system-the elements of language are not organized and combined at random, but rather according to certain rules.

2. Language is arbitrary-the absence of any natural or necessary connection between a word's meaning and its sound or form.

3. Language is vocal-sound is the primary medium for all languages.

4. Language is used for human communication—language is different from the communication systems animals possess.

Ⅴ. Origins of language

1. Ding-Dong Theory

Language began when humans started naming objects after a relevant sound that was already involved in their everyday life.

2. Sing-Song Theory

Language arose from rhythmic primitive chants associated with ritual dance.

3. Pooh-Pooh Theory

Language comes from the automatic vocal responses to pain, fear, surprise, or other emotions: a laugh, a shriek, a gasp.

4. Yo-He-Ho Theory

Language started with the rhythmic sounds people used when they worked together.

音系学
形态学
句法学
语义学
语用学

2. 宏观语言学

社会语言学
心理语言学
神经语言学
文体学
语篇分析
计算语言学
认知语言学
应用语言学

Ⅳ. 语言的定义

1. 语言是一个系统——其元素非任意排列，而是根据一定规则组合的。

2. 语言是任意的——一个词的意思和它的声音或形式之间没有任何自然或必要的联系。

3. 语言是口头的——是所有语言的基本交流形式。

4. 语言是人类用来交流的工具——不同于动物的交流系统。

Ⅴ. 语言的起源

1. 本能论

语言起源于人类用与日常生活相关的声音来命名物体。

2. 唱歌说

语言起源于与仪式舞蹈相联系的原始圣歌。

3. 感叹说

语言来源于对痛苦、恐惧、惊讶或其他情感的自动声音反应：大笑、尖叫、喘息。

4. 劳动喊声说

语言来源于共同劳动时发出的有节奏的声音。

5. Ta-Ta Theory Language came from the use of tongue and mouth gestures to mimic manual gestures.	**5. 模仿说** 语言来源于用舌头和嘴的手势来模仿手的手势。
6. Bow-Wow Theory Language developed as onomatopoeia, imitations of natural sounds.	**6. 摹声说** 语言起源于拟声词，即对自然声音的模仿。
Ⅵ. Design features of language 【重点、考点：论述语言的识别特征】	**Ⅵ. 语言的定义特征**
1. Arbitrariness This refers to the fact that there is no natural or necessary connection between a word's meaning and its sound or form. There is no explanation why English use the sounds /kæt/ to refer to the animal cat, or why Chinese use the word "mao" to refer to the same animal. The relation between the sounds and what they denote is entirely arbiturary.	**1. 任意性** 任意性是指某个符号的声音与意义之间没有逻辑或内在联系。例如，英文中用/ kæt /来指动物猫，而中文却用"mao"。单词的声音与其意义之间的关系是任意的。
2. Duality Language consists of two sets of structures. At the lower level is a structure of sounds which is meaningless in themselves. These sounds can be grouped and regrouped into a large number of units of meaning (morphemes and words etc.) at the higher level. These meaningful units at the higher level can be arranged and rearranged into an infinite number of sentences. Human language, for example, has a variety of sound units, called phonemes, but each phoneme is usually meaningless on its own. It only becomes meaningful when combined with other phonemes to form a morpheme.	**2. 二重性** 二重性指语言有两个系统的特征。在较低的层次上是无意义的声音系统。这些声音可以被分割并在较高层次上重新组合成大量的意义单位(语素和单词等)。这些有意义的单位可以被安排和重新安排成无限数量的句子。比如，人类语言中的音素，独立的音素本身通常是没有意义的，当与其他因素结合起来形成语素才有可能产生意义。
3. Productivity Productivity or creativity refers to man's ability of the users of languages in making and comprehending an infinite number of sentences including those that they have never heard before.	**3. 能产性** 能产性是指人们的一种语言能力，它能使人们说出或者理解无限多的句子，有些是我们以前从未听过的句子。
4. Interchangeability Interchangeability or reciprocity refers to the fact that humans can transmit and receive identical linguistic signals, and our positions as a speaker and a hearer can be easily switched.	**4. 互换性** 互换性是指人可以传递和接收相同的语言信号的能力，即人作为说话者和听话者的角色是可以随意更换的。
5. Displacement Displacement is the capability of language to communicate about things that are not immediately present, i. e., things that are either not here or are not here now.	**5. 移位性** 移位性是一种语言的能力，它能使人们谈论那些不可及的事物，也就是那些要么不在这里，要么现在不在这里的事物。

6. Specialization Specialization refers to the fact that man is not fully physically involved in the process of communication.	**6. 专门性** 专门性是指人们在交流过程中并非全身投入，而是只通过语言即可交流的能力。
7. Cultural transmission Language is culturally transmitted, i. e. , language is more learned after birth through a social setting instead of inherent. The story of wolf child show that a human being brought up in isolation is simply dose not acquire human language.	**7. 文化传递性** 语言是通过文化传递的，文化传递性指语言是后天通过社会环境习得的，而不是与生俱来的特征。狼孩的故事表明，一个在孤立环境中长大的人是根本学不到人类语言的。
Ⅶ. Functions of language	**Ⅶ. 语言功能**
1. Phatic function/communion Language is used to establish or maintain good interpersonal relationships between the addresser and addressee. Greetings, farewells, and addresses perform this function.	**1. 寒暄功能** 语言能用来在说话者和听者之间建立或维持良好的人际关系。如问候语、送别及称谓。
2. Directive function Language is used by the addresser to get the addressee to do something. Most imperative sentences fulfil directive function.	**2. 指示功能** 语言能使听话者按照听到的话去做。大部分祈使句都体现了这种功能。
3. Informative function Language is used to make statements, to communicate information, or to represent one's understanding of something. Declarative sentences perform this function.	**3. 信息功能** 语言用来陈述，交流信息，或表示一个人对某事的理解，一般出现在陈述句中。
4. Interrogative function Language is used to obtain information from those being asked. All questions that anticipate responses fulfil this function.	**4. 疑问功能** 语言用来向他人提问而获取信息。需回答的疑问句体现了此功能。
5. Expressive function Language is used to supply information about the speaker's values, feelings and attitudes. Ejaculations perform this function, such as "My God!" and "Hurrah!"	**5. 表达功能** 语言用来提供有关说话者的价值观、感情和态度的信息。感叹句体现了此功能，例如"天呐""万岁!"
6. Evocative function Language is used to elicit specific emotions in those who hear it. This function is served by jokes, ads, and propaganda.	**6. 唤起功能** 语言用来使听话者产生某种感情。开玩笑，广告还有宣传中的语言体现了这一功能。
7. Performative function Language is used to do things or to carry out actions. "I do."—as uttered in the course of the marriage ceremony; "I name this ship the 'Queen Elizabeth'".	**7. 施为功能** 语言用来实施一种行为。比如，"我愿意"——在婚礼上的宣誓；"我将此船命名为'伊丽莎白女王号'"。

Ⅷ. Some major concepts in linguistics	**Ⅷ. 语言学中的主要概念**
1. Descriptive and prescriptive grammar	**1. 描写式与规定式语法**
(1) Descriptive grammar objectively analyzes and describes how language is actually used; while prescriptive grammar attempts to establish rules defining correct usage of language.	（1）描写式语法旨在对语言进行描述，而规定式语法旨在规定语言应该如何使用。
(2) Traditional grammar is often referred to as prescriptive because it attempts to set down rules. Modern linguistics is descriptive.	（2）传统语法学家试图规定语言规则，这被称为规定式语法。现代语言学基本上是描写式语法。
2. Synchronic and diachronic linguistics	**2. 共时与历时语言学**
Synchronic linguistics aims at describing a language at any given time, while diachronic study refers to the study of how a language evolves over a period of time.	共时语言学指在任何特定的时间描述一种语言的语言学分类，而历时语言学是指研究一种语言在一段时间内是如何演变的学科分类。
Synchronic linguistics is concerned with the state of language at any point in history whereas diachronic linguistics is concerned with the variations between two or more states of language over times.	共时语言学集中研究历史任何时期点的语言现状，而历时语言学集中研究几十年或几百年的时期内两个或比两个更多的语言状况的差异。
3. Langue and parole	**3. 语言与言语**
(1) F. de Saussure made an important distinction between langue and parole.	（1）索绪尔对语言和言语做了重要区分。
(2) Langue refers to the abstract linguistic system shared by all the members of a speech community. Parole refers to particular realizations of langue.	（2）语言是指一个语言群体的所有成员所共有的抽象的语言系统。言语是指语言的具体实现和运用。
(3) Saussure analyzes language from a sociological perspective as a matter of social convention. Langue refers to the social, conventional side of language, while parole the speech of individuals.	（3）索绪尔从社会学的角度把语言作为一种社会习俗来分析。语言是社会的，约定性的，而言语是个人的话语。
4. Competence and performance	**4. 语言能力和语言应用**
According to Chomsky, competence is a set of rules internalized by speakers which enables them to produce and understand an infinite number of sentences and recognize the mistakes and ambiguities, while performance is the actual realization of the set of rules in linguistic communication.	根据乔姆斯基的理论，语言能力是指说话者内化的一套规则，它使说话者能产生和理解无数个句子，并能识别错误和歧义。语言运用是指语言交际中一系列规则的实际实现。
5. Syntagmatic and paradigmatic relations	**5. 组合与聚合关系**
Saussure also makes distinction between syntagmatic and paradigmatic relations. Syntagmatic relation is a type of sematic relations between words that co-occur in the same sentence or text. Paradigmatic relation is a different type of sematic relations between words that can be substituted with another word in the same categories.	索绪尔提出了另一对概念：组合与聚合关系。组合关系是指在同一句子或文本中同时出现的词之间的一种语义关系。聚合关系指一种不同类型的语义关系，一个词可以被同一范畴内的另一个词所替代。

6. Functionalism and formalism	6. 功能主义与结构主义
【重点、考点：区分功能观与句子观】 Functionalism or functional linguistics is an approach to the study of language in terms of its social functions in communication. Formalism or formal linguistics studies the abstract forms of language and the relationship between linguistic elements.	功能主义或功能语言学指对语言在交际中的社会功能的研究。 结构主义或结构语言学指对抽象的语言形式及内部关系的研究。

1.2 课后习题详解

1. Define the following terms briefly.

linguistics	language	arbitrariness
duality	competence	performance
stylistics	phatic communion	functionalism
formalism	synchronic linguistics	diachronic linguistics

2. If language is partially defined as communication, can we call the noises that dogs make language? Why or why not?
3. One of the main features of our human languages is arbitrariness. Can you briefly explain what this feature refers to? Support your argument with examples.
4. What kind of evidence supports the idea that language is culturally transmitted?
5. Point out three major differences between linguistics and traditional grammar.
6. What is the difference between a prescriptive and a descriptive approach to language?
7. Distinguish between synchronic and diachronic linguistics.
8. A wolf is able to express subtle gradations of emotion by different positions of the ears, the lips, and the tail. There are eleven postures of the tail that express such emotions as self-confidence, confident threat, lack of tension, uncertain threat, depression, defensiveness, active submission, and complete submission. This system seems to be complex. Suppose there were a thousand different emotions that the wolf could express in this way. Would you then say a wolf had a language similar to man's? If not, why not?

参考答案

1. **Linguistics:** The scientific study of language which is led by the three scientific canons: exhaustiveness, consistency and economy.

   Language: Language is a system of arbitrary vocal symbols used for human communication.

   Arbitrariness: Language is arbitrary. As a design feature of human language, arbitrariness refers to the the absence of any natural or necessary connection between a word's meaning and its sound or form. The relation between the sounds and what they denote is entirely arbiturary. Language is not entirely arbitrary and onomatopoeic words are exceptions.

   Duality: Duality is a design feature of human language. Language consists of two sets of structures. At the lower level is a structure of sounds which is meaningless in themselves. These sounds can be grouped and regrouped into a large number of units of meaning (morphemes and words etc.) at the higher level. These meaningful units at the higher level can be arranged and rearranged into an infinite number of sentences. Human language, for example, has a variety of sound units, called phonemes, but each phoneme is usually meaningless on its own. It only becomes meaningful when combined with other phonemes to form a morpheme.

Competence: According to Chomsky, competence refers to the knowledge that native speakers have of their language as a system of abstract formal relations.

Performance: According to Chomsky, performance refers to the actual linguistic behavior of native speakers.

Stylistics: Stylistics is a branch of linguistics and which is the study of how literary effects can be related to linguistic features. It usually refers to the study of written language; including literary texts, but it also investigate spoken language sometimes. It can be called the "science of literature" since it is the scientific study of literary style.

Phatic communion: Phatic communion is a function of language. Language is used to establish or maintain good interpersonal relationships between the addresser and addressee. Greetings, farewells, and addresses perform this function.

Functionalism: Functionalism or functional linguistics is an approach to the study of language in terms of its social functions in communication. Functionalism explains language types by attributing a deciding position to the function.

Formalism: Formalism or formal linguistics studies the abstract forms of language and the relationship between linguistic elements. It focuses on the forms of languages as proof of universals without taking into account how these forms function in social life.

Synchronic linguistics: Synchronic linguistics aims at describing a language at any given time. It is concerned with the state of language at any point of time in history.

Diachronic linguistics: Diachronic linguistics refers to the study of how a language evolves over a period of time. It focuses on the variations between two or more states of language over time.

2. No, we cannot call the noises that dogs make as language even though language is partially defined as communication. There are two reasons for that: first, language is human-specific, it is a system of arbitrary vocal symbols used only for human communication. Second, language has design features which distinguish human language from animal communication systems. For example, language consists of two sets of structures. At the lower level is a structure of sounds which is meaningless in themselves. These sounds can be grouped and regrouped into a large number of units of meaning (morphemes and words etc.) at the higher level. These meaningful units at the higher level can be arranged and rearranged into an infinite number of sentences. Human language, for example, has a variety of sound units, called phonemes, but each phoneme is usually meaningless on its own. It only becomes meaningful when combined with other phonemes to form a morpheme. Language can be used to communicate about things that are not immediately present, i. e., things that are either not here or are not here now.
3. Language is arbitrary. As a design feature of human language, arbitrariness means the absence of any natural or necessary connection between a word's meaning and its sound or form. For ex-

ample, we Chinese people use the sound "yizi" and Japanese use "isu" for the same meaning of "chair"; and we cannot explain why we use the letter symbol "book" for a book and "pen" for a pen. A dog may be called a pig if the first man happens to name it as a "pig". So, the relation between the sounds and what they denote is entirely arbitrary. However, the arbitrariness of language is a matter of degree, the onomatopoeic words and the compounding words, for instances, are motivated in a certain degree.

4. Language is culturally transmitted, i. e., language is more learned after birth through a social setting instead of inherent. Evidences are as follows: the story of wolf child show that a human being brought up in isolation is clearly does not acquire human language. Animals inherit their cries from parents, while human babies do not speak any language at birth. The society into which a baby is born determines the language he learns. A French baby born and brought up in Beijing by an Chinese family will speak Chinese, while an Chinese kid brought up in a French community will speak French.

5. Linguistics differs from traditional grammar at least in three basic ways:

   First, linguistics is descriptive while traditional grammar is prescriptive. Linguistics objectively analyzes and describes how language is actually used, rather than set out rule for correct behaviour in using language. Traditional grammar establishes rules defining correct usage of language. These rules may emphasize things such as spelling, pronunciation, vocabulary, syntax, and semantics.

   Second, modern linguistics believes that speech is prior to writing, which is another important point that differ linguistics from traditional grammar. Linguists agree that speech evolved first, and the writing system developed later.

   Third, traditional grammar analyzes language based on a Latin-based frame-work. Modern language thinks it's unthinkable to judge one language by the standard of another.

6. Descriptive linguistics objectively analyze and describe how language is actually used. Prescriptive linguistics attempts to establish rules defining correct usage of language. These rules may emphasize things such as spelling, pronunciation, vocabulary, syntax, and semantics. Modern linguistics believes that whatever occurs in the language people actually use should be described and analyzed. While traditional grammar is prescriptive which is based on "high" written language. Its task is to set models for language users to follow.

7. Synchronic linguistics aims at describing a language at any given time, while diachronic study refers to the study of how a language evolves over a period of time. Synchronic linguistics is concerned with the state of language at any point in history whereas diachronic linguistics is concerned with the variations between two or more states of language over time.

8. No, we can not say a wolf has a language similar to that of men even though there were a thousand different emotions that the wolf could express with his positions of body parts. There are two reasons for that:

   First, language is a system of arbitrary vocal symbols used only for human communication. The primary medium for human communication is speech, so the kind of communication system composed by positions of body parts are different from human language fundamentally.

   Second, language has design features which distinguish human language from animal communication systems. For example, language consists of two sets of structures. At the lower level is a structure of sounds which is meaningless in themselves. These sounds can be grouped and regrouped into a large number of units of meaning (morphemes and words etc.) at the higher level. These meaningful units at the higher level can be arranged and rearranged into an infinite number of sentences. However, those positions owned by wolf have no such features. Therefore, wolf's system is not so productive as human languages.

1.3 考研真题与典型题详解

Ⅰ. Fill in the blanks.

1. Human language is arbitrary. This refers to the fact that there is no logical or intrinsic connection between a particular sound and the ________ it is associated with. (人大 2007 研)
2. Human languages enable their users to symbolize objects, events and concepts which are not present (in time and space) at the moment of communication. This quality is labeled as ________. (北二外 2003 研)
3. By duality is meant the property of having two levels of structures, such that units of the ________ level are composed of elements of the ________ level and each of the two levels has its own principles of organization. (北二外 2006 研)
4. The features that define our human languages can be called ________ features. (北二外 2006 研)
5. The term ________ originates from Malinowski's study of the functions of language performed by Trobriand Islanders. It refers to the social interaction of language. (中山大学 2006 研)
6. Halliday proposes a theory of metafunctions of language, that is, language has ________, interpersonal and textual functions. (中山大学 2008 研)
7. Our language can be used to talk about itself. This is the ________ function of language. (中山大学 2005 研)
8. Linguistics is usually defined as the ________ study of language. (北二外 2003 研)
9. ________ studies how the speech sounds are made, transmitted, and received, and ________ studies the rules governing the structure, distribution and sequencing of speech sounds and the shape of syllables. (人大 2006 研)
10. ________ studies meaning in language, ________ is about principles of forming and understanding correct English sentences, and ________ is concerned with the internal organization of words. They are all among the main branches of linguistics. (人大 2006 研)
11. In Saussure's view, the relationship between signifier (sound image) and signified (concept) is ________. (北二外 2003 研)
12. ________ is the study of the language-processing mechanisms. It is concerned with the storage, comprehension, production and acquisition of language; ________ on the other hand, attempts to show the relationship between language and society. They both belong to branches of macrolinguistics. (人大 2006 研)
13. Saussure distinguished the linguistic competence of the speaker and the actual phenomena or

data of linguistics (utterances) as ________ and ________. The former refers to the abstract linguistic system shared by all the members of a speech community, and the latter is the concrete manifestation of language either through speech or through writing.（人大 2006 研）

14. ________ grammars attempt to tell what is in the language, while ________ grammars tell people what should be in the language. Most contemporary linguists believe that whatever occurs naturally in the language should be described.（人大 2006 研）

15. One of the important distinctions in linguistics is ________ and performance.（人大 2006 研）

16. Theory that primitive man made involuntary vocal noises while performing heavy work has been called the ________ theory.

17. The description of a language as it changes through time is a ________ study.

18. Language is a means of ________ communication.（暨南大学 2018 研）

Ⅱ. Multiple Choices

1. Which of the following statement is NOT true?（大连外国语学院 2008 研）
   A. Language is a means of vocal communication.
   B. Language is instrumental.
   C. Language is social and conventional.

2. Which of the following is NOT a frequently discussed design feature?（大连外国语学院 2008 研）
   A. Arbitrariness B. Convention C. Duality

3. By ________ we mean language is resourceful because of its duality and recursiveness.（西安外国语学院 2006 研）
   A. arbitrariness B. duality C. creativity D. displacement

4. Which of the following words is entirely arbitrary?（西安交大 2008 研）
   A. tree B. crash C. typewriter D. bang

5. The functions of language do NOT include ________.（大连外国语学院 2008 研）
   A. informative function B. interpersonal function
   C. metacognitive function

6. The most important sociological use of language is the ________ function, by which people establish and maintain their status in a society.（西安外国语学院 2006 研）
   A. performative B. interpersonal
   C. phatic D. metalingual

7. Saussure took a(n) ________ view of language, while Chomsky looks at language from a ________ point of view.（西安交大 2008 研）
   A. sociological... psychological B. psychological... sociological
   C. applied... pragmatic D. semantic... linguistic

8. According to F. de Saussure, ________ refers to the abstract linguistic system shared by all the members of a speech community.（西安交大 2008 研）
   A. parole B. performance C. langue D. Language

9. The study of physical properties of the sounds produced in speech is closely connected with

__________.（大连外国语学院 2008 研）

A. articulatory phonetics

B. acoustic phonetics

C. auditory phonetics

10. Study the following dialogue. What function does it play according to the functions of language?

—A nice day, isn't it?

—Right! I really enjoy the sunlight.

A. Emotive.

B. Phatic.

C. Performative.

D. Interpersonal.

11. __________ deals with language application to other fields, particularly education.

A. Linguistic geography

B. Sociolinguistics

C. Applied linguistics

D. Comparative linguistics

12. Verbal dueling, the use of language for the sheer joy of using it, is mainly to do with the __________ function of language.（武汉大学 2011 研）

A. performative

B. interpersonal

C. informative

D. recreational

Ⅲ. True or False

1. The phatic function refers to language function for establishing or maintaining social contact rather than for exchanging information or ideas.（清华 2001 研）
2. Syntax refers to the study of the rules governing the way words are combined to form sentences in a language.（大连外国语学院 2008 研）
3. "Competence" and "performance" are two distinctive terms proposed by Saussure.（北二外 2005 研）
4. The concept competence originally refers to the grammatical knowledge of the ideal language user and has nothing to do with the actual use of language in concrete situation.（南开大学 2004 研）
5. Prescriptive linguistics is more popular than descriptive linguistics, because it can tell us how to speak correct language.
6. By diachronic study we mean to study the changes and development of language.
7. Onomatopoeic words are totally arbitrary.
8. There are many languages in today's world that can only be spoken, but not written.（暨南大学 2018 研）

Ⅳ. Explain the following terms.

1. arbitrariness（四川大学 2006 研）
2. duality（四川大学 2006 研）
3. displacement（南开大学 2010 研；南京师大 2018 研）
4. performative function（武汉大学 2004 研）
5. parole（北师大 2004 研）
6. descriptive study of linguistics（四川大学 2007 研）
7. langue（北外 2010 研）
8. Cultural transmission（山东科技大学 2018 研）

Ⅴ. Short answer questions

1. Cite an example to explain synchronic linguistics.（人大 2005 研）
2. How well, in your opinion, does the word "communication" represent the function of human language?（北二外 2008 研）
3. What are linguistic competence and communicative competence?（武汉大学 2007 研）
4. One of the design features of human language is creativity. What is it? And what makes it possible?（浙江大学 2007 研）
5. What is the directive function?（西安交大 2008 研）

Ⅵ. Essay questions

1. Linguistics is not the only field concerned with language. Other disciplines such as sociology, psychology, ethnography are also preoccupied with language.（中山大学 2008 研）
2. There are two kinds of grammar based on different linguistic points of view. They are prescriptive grammar and descriptive grammar. A grammar may describe how language is actually spoken and/or written, and may not state or postulate how it ought to be spoken or written. But a grammar may also state the rules for what is considered the best or most correct usage. Which grammar is descriptive grammar, and which grammar is prescriptive grammar? Cite some examples to give your reasons.（北师大 2003 研）
3. Saussure puts forward the concept of langue and parole, and Chomsky puts forward the concept of competence and performance. Please dwell upon the differences and similarities, if any, of the two pairs: langue and parole vs. competence and performance.（北京交通大学 2007 研）
4. Examine the following two statements about language, and discuss the similarities and differences between them. Do you agree with the two statements? Explain your answer.

   (1) Sapir (1921: Language): "Language is a purely human and non-instinctive method of communicating ideas, emotions and desires by means of voluntarily produced symbols."

   (2) Bloch and Trager (1942: Outline of Linguistic Analysis): "A language is a system of arbitrary vocal symbols by means of which a social group co-operates."
5. It is widely known that animals have their own ways of communicating with each other. For example, bees can dance very complicated dances and some birds can sing very complicated songs. It is also generally agreed that there are fundamental differences between human language and other animals' ways of communicating.

   i. What is your view on this point?

   ii. If you also think that there are fundamental differences between human language and other animals' ways of communicating, according to you, what are the differences? Please give short explanations. If you don't think that there are fundamental differences between human language and other animals' ways of communicating, please also defend your position. Illustrate your points with examples if necessary.
6. Why do we say linguistics is a science?（北外 2011 研）
7. What are the three metafunctions of Systemic Functional Grammar? Illustrate each of them with specific examples.（武汉大学 2011 研；华南理工大学 2018 研）

参考答案及解析

Ⅰ. Fill in the blanks.

1. meaning

（语言具有任意性，其所指与其形式没有逻辑或内在的联系。）

2. displacement

（移位性是指人类语言可以让使用者在交际时用语言符号代表时间和空间上不可及的物体、事件和观点。）

3. primary，secondary

（二重性是指拥有两层结构的这种属性，底层结构是上层结构的组成成分，每层都有自身的组合规则。）

4. design

（人类语言区别于其他动物交流系统的特点是语言的区别特征，是人类语言特有的特征。）

5. phatic communion

（寒暄功能是指那些有助于确立和维持人际关系的表达，最先由 Malinowski 提出。）

6. ideational

（韩礼德将儿童的语言功能范围逐渐缩小，简化成为一套高度符号化和抽象化的功能：概念、人际、语篇功能。）

7. metalingual

（语言的元语言功能是指语言可以用来讨论语言本身。）

8. scientific

（语言学通常被定义为研究科学的语言，或对语言的科学研究。）

9. Phonetics；phonology

（语音学研究语音是如何产生，传播以及接收的；音系学研究支配语音分布和排列的规则以及音节的形式。）

10. Semantics；syntax；morphology

（语义学研究语言的意义，句法学研究构成句子的规则，形态学研究词汇的内部结构。三者都是语言学的分支。）

11. arbitrary

（索绪尔认为符号的形式或声音与其意义之间没有逻辑联系，所以两者之间的关系是任意的。）

12. Psycholinguistics；sociolinguistics

（心理语言学研究语言处理机制，如语言的记忆，理解及习得等；社会语言学研究语言与社会之间的关系。）

13. langue；parole

（索绪尔用语言和言语来区分说话者的语言能力和言语上（表达的）的实际表现或语料。）

14. Descriptive；prescriptive

（描述性语言记录语言共同体的成员所遵循的规则，规定式的语言学目的在于为正确使用语言定下各种规则。）

15. competence

（语言能力指理想的语言使用者关于语言规则的语言知识，语言应用指语言交际中关于语言规则知识的实际使用。）

16. yo-he-ho

（语言的起源有摹声说、感叹说和劳动喊声说。劳动喊声说认为语言起源于原始人共同劳动时发出的有节奏的哼哟声。）

17. diachronic linguistic

（历时语言学集中研究几十年或几百年的时期内两个或比两个更多的语言状况的差异。）

18. human

（语言是人类用来交际的任意性的语音符号系统。）

Ⅱ. Multiple Choices

1. B （语言不是机械的、工具的，而是一种交流方式。）
2. B （语言的区别性特征主要是指任意性二重性、创造性和移位性。）
3. C （创造性指语言的能产性，它能够使人造出和理解无穷的长句，其中很多句子是以前从未听过的。）
4. A （crash 是一个缩略语，typewriter 是复合词，bang 是拟声词，所以只有 tree 的形成是完全任意的。）
5. C （语言的主要功能包括寒暄功能、指示功能、信息功能、疑问功能、表达功能、施为功能和劝说功能。）
6. B （语言最重要的社会功能是人际功能。）
7. A （索绪尔的语言指语言社团中的语言，所以是从社会的角度研究语言。乔姆斯基是从使用者本身掌握的语言知识研究语言，是从心理的角度研究语言。）
8. C （索绪尔的语言指语言社团中的语言。）
9. B （声学语音学研究语音的物质特征。）
10. B （谈论天气的问候语体现了语言的寒暄功能。）
11. C （应用语言学研究语言在其他领域的使用，尤其是教育方面。）
12. D （如果运用语言仅仅是为了开心好玩，那就是运用了语言的娱乐功能。）

Ⅲ. True or False

1. T （寒暄功能是指建立与保持社交联络而不是交换信息。）
2. T （句法学研究词汇构成句子的规则。）
3. F （语言能力与语言表现的区别是由乔姆斯基提出的。）
4. T （语言能力与语言在具体情况下的应用无关，语言表现是语言在具体情况下的表现。）
5. F （描写式和规定式的语言学是分析语言的两种不同的方法，不能简单地说谁好谁坏。）
6. T （历时研究是研究语言的变化与发展。）
7. F （拟声词并不完全是任意的，与其表达的声音具有一定的相似性。）
8. T （语言学研究主要以口语为主，口语形式先于书面语出现，而且世界上有的语言只有口语形式没有书面形式。）

Ⅳ. Explain the following terms.

1. Arbitrariness refers to the fact that the forms of linguistic signs bear no natural relationship to their meaning. Arbitrariness of language makes it potentially creative; a conventionality of lan-

guage makes a language be passed from generation to generation. For example, it is unable to explain why a book is called a /buk/ and a pen a /pen/.

2. Duality refers to the fact that in all languages so far investigated there are two levels of structure or patterning. At the first, higher level, language is analyzed in terms of combinations of meaningful units (such as morphemes, words etc.); at the second, lower level, it is seen as a sequence of segments which lack any meaning in themselves, but which combine to form units of meaning. For example, a syllable is the smallest unit that is normally spoken by itself, and scores of syllables become the carriers of hundreds of meaningful segments of words that are called morphemes.
3. Language can be used to refer to what is present, what is absent, what happens at present, what happened in the past, what will happen in the future or what happens in a far-away place. This property of language enables language users to overcome the barriers caused by time and place. For example, scientists can predict the "future" of certain planets that are several billions of light years away from us.
4. The performative function of language is primarily to change the social status of persons and it can extend to the control of reality as on some magical or religious occasions. The kind of language employed in performative verbal acts is usually quite formal and even ritualized. For example, in Chinese when someone breaks a bowl the host or the people present are likely to say *sui sui ping an* (every day be safe and happy) as a means of controlling the forces which the believers feel might affect their lives.
5. Parole refers to the realization of langue in actual use. It varies enormously according to individuals. The speeches, the idiosyncratic utterances made by individuals are all examples of parole.
6. To say that linguistics is a descriptive study is to say that the linguist tries to discover and record the roles to which the members of a language-community actually conform and does not seek to impose upon them other rules, or norms, of correctness, which are in the scope of prescriptive linguistics.
7. 参见 1.1 复习笔记。
8. Language is culturally transmitted, i.e., language is more learned after birth through a social setting instead of inherent. The story of wolf child show that a human being brought up in isolation is clearly does not acquire human language.

V. Short answer questions

1. Synchronic Linguistics is the description of a language at some point of time in history. It focuses on the characteristics of the language at a certain time. For example, when we study English, we learn about the vocabulary, the language points and oral English etc. At this time, we are learning English of current time in synchronic method.
2. We use language for numerous purposes, from writing letters to discuss with our friends, delivering speeches and talking to ourselves. However, the primary function of language is to convey information and commands, as well as feelings and emotions. That is, language is a medium of communication. The term "communication" indicates much of the function of language. This function can be further divided into more specific functions, such as phatic function/communion,

directive function, informative function, interrogative function, expressive function, evocative function, performative function etc.

3. Linguistic competence was originally proposed by Noam Chomsky. It is defined as a language user's underlying knowledge about the system or rules. In Chomsky's view, the native speaker's competence can be characterized as a set of rules for producing an understanding of sentences in his language. To acquire the native speaker's competence is to obtain the ability of recognizing and producing grammatical sentences in a language.

   Communicative competence, on the other hand, was proposed by Dell Hymes as an effort to refine the original notion by Chomsky. He pointed out that Chomsky's competence is necessary but not sufficient for a learner to communicate with others successfully in a speech community. In addition to grammatical accuracy, a successful communication requires appropriacy in the sense that he knows when he speaks what to whom. Thus, he extended the notion of competence by incorporating the pragmatic ability for language use. This extended idea of competence is called communicative competence.

4. The creativity or productivity refers to man's ability that of the users of languages in making and comprehending an infinite number of sentences including those that they have never heard before. It is human-specific. It combines the basic linguistic units to form an infinite set of sentences, most of which are never heard before. Human language is resourceful because of its duality and its recursiveness. The speaker is able to understand the sentences before produced or heard. The fact that human language is recursive could be shown in that words can be used in new ways to mean new things, and can be instantly understood by people who have never come across that word before. For example, I could make a sentence like "The man who is waiting for the lady who is talking to the boy who is playing with a girl...is my uncle."

5. Directive function is one of functions of language. Language is used by the addresser to get the hearer to do something. Most imperative sentences fulfil directive function. For example, the sentence "Open the window and let the air in!" performs a directive function. Other syntactic structures or sentences of other sorts can, according to J. Austin and J. Searle's "Indirect speech act theory" at least, serve the purpose of direction too, e. g., "If I were you, I would have blushed to the bottom of my ears!"

Ⅵ. Essay questions

1. Since language has both individual and social aspects, it is naturally of interest to psychologists and sociologists among others.

   Many psychologists are interested to investigate the interrelation of language and mind, in processing and producing utterances and in language acquisition for example, language development in the child, such as the theories of language acquisition; biological foundations of language, and a big topic—the relationship between language and cognition, so there is psycholinguistics.

   Socialists who are interested in the relations between language and society do researches concerned both sociology and linguistics, including the social functions of language and the social characteristics of its users.

When anthropologists enlisted the help of linguists to study unwritten languages, anthropology and linguistics became closely associated in the early days of anthropological fieldwork. In contrast to other linguists, anthropological linguists are interested primarily in the history and structure of formerly unwritten languages. They are concerned with the emergence of language and also with the divergence of languages over thousands of years.

Therefore, it is not surprising there are some branches of macrolinguistics that show an interdisciplinary nature.

2. The first one is typical of descriptive grammar, while the second one is prescriptive grammar. The descriptive grammar aims to describe how people speak and detail the underlying knowledge. It is believed in descriptive grammar that whatever occurs in natural speech, such as hesitation, incomplete utterance, should be described in the analysis, and not be marked as incorrect, abnormal, or corrupt; modern linguistics is mostly descriptive. Whereas, the prescriptive approach aims to teach people how to speak, read, and write a particular language; in the 18th century, all the main European languages were studied prescriptively.

   For example, the statement that "in standard English, a double negative is rarely used" is a description, showing how the language is used in standard English, regardless of whether it is correct or not. "You should never use a double-negative" is a typical grammar rule that prescribes what should be grammatically correct in the Standard English. As for the spelling, prescription says "judgment" is correct, but description accurately points out that "judgement" is considered by Edited English to be correct too, and a descriptive account for these two different spellings will show how the later one is used and who uses it.

3. According to F. de Saussure, langue refers to the abstract linguistic system shared by all members of a speech community; while parole refers to the realization of langue in actual use.

   For Chomsky, a fundamental distinction between linguistic competence and performance should be made. A language user's underlying knowledge about the system of rules is called linguistic competence. And performance refers to the actual use of language in concrete situations. In light with this, competence enables a speaker to produce and understand an indefinite number of sentences and to recognize grammatical mistakes and ambiguities. A speaker's competence is stable but his performance is often influenced by psychological and social factors, and thus would involve imperfections such as slips of tongue, false starts, unnecessary pauses, and so on. Thus, the point is that a speaker's performance does not always match his competence.

   Saussure's distinction is somewhat similar with Chomsky's in the sense that they both refer to the constant factor which underlies the utterances that constitute parole/performance. However, their difference is quite obvious. Saussue's language is a social product, a set of conventions for a speech community. Chomsky regards competence as a property of the mind of each individual. Saussrue looks at language more from a sociological point of view while Chomsky looks at it more from a psychological point of view.

4. Similarities:

   (1) Both definitions stick to the fact that language is primarily a matter of speech because the primary medium of language is sound. Sapir illustrates this idea by implying that the pro-

duced symbols are auditory and Bloch and Trager by explicitly using the word 'vocal'.

(2) Both definitions allude to the fact that the association between the words and the things that they denote is rarely inherent, Sapir by using the word "symbols" and Bloch and Trager by placing emphasis on "arbitrary" and "symbols".

Differences:

(1) Sapir's definition emphasizes that language relates to communication between human beings. It is very different from the communication systems of other creatures, such as bird songs and bee dances. Bloch and Trager do not clearly indicate this property, only saying that it is possessed by a social group.

(2) Sapir also considers that language is 'non-instinctive' and 'voluntarily produced'. Thus, for him language does not include such instinctive forms of communication as smiling and cries of pain, etc. However, Bloch and Trager's definition does not include this feature.

(3) The element 'system' in Bloch and Trager's definition reflects the fact that language provides us with the framework for generating appropriate utterances rather than providing us with an infinite store of ready-made utterances. Still elements of lacunae are combined according to rules.

(4) The function of language is indicated differently in two definitions. Sapir sees language as for communicating ideas, emotions and desires, while Bloch and Trager consider it for a social group's co-operation. Sapir's definition proposes 'communication' as the principal function of language and specifies what is communicated; Bloch and Trager only vaguely point out that language can be used for co-operation.

Each of the two definitions has its own special emphasis and it not totally free from limitations. We think the two definitions grasp some defining properties of language that distinguish it from any animal system of communication, for example, 'vocal', 'arbitrary', 'symbol', 'purely human', 'a system'. But either has some limitation. As for Sapir's definition, whether one considers language to be instinctive or not is an issue. Language is instinctive insofar as we are all born with a predisposition to speak, we all acquire a language without tuition and when we speak, we do not consciously convert our thoughts into speech. Language is, however, non-instinctive in that we can choose what to say or whether to say anything at all. Both descriptions of language's function are not precise. Sapir's definition confines language only to communicating ideas, emotions and desires, and Bloch and Trager's definition does not point it out at all.

5. i. There are fundamental differences between human language and other animal's ways of communicating. All creatures, not only the "clever" ones like apes and dolphins but also such "lower" ones as bees and birds, are able to communicate with each other. We have been careful in using the term "animal communication system" to indicate this ability. But language is human-specific which is not merely a tool used to transmit information but also a means of social communication. Linguists made a list of "design features", which are found utterly absent in animal communication and thus distinguish human language from animal's cry.

ii. There are fundamental differences between human language and other animals' ways of communicating, such as the "design feature", which could distinguish human language from other systems of communication. For instance, 1) Duality, Duality, animals that communicate using vocal signals have a repertoire of simple sounds that varies among species. A cow has less than ten, and a chicken has about twenty, but most animals can only use each simple sound for one thing at a time, limiting the communicative ability of animal language. However, human language consists of two sets of structures. At the lower level is a structure of sounds which is meaningless in themselves. These sounds can be grouped and regrouped into a large number of units of meaning (morphemes and words etc.) at the higher level. These meaningful units at the higher level can be arranged and rearranged into an infinite number of sentences. 2) Productivity or creativity, it means that human beings can produce novel utterances whenever they want. The robin is creative in its ability to sing the same thing in many ways, but not creative in its ability to use the same units of the system to express many different messages with different meanings. 3) Displacement, it is the capability of language to communicate about things that are not immediately present, i. e., things that are either not here or are not here now. The majority of animals can only communicate about things that are happening right now.

（本题主要考查语言的本质特征。结合所学知识和自己对这一组特征的理解，先给出自己的观点，再阐释动物语言系统和人类语言系统的区别。）

6. Linguistics is generally defined as the scientific study of language. It tries to answer the basic questions "What is language?" and "How does language work?" Linguistics studies not any particular language, e. g., English, Chinese, Arabic, and Latin, but it studies languages in general.

It is a scientific study because it is based on the systematic investigation of linguistic data, conducted with reference to some general theory of language structure. In order to discover the nature and rules of the underlying language system, what the linguist has to do first is to collect and observe language facts, which are found to display some similarities, and generalizations are made about them; then he formulates some hypotheses about the language structure. But the hypotheses thus formed have to be checked repeatedly against the observed facts to fully prove their validity. In linguistics, as in any other discipline, data and theory stand in a dialectical complementation; that is, a theory without the support of data can hardly claim validity, and data without being explained by some theory remain a muddled mass of things.

（此题考查语言学作为一门学科其科学性，为开放性试题，从其研究内容及方法角度作答即可。）

7. According to Halliday, the adult's language becomes much more complex and it has to serve many more functions, and the original functional is gradually reduced to a set of highly coded and abstract functions, which are three metafunctions: the ideational, the interpersonal, and the textual functions.

First, the ideational function ("experiential" and "logical") is to convey new information, to communicate a content that is unknown to the hearer. Present in all language uses, the ideational function is a meaning potential, because whatever specific use one is making of language, he has to refer to categories of his experience of the world.

The ideational function mainly consists of "transitivity" and "voice". This function not only specifies the available options in meaning but also determines the nature of their structural realisations. For example, "John built a new house" can be analysed as a configuration of the function roles:

Actor: John

Process: Material: creation: built

Goal: affected: a new house

Second, the interpersonal function embodies all uses of language to express social and personal relations. This includes the various ways the speaker enters a speech situation and performs a speech act. Because the clause is not confined to the expression of transitivity, there are non-ideational elements in the adult language system.

Interpersonal function is realised by mood and modality. Mood shows what role the speaker selects in the speech situation and what role he assigns to the addressee. If the speaker selects the imperative mood, he assumes the role of one giving commands and puts the addressee in the role of one expected to obey orders. Modality specifies if the speaker is expressing his judgement or making a prediction. For example, "Give me that teapot!"

Mood is made up of two parts: the "Subject" and the "Finite" element. The subject can be a noun, a noun phrase, or a clause.

Third, the textual function refers to the fact that language has mechanisms to make any stretch of spoken or written discourse into a coherent and unified text and make a living passage different from a random list of sentences. Although two sentences may have exactly the same ideational and interpersonal functions, they may be different in terms of textual coherence.

The textual function fulfils the requirement that language should be operationally relevant, having texture in a real context of situation that distinguishes a living passage from a mere entry in a grammar or a dictionary. It provides the remaining strands of meaning potential to be woven into the fabric of linguistic structure.

For example, analyze the sentence "John likes linguistics." on three levels of metafunctions.

Ideational Mental Process Reaction	John	likes	linguistics
	Senser	Mental reaction	Mental reaction
Interpersonal Declarative	Mood	Residue	
	Subject	Predicator	Adjunct
Textual Unmarked Theme	Theme	Rheme	
	Given		New

(考查韩礼德功能语法中三项元功能，并举例说明。)

第2章　语音

2.1　复习笔记

本章要点：

1．Speech organs

发音器官

2．Distinction, classification and the criteria of description between consonant and vowels

辅音和元音的区别、分类及描写规则

3．Variations of sounds

语音的变化

4．Phonemes, minimal pairs and sets and free variation

音位，最小对立、集合体和自由变异

5．Distinctive features and consonant cluster

区别特征和辅音连缀

6．Syllable structure, stress and intonation

音节结构、重音和语调

常考考点：

1．语音学

语音学的定义；发音器官的英文名称；英语辅音的定义、发音部位、发音方法和分类；英语元音的定义和分类、基本元音；发音语音学；听觉语音学；声学语音学。

2．音系学

音系学的定义；音系学与语音学的联系和区别；音素、音位、最小对立体、自由变异；音位理论；区别性特征；超切分特征；音节；重音（词重音、句子重音）；音高和语调。

本章内容索引：

Ⅰ．Phonetics

1．Phonetics

2．Three major research fields of phonetics

Ⅱ．Articulators

1．Articulators

（1）Seven major articulators

（2）Three notices

2．Voiceless and voiced sounds

3．Nasal and oral sounds

Ⅲ．Classification of English Speech Sounds

1．Consonants

(1) Manner of Articulation and Place of Articulation

(2) Classification of Consonants

2. Vowel

(1) The Height of the Tongue

(2) The Shape of the Lips

(3) The Width of the Mouth

(4) Monophthongs and Diphthongs

Ⅳ. Variations of Sounds

1. Liaison
2. Elision
3. Assimilation

Ⅴ. Phonology

1. Phonology
2. Phoneme
3. Minimal Pairs and Sets
4. Free Variation
5. Distinctive Features

Ⅵ. Syllables and Consonant Cluster

1. Syllables
2. Consonant Cluster

Ⅶ. Suprasegmentals

1. Suprasegmental features
2. Stress
3. Intonation

Ⅰ. Phonetics

1. Phonetics

Phonetics refers to the study of the speech sounds that appeared in all human languages.

2. Three Major Research Fields of Phonetics

(1) Articulatory phonetics refers to the study of how speech sounds are produced, or "pronounced".

(2) Acoustic phonetics focuses on the process of the speech's propagation in the air.

(3) Auditory phonetics involves how listeners perceive speech sounds.

Ⅱ. Articulators

1. Articulators

【考点：根据图指出发音器官名称】

(1) Seven Major Articulators

Ⅰ. 语音学

1. 语音学

语音学研究所有人类语言的声音。

2. 语音学研究的三大领域

(1) 发音语音学研究语音的产生。

(2) 声学语音学研究语音的物质特征。

(3) 感知语音学(或听觉语音学)研究语音的感知。

Ⅱ. 发音器官

1. 发音器官

(1)七个主要的发音器官

There are seven major articulators: pharynx, velum or soft palate, hard palate, alveolar ridge or alveolum, tongue, teeth and lips.

咽腔、软腭、硬腭、齿龈、舌、齿、唇。

(2) Three Key Points

①Larynx is also an organ of articulator.

②Jaws are sometimes called articulators, but it is different from other articulators.

③The nose and the nasal cavity are different from other articulators.

(2)三个注意的点

① 喉也是发音器官。

② 下颌有时也称作发音器官，但它与其他的发音器官不一样。

③ 鼻子和鼻腔和其他的发音器官也不一样。

2. Voiced and Voiceless Sounds

2. 浊音和清音

(1) **Voiceless sounds** refers to those sounds pronounced in the way that the vocal cords do not vibrate during the pronunciation process (the vocal cords are spread apart, the airstream from the lungs is not obstructed at the space between vocal cords and passes freely).

(1)在发音过程中，发音时声带不振动，这样所发出的音叫做清音。

(2) **Voiced sounds** refers to those sounds pronounced in the way that the vocal cords vibrate during the pronunciation process (the vocal cords are drawn together, the airstream forces its way through and causes them to vibrate).

(2)在发音过程中，发音时声带振动，这样所发出的音叫做浊音。

3. Nasal and oral sounds

3. 鼻音和口腔音

(1) **Nasal sounds** refers to sounds pronounced in the way that the velum droops and thus the nasal cavity and oral cavity are ventilated at the same time.

(1)软腭下垂，使鼻腔和口腔同时通气，这样发出的音为鼻音。

(2) **Oral sounds** refers to sounds pronounced in the way that the velum rises to the back of the throat, and at the same time, a blockage of the nasal cavity is formed, releasing the airstream from the mouth.

(2)软腭上升直到喉咙后部，同时形成鼻腔阻塞，气流从口腔中释放，这样发出的音为口腔音。

Ⅲ. Classification of English speech sounds

Ⅲ. 辅音和元音

1. Consonants

1. 辅音

【考点：名词解释】

Consonants are sounds produced due to certain parts of the vocal tract are compressed or obstructed, causing the airstream in the oral cavity to be deflected, obstructed or completely blocked in the process of pronunciation.

发音时，声道的某些部位受到压缩或阻碍后，使得气流在口腔里转向、受阻或完全被阻塞，由此产生的音叫做**辅音**。

(1) Manner of articulation and place of articulation

(1) 发音方式和发音部位

① **Manner of articulation** refers to the type of stricture involved in the production of a consonant (the way the airstream passes through certain parts of the vocal tract).

① **发音方式**指发音器官之间的关系，以及气流经过声道的某些部位时的方式。

② **Place of articulation** refers to the involvement of the articulators in the production of a particular consonant (where the airstream friction, narrowing or obstruction occurs).

②**发音部位**指声道的那些发生气流摩擦、狭窄化或阻碍的部位。

(2) Classification of consonants

【考点：描述给定辅音 & 根据描述指出辅音名称】

① According to the manner of articulation, consonants are divided into stops, fricatives, affricates, liquids, nasals and glides.

stops: [p, b, t , d, k, g]

fricatives: [f, v, θ, ð, s, z, ʃ, ʒ, h]

affricates: [dʒ, tʃ]

liquids: [l, r]

nasals: [m, n, ŋ]

glides: [j, w]

② According to the place of articulation, the consonants are classified as bilabials, labiodentals, dentals, alveolars, palatals, velars and glottal.

bilabials: [p, b, m, w]

labiodentals : [f, v]

dentals: [θ, ð]

alveolars: [t, d, n, s, z, r, l]

palatals: [j, ʃ, ʒ, dʒ, tʃ]

velars: [k, g, ŋ]

glottal: [h]

2. Vowel

【考点：描述给定元音 & 根据描述指出元音名称】

Vowels are sounds produced when the vocal tract is not compressed or obstructed, so there will be no turbulence or stagnation of airstream.

(1) The Height of the Tongue

Front vowels: [iː] [ɪ] [e] [ɛ] [æ] [ɑ]

Central vowels: [3ː] [ə] [ʌ]

Back vowels: [uː] [u] [ɔː] [ɔ] [ɑː]

(2) The Shape of the Lips

Rounded vowels: [uː] [u] [ɔː] [ɔ]

Unrounded vowels: [iː] [ɪ] [e] [ɛ] [æ] [ɑ] [3ː] [ə] [ʌ] [ɑː]

(3) The Width of the Mouth

Open vowels: [æ] [ɑ] [ɔ] [ɑː]

Close vowels: [iː] [ɪ][uː] [u]

Semi-open vowels: [ɔː] [e] [ɛ] [3ː] [ə] [ʌ]

(2) 辅音的分类

①按发音方式分类，辅音可分为爆破音、擦音、塞擦音、流音、鼻音、滑音。

爆破音：[p, b, t, , d, k, g]

擦音：[f, v, θ, ð, s, z, ʃ, ʒ, h]

塞擦音：[dʒ, tʃ]

流音：[l, r]

鼻音：[m, n, ŋ]

滑音：[j, w]

②按发音部位分类，辅音可分为双唇音、唇齿音、齿音、齿龈音、硬腭音、软腭音和声门音。

双唇音：[p, b, m, w]

唇齿音：[f, v]

齿音：[θ, ð]

齿龈音：[t, d, n, s, z, r, l]

硬腭音：[j, ʃ, ʒ, dʒ, tʃ]

软腭音：[k, g, ŋ]

声门音：[h]

2. 元音

发音时，声道不受任何压缩或阻碍，因此不会有气流的紊乱或停滞，由此产生的音叫做元音。

(1) 舌头最高部分的高度

前元音：[iː] [ɪ] [e] [ɛ] [æ] [ɑ]

中元音：[3ː] [ə] [ʌ]

后元音：[uː] [u] [ɔː] [ɔ] [ɑː]

(2)唇的圆展度

圆唇音：[uː] [u] [ɔː] [ɔ]

展唇音：[iː] [ɪ] [e] [ɛ] [æ] [ɑ] [3ː] [ə] [ʌ] [ɑː]

(3)开口的宽度

开元音：[æ] [ɑ] [ɔ] [ɑː]

闭元音：[iː] [ɪ][uː] [u]

半开元音：[ɔː] [e] [ɛ] [3ː] [ə] [ʌ]

(4) **Monophthongs and Diphthongs** **Monophthong** refers to those pure vowels that are constant both in number and quality. **Diphthong** refers to a resulting combination of sounds from a sequence of two sounds produced from one vowel position to another.	(4) **单元音与双元音** **单元音**指在数量上和性质上都恒定不变的纯元音。 如果在发音时通过舌头的一次运动，由第一个单元音滑向第二个单元音，所产生的音的组合就叫做**双元音**。
Ⅳ. Variations of Sounds	**Ⅳ. 音的变化**
1. Liaison refers to the phenomenon that two words are pronounced together in the actual discourse process, especially when the second word begins with a vowel.	**1. 连读** 指在实际话语过程中把两个词连到一起读，尤其是第二个单词以元音开始时，这种现象叫做连读。
2. Elision is the phenomenon of missing one or several sounds in the actual speech.	**2. 省音** 在实际话语中漏掉一个音或几个音，这种现象叫做省音。
3. Assimilation refers to the process in which a sound changes and gets some or all of the characteristics of neighboring sounds or syllables.	**3. 同化** 同化指一个音具有了邻近音的一部分或者全部特征的这一过程。
Ⅴ. Phonology	**Ⅴ. 音系学**
1. Phonology Phonology is study of the systems and patterns of speech sounds in a language.	**1. 音系学** 音系学研究的是语言的语音系统。
2. Phoneme **Phoneme** is a basic unit of phonology research, and it is an abstract collection of a set of phonetic features, which has the function of distinguish meaning.	**2. 音位** **音位**是音系学研究的一个基本单位，是一组语音特征的抽象集合体，具有区别意义的作用。
3. Minimal Pairs and Sets **Minimal Pairs** refers two words that can be distinguished by only by one sound. **A minimal set** refers to a group of words that can be distinguished in meaning by changing a phoneme in the same position (always in the same position).	**3. 最小对立体** 能够用一个音区别意义的两个词叫做最小的对立体。 当一组词能够通过改变其中同一位置的一个音素来区别意义时，这组词就叫做**最小集合体**。
4. Free Variation 【考点：名词解释】 If two or more phonemes occur in the same position without distinguishing their meanings, then these two phonemes can be regarded as **free variation**.	**4. 自由变体** 如果两个或两个以上音素出现在一个相同的语音环境中，并不区别意义，那么这两个音素就可被视为自由变体。
5. Distinctive features refers to a feature that can distinguishes one phoneme from another.	**5. 区别特征** 区别性特征是指能够区别意义的语音特征。

Ⅵ. Syllables and Consonant Cluster

1. Syllables

Those units, which are often longer than one sound and smaller than a whole word, are called syllables. For example, the English word "beautiful" consists of three speech units: beau-ti-ful.

Syllable structure

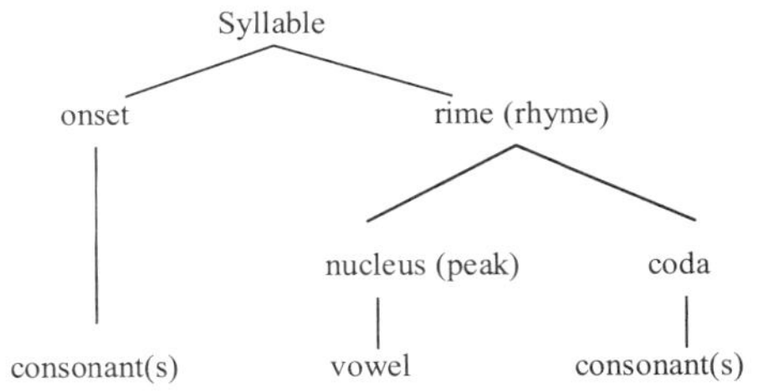

【考点：判断一个音节的节首、韵基和节尾】

2. Consonant Cluster

In English some words may have two or more consonants in one syllable, such as [spl] in ['splendid]. Such phonetic sequences are called are called consonant clusters.

Ⅶ. Suprasegmentals

1. Suprasegmental features

refers to the features that are broader than the segment level and can distinguish meaning, which mainly include accent, tone and intonation etc.

2. Stress

refers to a certain syllable in a word or certain syllables in a sentence that are read more heavily and stronger.

3. Intonation

involves recurring rising and falling patterns of pitch, refers to speech sounds which are identical as to their place or manner features may differ in length, pitch or loudness.

Ⅵ. 音节和辅音连缀

1. 音节

英语单词"beautiful"由三部分组成 beau-ti-ful，这样的比一个音长但又比一个词的音短的单位就叫做音节。

音节的结构

2. 辅音连缀

在英语中一些词在一个音节中会有两个或多个辅音，例如['splendid]中的[spl]，这样的语音序列叫做辅音连缀。

Ⅶ. 超切分特征

1. 超切分特征

指的是大于音段层面上的，能够区别意义的特征，其主要包括重音、声调和语调等。

2. 重音

重音指单词中的某个音节或语句里的某几个音节被读得重些、强些。

3. 语调

语调涉及重复出现的升降模式，是指声调高低抑扬轻重的配制和变化。

2.2 课后习题详解

1. Define the following terms briefly.

articulator	assimilation	consonant	elision
intonation	phoneme	phonetics	phonology
stress	voicing	voiceless	vowel

2. What is the test most often used for determining phonemes in a language? Illustrate how the test works with examples.

3. What's the difference between an open and a closed syllable?

4. For each group of sounds listed below, state the phonetic feature or features which they share.

Example: [p] [b] [m]   Feature: bilabial, stop, consonant

(1) [g][p][t][d][k][b]

(2) [u][u:][ɔ]

5. Name the single feature that distinguishes the following pairs of sounds.

(1) [ð] : [θ]

(2) [p] : [f]

(3) [I] : [e]

(4) [b] : [m]

(5) [s] : [ʃ]

(6) [s] : [ð]

6. The following sets of minimal pairs show that English [p] and [b] contrast in initial, medial and final positions.

Initial	Medial	Final
pit/bit	*rapid/rabid*	*cap/cab*

Find similar sets of minimal pairs for each pair of consonants given:

(1) [k] – [g]

(2) [m] – [n]

(3) [b] – [v]

(4) [b] – [m]

(5) [p] – [f]

7. The English data below provide examples of stress placement on certain verbs.

A	B	C
ap'pear	a'dapt	as'tonish
col'lide	col'lapse	con'sider
e'rase	e'lect	i'magine
ca'rouse	ob'serve	de'termine
cor'rode	tor'ment	'promise

(1) Describe in words the stress placement on these verbs. Make sure you refer to syllable structure in your statement.

(2) Provide syllable representations of the words *col'lide*, *e'lect*, and *con'sider* in order to illustrate your conclusion about stress placement in these forms.

参考答案

1. **Articulator**: Different parts of the vocal tract involved in the production of speech sound are called organs of speech or articulators, including lips, teeth, alveolar ridge, hard palate, soft palate, tongue, uvula and vocal cords.

Assimilation: Assimilation refers to the process in which a sound changes and gets some or all of the characteristics of neighboring sounds or syllables. There are two kinds of assimilation. One is regressive assimilation which means the changes are brought about by the following sound; and the other is progressive assimilation, which means changes brought about by the preceding sound.

Consonant: Consonants are sounds produced due to certain parts of the vocal tract are compressed or obstructed, causing the airstream in the oral cavity to be deflected, obstructed or completely blocked in the process of pronunciation. There are altogether 24 consonants in English.

Elision: Elision is the phenomenon of missing one or several sounds in the actual speech.

Intonation: Intonation involves recurring rising and falling patterns of pitch, refers to speech sounds which are identical as to their place or manner features may differ in length, pitch or loudness.

Phoneme: Phoneme is a basic unit of phonology research, and it is an abstract collection of a set of phonetic features, which has the function of distinguish meaning.

Phonetics: Phonetics refers to the study of the speech sounds that appeared in all human languages. Articulatory phonetics, auditory phonetics and acoustic phonetics are three major research fields of phonetics.

Phonology: Phonology is study of the systems and patterns of speech sounds in a language.

Stress: Stress refers to a certain syllable in a word or certain syllables in a sentence that are read more heavily and stronger.

Voicing: Voicing is a distinctive phonetic feature of speech sound that can distinguish one word from another, which refers to the vibration in the larynx caused by air from the lungs passing through the vocal cords when they are partly closed. A speech sound can be defined as voiced or voiceless. For example, the only difference between [z] and [s] is voicing.

Voiceless: One of the two branches in voicing. Voiceless sounds refers to those sounds pronounced in the way that the vocal cords do not vibrate during the pronunciation process (the vocal cords are spread apart, the airstream from the lungs is not obstructed at the space between vocal cords and passes freely).

Vowel: Vowels are sounds produced when the vocal tract is not compressed or obstructed, so there will be no turbulence or stagnation of airstream. There are altogether 21 vowel sounds in English.

2. The minimal pair test or substitution test is the first rule of thumb to determine the phonemes of any language, that is, to see whether substituting one sound for another results in a different word. If it does, the two sounds represent different phonemes. For example, we see from the contrast between *fine* and *vine* and between *chunk* and *junk* that [f], [v], [tʃ] and [dʒ] must be phonemes in English because substituting [v] for [f], or [dʒ] for [tʃ] produces a different word.
3. The units, which are often longer than one sound and smaller than a whole word, are called syllables. Syllables can be divided into two sorts: the open syllables and the closed syllables. Syllables like *me*, *by* or *no that* have an onset and a nucleus, but no coda are called open syllables; while the coda is present in the syllables like *up*, *cup* or *hat*, which is called closed syllables.
4. (1) [g][p][t][d][k][b] shared features: stop, consonant.

(2) [u][u:][ɔ] shared features: back, rounded, vowel.

5. (1) [ð] : [θ] voicing. (voiced vs. voiceless)

(2) [p] : [f] place of articulation. (bilabial vs. labiodental)

(3) [ɪ] : [e] the height of the tone rising. (high vs. mid)

(4) [b] : [m] manner of articulation. (stop vs. nasal)

(5) [s] : [ʃ] place of articulation. (alveolar vs. palatal)

(6) [s] : [ð] place of articulation. (alveolar vs. dental)

6.

	Initial	Medial	Final
(1)	kook/gook	raking/raging	lak/lag
(2)	moon/noon	dime/dine	beam/bean
(3)	berry/very	dribble/drivel	dub/dove
(4)	be/me	ribbed/rimmed	rib/rim
(5)	pat/fat	depend/defend	rap/raff

7. (1) Stress in languages may be predictable by rules: lexical category, morphological structure and number of syllables all seem to be relevant factors for the placement of stress in English words.

For two-syllable verbs, the final (ultimate) syllable will receive main stress if it has a long vowel or ends in at least two consonants. In this case, the first (penultimate) syllable may have secondary stress, contain an unstressed full vowel, or contain a reduced vowel. For example, *a'dapt*, *e'lect*.

If the ultimate syllable does not have a long vowel or end in two or more consonants, the penultimate syllable is stressed, as in *'promise*. Otherwise, the main stress will be put on the second syllable. For example, *ca'rouse*, *ob'serve*, *as'tonish*, *de'termine*.

If there is a double-letter in the word, the main stress should be put between them, or in other words, on the second one of the two. Such as *ap'pear*, *cor'rode*, *col'lide*, *col'lapse*.

(2) They are two-syllable words; therefore the final (ultimate) syllable will receive main stress, as *col'lide*, *e'lect and con'side*.

2.3 考研真题与典型题详解

Ⅰ. Fill in the blanks.

1. The sound [b] can be described with "__________, bilabial, stop". (北二外 2004 研)
2. Consonant articulations are relatively easy to feel and as a result are most conveniently described in terms of __________ and manner of articulation. (北二外 2004 研)
3. __________ are produced by constricting or obstructing the vocal tract at some place to divert, impede, or completely shut off the flow of air in the oral cavity. (中山大学 2006 研)
4. Consonant articulations are relatively easy to feel, and as a result are most conveniently described in terms of place and __________ of articulation. (北二外 2008 研)
5. The sound [k] can be described with "voiceless, __________, stop". (北二外 2003 研)
6. __________ refers to the change of a sound as a result of the influence of an adjacent sound.

（中山大学 2005 研）

7. Stress refers to the degree of ________ used in producing a syllable.（中山大学 2006 研）

8. In phonological analysis the words *fail-veil* are distinguishable simply because of the two phonemes/f/-/v/. This is an example for illustrating ________.

9. In English there are a number of ________, which are produced by moving from one vowel position to another through intervening positions.

10. The different members of a phoneme, sounds which are phonetically different but do not make one word different from another in meaning, are ________.

11. Phonetic similarity means that the ________ of a phoneme must bear some phonetic resemblance.（中山大学 2011 研）

Ⅱ. Multiple Choice

1. All syllables contain a ________.（北二外 2004 研）

A. nucleus　　B. coda　　C. onset

2. Of the three cavities. ________ is the most variable and active in amplifying and modifying speech sounds.（北二外 2004 研）

A. nasal cavity　　B. pharynx cavity　　C. oral cavity

3. Of the consonants /p/, /t/, /k/, /f/, /m/, /z/ and /g/, which has the features of voiceless and velar?（对外经贸 2005 研）

A. /k/　　B. /p/　　C. /g/　　D. /t/

4. The consonant(s) in the word "smile" can be described as:（对外经贸 2006 研）

A. voiceless oral alveolar fricative

B. voiceless nasal bilabial liquid

C. voiced oral alveolar plosive

D. voiced oral bilabial fricative

5. The vowel ________ is a low back vowel.（西安外国语学院 2006 研）

A. /iː/　　B. /u/　　C. /e/　　D. /aː/

6. The categories of consonant are NOT established on the basis of ________.（大连外国语学院 2008 研）

A. manners of articulation　　B. place of articulation

C. narrow transcription

7. Point out which item does not fall under the same category as the rest, and explain the reason in ONE sentence.（南京大学 2008 研）

A. /f/　　B. /z/　　C. /ʒ/　　D. /k/

(Focus on manner of articulation)

8. Which of the following is not a minimal pair?（对外经贸 2006 研）

A. (liːf) (fiːl)　　B. (sip) (zip)

C. (sai) (sei)　　D. (keit) (feit)

9. In a syllable, a vowel often serves as ________.（大连外国语学院 2008 研）

A. Peak or Nucleus　　B. Onset　　C. Coda

10. Classification of English speech sounds in terms of manner of articulation involves the following

EXCEPT ________.

A. fricatives　　B. lateral　　C. affricates　　D. bilabial

11. The most recognizable differences between American English and British English are in ________ and vocabulary.

A. usage　　B. grammar　　C. pronunciation　　D. structure

12. Which one is different from the others according to places of articulation?

A. [n]　　B. [m]　　C. [b]　　D. [p]

13. As the vowel within the rhyme is the nucleus, the consonant(s) after it will be termed as ________.（长沙理工大学 2019 研）

A. the coda　　B. the onset　　C. the stress　　D. the stem

Ⅲ. True or False

1. When the vocal folds are apart, the air can pass through easily and the sound produced is said to be voiced.（大连外国语学院 2008 研）
2. Of the three cavities, pharynx cavity is the most variable and active in amplifying and modifying speech sounds.（北二外 2007 研）
3. English consonants can be classified into two categories: voiced and voiceless consonants.（对外经贸 2006 研）
4. Bilabial consonant is produced when the obstruction is partial and the air is forced through a narrow passage.（对外经贸 2006 研）
5. The sound segments are grouped into consonants and vowels.（大连外国语学院 2008 研）
6. Uvular is made with the back of the tongue and the uvula.（大连外国语学院 2008 研）
7. A syllable can be divided into two parts, the NUCLEUS and the CODA.（大连外国语学院 2008 研）
8. Auditory phonetics studies how sounds are perceived by the speaker.（清华 2001 研）
9. The last sound of "top" can be articulated as an unreleased or released plosive. These different realizations of the same phoneme are not in complementary distribution.
10. The speech sounds we hear and produce during linguistic communications are all phonemes.
11. Two sounds are in free variation when they occur in the same environment and do not contrast, namely, the substitution of one for the other does not produce a different word, but merely a different pronunciation.
12. In most cases, the number of syllables of a word corresponds to the number of morphemes.（暨南大学 2018 研）

Ⅳ. Explain the following terms.

1. Glottal Stop（四川大学 2006 研）
2. Voiceless（西安交大 2008 研）
3. Minimal pairs（北航 2008 研；北二外 2006 研）
4. Phoneme（人大 2006 研；上海交大 2007 研）
5. Free variation（武汉大学 2004 研）
6. Assimilation（武汉大学 2008 研；上海交大 2005 研）
7. Suprasegmental features（中山大学 2005 研；南开大学 2004 研）

8. Syllable(四川大学 2006 研)
9. Complementary distribution
10. Narrow transcription (南京师大 2018 研)

V. Short answer questions

1. What is acoustic phonetics? (人大 2003 研)
2. What are the three parts of the vocal organs? (清华 2001 研)
3. Give the phonetic term for each of the following descriptions. (北二外 2006 研)
 (1) the sound produced by the lower lip and the upper front teeth
 (2) the sound produced with a complete closure in the mouth so that the air stream cannot escape through the mouth
4. How are the vowels described usually? (北二外 2009 研)
5. What are suprasegmental features? How do the major suprasegmental features of English function in conveying meaning?
6. What is assimilation? Is it similar to coarticulation? What does it include?
7. In the African language Manika, the affix, the meaning of which is similar to that of the suffix -ing in English, has two phonetic forms, as shown in the data given below. You are required to
 (1) give the two phonetic forms of the affix;
 (2) give the underlying form of the affix;
 (3) write a formal phonological rule to derive the underlying form of the affix to its phonetic forms, using the words [dumuni] "eating" and [sungoli] "sleeping" to illustrate the process of derivation. (南开大学 2011 研)

bugo	*hit*	bugoli	*hitting*
dila	*repair*	dilali	*repairing*
don	*come*	donni	*coming*
dumu	*eat*	dumuni	*eating*
gwen	*chase*	gwenni	*chasing*
da	*lie down*	dali	*lying down*
famu	*know*	famuni	*knowing*
men	*hear*	menni	*hearing*
sungo	*sleep*	sungoli	*sleeping*

8. Transcribe the following words into IPA symbols, with stress marking where necessary. (中山大学 2011 研)
 Example: find—/faind/, beneath—/bi'ni:θ/
 (1) corpora
 (2) sociologist
 (3) chef
 (4) debris
 (5) nasal
 (6) embedding
 (7) antonymy

(8) facial

(9) annotated

(10) phonetics

9. In English, the phoneme /p/ is pronounced differently in words such as *pat*, *spat*, or *tap*. Can you form a rule that can generalize this linguistic phenomenon?（南开大学 2010 研）

10. What are the criteria used in phonetic description of vowels?（厦门大学 2010 研）

Ⅵ. Essay questions

1. What are the differences between voiced sounds and voiceless sounds in terms of articulation?（南开大学 2004 研）

2. What are suprasegmental features?（西安外国语学院 2006 研）

3. In Chinese tone changes are used in the way that affects the meanings of individual words.（中山大学 2011 研）

参考答案及解析

Ⅰ. Fill in the blanks.

1. voiced

（/b/是双唇音，爆破音，浊音。）

2. place

（辅音根据发音方式和发音部位进行分类。）

3. consonants

（发音时，声道的某些部位受到压缩或阻碍后，使得气流在口腔里转向、受阻或完全被阻塞而产生的音叫做辅音。）

4. manner

（辅音根据发音方式和发音部位进行分类。）

5. velar

（/k/是清音，软腭音，爆破音。）

6. Assimilation

（同化指一个音具有了邻近音的一部分或者全部特征的这一过程，包括鼻化、齿化、鄂化。）

7. force

（重音指在音节发音时所用的力度。）

8. minimal pairs

（如果有两个词，它们除了出现在同一位置上的一个音外，其余的音都一样，那么这两个词就构成了一个最小的对立体，所以 *fail-veil* 是最小对立体。）

9. diphthongs

（如果在发音时通过舌头的一次运动，由第一个单元音滑向第二个单元音，这样产生的音的组合就叫做双元音。）

10. allophones

（同一个音位在不同语音环境中的实现方式被称为该音位的音位变体。音位变体是互补分布的，而且发音相似。）

11. allophones
（语音的相似性指一个音位的音位变体必须具备某些语音相似性。）

Ⅱ. Multiple Choice

1. A （一般的音节由节首、节核和节尾构成，一个音节中可以没有节首或节尾，但一定有节核。）
2. C （在三大发音器官中，气流在口腔中受挤或转向从而产生不同的声音。）
3. A （/k/是清音，软腭音，爆破音；/t/是清音，齿龈音，爆破音；/g/是浊音，软腭音，爆破音，/p/是清音双唇音，爆破音。）
4. A （/s/是清音，摩擦音，齿龈音。）
5. D （/a/是低元音，后元音，紧元音。）
6. C （划分辅音的两个根据是发音位置和发音方式。）
7. D （A、B、C 都是摩擦音，但 D 是爆破音。）
8. A （能够用一个音区别意义的两个词叫做最小的对立体。A 需要两个音来区分，不是最小对立体。）
9. A （在音节中，节核通常由元音来担当。）
10. D （bilabial 是根据发音部位划分的。）
11. C （英音和美音最大的区别就是发音和词汇，比如发音方面，美音有儿化音。）
12. A （[m]，[b]，[p]都是双唇音，[n]是齿龈音。）
13. A （一个音节(syllable)可以分成两个部分，韵基(rhyme)和节首(onset)。韵基中的元音是核心，它后面的辅音用术语韵尾(coda)来表示。）

Ⅲ. True or False

1. F （在发音过程中，发音时声带不振动，这样所发出的音叫做清音。）
2. F （在三大发音腔中，口腔是在发音中最灵活的。）
3. T （英语辅音可分为清辅音和浊辅音。）
4. F （双唇音是由上唇和下唇接触，使语流受阻而构成的一种辅音。）
5. T （音段可分为元音和辅音。）
6. T （小舌音是由舌后部与小舌共同作用产生的音。）
7. F （音节中必不可少的就是节核，即元音，节首和节尾可有可无。）
8. F （感知语音学(或听觉语音学)研究语音的感知。）
9. F （同一个音位的不同变体在语音组合中不区别意义，并且出现在不同的语音环境中，那么它们就被称作处于互补分布。）
10. F （我们所听见和说出的声音并不总是音位，有可能是音素，只有那些能区别意义的才是音位。）
11. T （自由变体是指两个音素出现在一个相同的语音环境中，并不区别意义，即用一个音素替换另一个音素不产生新词，只产生同一个词的不同读音。）
12. F 音节的数量和音素的数量并没有直接关系。音节的数量取决于节核的数量。

Ⅳ. Explain the following terms.

1. Glottal Stop: Vocal tract is composed of oral cavity, nasal cavity and pharynx. When the vocal folds are totally closed, no air can pass between them. The result of this gesture is the glottal stop.

2. When the vocal folds are apart, the air can pass through easily and the sound produced is said to be voiceless. For example, consonants (p, s, t) are produced this way, so they are voiceless consonants. "Voiceless" is defined in contrast to "voiced". Consonants (b, z, d) are voiced consonants.
3. Minimal Pairs refers two words that can be distinguished by only by one sound. For example, the English words "bear" and "pear" constitute a minimal pair as they differ in meaning and in their initial phonemes /b/ and /p/.
4. Phoneme is a basic unit of phonology research, and it is an abstract collection of a set of phonetic features, which has the function of distinguish meaning. For example, in English, /p/ is described as a phoneme.
5. If two or more phonemes occur in the same position without distinguishing their meanings, then these two phonemes can be regarded as free variation. For example, the final consonant of *cup* may not be released by some speakers, so there is no audible sound at the end of this word. In this case, it is the same word pronounced in two different ways: (k^{h}ʌp^h) and (k^{h}ʌp˺). (The diacritic "˺" indicates "no audible release" in IPA symbols.)
6. The way that sounds belonging to one word or one syllable can cause changes in sounds belonging to neighboring words or syllables is called assimilation. For example, in "mink", "n", which is originally pronounced as /n/, will be velarized by the following "k" /k/, and therefore the word will be pronounced as /miŋk/
7. Suprasegmental features refers to the features that are broader than the segment level and can distinguish meaning. The principal suprasegmental features are stress, tone and intonation.
8. Syllable: These units, which are often longer than one sound and smaller than a whole word, are called syllables. For example, the English word *beautiful* consists of three speech units: beau-ti-ful.
9. When two sounds never occur in the same environment, they are in complementary distribution. For example, the aspirated English stops never occur after (s), and the unaspirated ones never occur initially. Allophones of the same phoneme are usually in complementary distribution. The allophones of /p/, for instance, are also in complementary distribution. The unaspirated (p) occurs after /s/, while the aspirated (p^h) occurs in all other environments except after /s/.
10. When we try to symbolize all the possible speech sounds, including even the minutest shades of pronunciation, it is called narrow transcription. In narrow transcription, there are diacritics added to the one letter symbols to show the finer differences between sounds.

V. Short answer questions

1. Acoustic phonetics is a technical area of linguistics. It is the study of sound waves made by the human vocal organs for communication.
2. The pharynx, the mouth and the nose are the three parts of the vocal organs.
3. (1) labiodental (2) nasal
4. Usually, the description of the vowels needs to fulfill four basic requirements:
   (1) The height of tongue raising (high, mid, low);
   (2) The position of the highest part of the tongue (front, central, back);

(3) The length or tenseness of the vowel (tense vs. lax or long vs. short);

(4) lip-rounding (rounded vs. unrounded).

5. Suprasegmental features refers to the features that are broader than the segment level and can distinguish meaning. The principal suprasegmental features are stress, tone and intonation. The location of stress in English distinguishes meaning.

For example, a shift of stress may change the part of speech of a word from a noun to a verb although its spelling remains unchanged. Tones are pitch variations, which are caused by the differing rates of vibration of the vocal cords. Pitch variations can distinguish meaning just like phonemes. When pitch, stress and sound length are tied to the sentence rather than the word in isolation, they are collectively known as intonation. Intonation plays an important role in the conveyance of meaning in almost every language, especially in a language like English.

6. Assimilation is a process by which one sound takes on some or all the characteristics of a neighbouring sound. It is often used synonymously with coarticulation. Nasalization, dentalization and velarization are all instances of assimilation. There are two possibilities of assimilation: if a following sound is influencing a preceding sound, it is regressive assimilation; the converse process, in which a preceding sound is influencing a following sound, is known as progressive assimilation.

7. (1) The two phonetic forms are: [ni] and [li].

(2) The underlying form is [ni].

(3) [ni] → [ni] / [– vowel] ________

[ni] → [li] / [+ vowel, -u] ________

In the word sungo, the last sound [o] is vowel, so -ing form of the word is sungoli. While the last sound of the word dumu is [u], which is quite an exception, the -ing form of the word is dumuni.

8. (1) corpora —/'kɔ: pərə/

(2) sociologist—/səusi'ɔlədʒist/

(3) Chef—/ʃef/

(4) debris—/də'bri: /

(5) nasal—/'neizəl/

(6) embedding—/im'bediŋ/

(7) antonymy—/'æntɔnəmi/

(8) facial—/'feiʃəl/

(9) annotated—/'ænəuteitid/

(10) phonetics—/fəu'netiks/

9. In English, there is a rule that /p/ is unaspirated after /s/ but aspirated in other places. So /p/ in "pat" and "tap" is aspirated but unaspirated in "spat" since it is after /s/. To bring out the phonetic difference, an aspirated sound is transcribed with a raised "h" after the symbol of the sound. So a phonetic transcription for "peak" is [p^hi: k] and that for "speak" is [spi: k]. So [p, p^h] are two different phones and are variants of the phoneme /p/. Such variants of a phoneme are called allophones of the same phoneme. The allophones are said to be in comple-

mentary distribution because they never occur in the same context: [p] occurs after [s] while [p^h] occurs in other places. We can present this rule as:

/p/ → [p] / [s]__________

[p^h] elsewhere

(note: __________ is the position in which /p/ appears)

In addition, sometimes a phoneme may also have free variants. Some speakers may not realize the final consonant of tap so there is no audible sound at the end of this word. Such phenomenon is called free variation.

10. As the vowels can not be described in the same way as the consonants, a system of cardinal vowels has been suggested to get out of this problem. The cardinal vowels are a set of vowel qualities arbitrarily defined, fixed and unchanging, intended to provide a frame of reference for the description of the actual vowels of existing languages. The cardinal vowels are abstract concept. The cardinal vowel diagram is a set of hypothetical positions for vowels used as reference points.

    The description of English vowels needs to fulfill four basic requirements: (1) the height of tongue raising (high, middle or low); (2) the position of the highest part of the tongue (front, central, back); (3) the length or tenseness of the vowel (tense vs. lax or long vs. short); (4) lip-rounding (rounded vs. unrounded). For example,

    [i:]: high, front, tense, unrounded vowel.

    [u]: high, back, lax, rounded vowel.

Ⅵ. Essay questions

1. Voiceless sounds refers to those sounds pronounced in the way that the vocal cords do not vibrate during the pronunciation process, to be specific, the vocal cords are spread apart, the air from the lungs passes between them unimpeded, consonants (p, s, t) are produced in this way; but when the vocal cords are drawn together, the airstream forces its way through and causes them to vibrate, such sounds produced in this way are described as voiced (b, z, d) are voiced consonants.

2. Suprasegmental features refers to the features that are broader than the segment level and can distinguish meaning. They are the phonological properties of such units as the syllable, the word, and the sentence. The principal suprasegmental features are stress, tone and intonation.

    The syllable refers to the phonological unit that is composed of one or more phonemes. Every syllable has a nucleus, which is usually a vowel. The nucleus may be preceded by one or more consonants called the onset and followed by one or more consonants called the coda.

    Stress refers to a certain syllable in a word or certain syllables in a sentence that are read more heavily and stronger. For words of more than one syllable, one is more stressed than the other. The more stressed syllable is the primary stress while the less stressed syllable is known as the secondary stress.

    Tones are pitch variations, which are caused by the differing rates of vibration of the vocal cords. Different rates of vibration produce what is known as different frequencies, and in auditory terms as different pitches. Pitch variations may be distinctive like phoneme, that is, when they may contribute to distinguish between different words.

When pitch, stress and sound length are tied to the sentence rather than the word in isolation, they are collectively known as intonation. When we speak, we change the pitch of our voice to express ideas. The same sentence uttered with different intonation may express different attitudes of the speaker. In English, there are four intonation patterns: the falling tone, the rising tone, the fall-rise tone, and the rise-fall tone.

3. Tones are pitch variations, which are caused by the differing rates of vibration of the vocal cords. Pitch variations can distinguish meaning just like phonemes; therefore, the tone is a suprasegmental feature. The meaning-distinctive function of the tone is especially important in what we call tone languages. English is not a tone language. Chinese is a typical tone language. It has four tones. The first tone is level(阴平), the second rise(阳平), the third fall rise(上声), and the fourth fall(去声). The role of the tone can be well illustrated by pronouncing the same sound combination such as [ba] in the four different tones and have different meanings:

bā(八)	High level	'eight'
bá(拔)	High rising	'pull out'
bǎ(靶)	Low falling rising	'target'
bà(坝)	High falling	'dam'

(考查汉语为声调语言，在解释时一定要举例子说明声调是如何改变意义的。)

第 3 章　形态学

3.1　复习笔记

本章要点：

1. Definition of Morphology
   形态学的定义
2. Definition and Classification of Morphemes
   语素的定义及分类
3. Morphs and Allomorphs
   形素与语素变体
4. Types of Word Formation
   词语构成的分类

常考考点：

词法的定义；屈折词与派生词；构词法(合成与派生)；语素的定义；语素变体；自由语素；粘着语素(词根，词缀和词干)。

本章内容索引：

Ⅰ. Morphology

Definition of Morphology

Ⅱ. Morphemes

1. Definition
2. Types of Morphemes
   (1) Free morpheme
   (2) Bound morpheme

Ⅲ. Morphs and Allomorphs

Definition of Morphs and Allomorphs

Ⅳ. Types of Word Formation

1. Compounding
2. Derivation
3. Other ways of word formation
   (1) Conversion
   (2) Backformation
   (3) Clipping
   (4) Blending
   (5) Acronym
   (6) Initialism

Ⅰ. Morphology

【考点：名词解释】

Morphology is a branch of linguistics which studies the internal structure of words, and the rules by which words are formed, including inflection and word formation.

Ⅱ. Morpheme

1. Definition

Morpheme is the basic unit in the study of morphology. It is the smallest unit of language that carries information about meaning or function. A morpheme is neither a meaning nor a stretch of sound, but a meaning and a stretch of sound joined together.

2. Types of Morphemes

(1) Free morpheme

【考点：名词解释】

① Free morpheme is an element of meaning which takes the form of an independent word. All monomorphemes belong to free morphemes and polymorphemic words, which are made up of free morphemes, are compounds.

② A word must contain a free morpheme which can constitute a word by it self, such as "talk". Root is used to refer to such this free morpheme. Root is the core of the word as it carries the major component of its meaning. A word may contain more than one root.

③ When free morphemes are combined with bound morphemes, the basic word form is known as the stem. Affixes can be added to the stem.

④ There are two categories of free morphemes. The first is a set of nouns, verbs, and adjectives that bear the main information. They are called lexical morphemes. They are also called open class words since we can regularly add new words to these classes.

⑤ The second category contains functional morphemes. A functional morpheme is a morpheme which simply modifies the meaning of a word, rather than supplying the root meaning. Functional morphemes are generally considered closed-class words, which means that new functional morphemes cannot normally be created.

Ⅰ. 形态学

形态学是语言学的一个分支，研究词的内部结构以及构词规则，它包括屈折变化和构词法两个领域。

Ⅱ. 语素

1. 定义

语素是形态学研究的基本单位。它是承载意义或功能信息的最小语言单位。语素既不是意思也不是语音，而是意思和语音的结合。

2. 语素的类型

(1) 自由语素

① 自由语素指能够单独出现或独立成词的语素。所有的单语素词都是自由语素，由自由语素构成的多语素词为复合词。

② 词根指词汇中能单独成词的自由语素。词根是词汇的核心，它承载着词汇的主要意义。一个词可以包含多个词根。

③ 词干指当自由语素和粘着语素连用时最基本的部分。词缀可以加在词干上。

④ 自由语素分为两类。一类是表达实义的名词，动词和形容词。它们被称作词汇语素。它们也被称为开放式词汇，因为我们可以定期地向这些类中添加新词汇。

⑤ 第二类叫做功能语素。功能语素是修饰一个词的意义，而不是提供词根意义的语素。功能语素通常被认为是一个封闭式词汇，这意味着新的功能语素几乎无法产生。

(2) Bound morphemes 【考点：名词解释】 ①Bound morpheme is one that cannot occur on its own as a separated word. It must be attached to another one to form word. E. g. , -s, -er, -ed and -ing. ②All affixes are bound morphemes. Affixes added to the beginning of the root or stem are called prefixes. Prefixes can change the meaning or grammatical class of words. ③Affixes may also be attached to the end of a root or stem, in which case they are referred to as suffixes. Suffixes may also alter a word's context or purpose. ④Bound morphemes can be divided into two categories. The first category is derivational morphemes. Derivational morphemes, when combined with a root, change the semantic meaning or the part of speech of the affected word. ⑤The other category is inflectional morphemes. Inflectional morphemes are purely grammatical markers to indicate grammatical relations.	**(2) 粘着语素** ① 一些语素不能够单独成词，但会起到一定的功能作用。这种语素叫做粘着语素。 ② 粘着语素相当于词缀。英语中所有的词缀都是粘着的。附着在词根或词干前面的词缀叫做前缀，前缀可以改变词义或词语功能。 ③ 词缀还可以放到词根或词干的后边，形成后缀，后缀也可以改变词义或功能。 ④ 粘着语素可以分为两类。一类叫做派生语素。派生语素指与一个词根结合，能改变语义意义或影响词的词性的语素。 ⑤ 另一类叫做屈折语素。屈折语素是表示语法关系的纯语法标记。
Ⅲ. Morphs and Allomorphs Morphs are the phonetic realizations of morphemes in general. Allomorphs are the variant realizations of a particular morpheme in different environments.	**Ⅲ. 形素和语素变体** 形素是语素的语音实现。 语素变体指一个语素在不同环境下的变体实现。
Ⅳ. Types of Word Formation 【考点：词的形成方法】 **1. Compounding** Compounding is the process of combining two free morphemes to produce new words known as compounds. Compounds have strict patterns. Stress of the compound always fall on the first element, and the grammatical category of the compound will be determined by the final word.	**Ⅳ. 构词法** **1. 复合** 复合是指将两个自由语素组合成一个复合词的过程。复合词有严格的形式。复合词的重音在前一部分，但词义通常由最终部分决定。
2. Derivation Derivation refers to the process that new words are formed by the addition of affixes to other words or morphemes. Different from a compound, at least a free morpheme and a bound morpheme must be contained in a derivational word.	**2. 派生** 派生是指将词缀加到其他词或语素上形成新词的过程。和复合词不同的是，派生词至少包含一个自由语素和一个粘着语素。
3. Other ways of word formation **① Conversion** Conversion refers to the process of changing or converting the class of a word without changing its form. Conversion is also called zero derivation.	**3. 其他构词法** **① 转类构词法** 转类构词法是指在不改变单词形式的情况下改变或转换单词的类的过程。转类构词法又叫做零派生。

Conversion is also called zero derivation.

② **Back-formation**

New words may be coined by removing its suffix. For example, as we have "beggar", we get "beg" by removing "gar". This process is called back-formation.

③ **Clipping**

Clipping is a term used to describe the process of removing parts of a word. Clipping occurs when a multi-syllabic word is simplified to a shorter form. Clipped words often seen in casual speech. E. g, gym = gymnasium, burger = hamburger.

④ **Blending**

Blending is the process of combining parts of other words to form a new word. Typically, blending is usually completed by taking just the beginning of one word and attaching it to the end of another. E. g, smog = smoke + fog, motel = motor + hotel.

⑤ **Acronym**

An acronym is a word or name formed from the initial letters of several words. They are pronounced as a single word. Words of this kind such as APEC, AIDS are called acronyms.

⑥ **Initialism**

Initialism are words made up of the first letters of a sequence of words and are pronounced one by one. E. g, WHO = World Health Organization, WTO = World Trade Organization.

转类构词法又叫做零派生。

② **逆向构词法**

有些时候我们可以通过去除后缀来得到新词，这个过程叫做逆向构词法。

③ **截短构词法**

把词语的一部分省略掉叫做截短构词法。多音节词汇变成形式较短的词汇，这种形式通常出现在非正式用语中。例如 gym = gymnasium, burger = hamburger。

④ **混成构词法**

混成构词法指将其他单词的部分组合成一个新词的过程。通常，混成构词法是结合了一个单词的开头和另一个单词的结尾。例如，smog = smoke + fog, motel = motor + hotel。

⑤**首字母拼音词**

通过几个单词的首字母结合而成的单词叫做首字母拼音词。这类词可以以词的形式发音。例如，APEC, AIDS。

⑥ **首字母拼写词**

首字母拼写词由几个单词的首字母组成，要以单个字母来发音。例如，WHO = World Health Organization, WTO = World Trade Organization。

3.2 课后习题详解

1. Define the following terms briefly.

   morphology　　morpheme　　free morpheme　　bound morpheme
   morph　　allomorph　　derivation　　clipping　　acronym
   initialism　　blending　　root　　stem　　prefix　　suffix

2. Which of the following forms are possible words of English?

   (1) mbood　　(2) coofp　　(3) sproke　　(4) worpz
   (5) frail　　(6) ktleem　　(7) fluke　　(8) bsarn

3. Consider the following words and finish two tasks:

   (1) For each word, determine whether it is simple or compound.
   (2) Circle all of the bound morphemes. Underline all of the roots.

   fly　　reuse　　spiteful　　preplan

desks	triumphed	suite	optionality
untie	delight	fastest	prettier
tree	justly	deform	mistreat
dislike	payment	disobey	premature

4. Each of the following columns illustrates a different morphological process.

Column I	Column II	Column III
mouse/mice	go/went	're cord/re'cord
ride/rode	is/was	'import/im'port
take/took	good/better	'convict/con'vict
man/men	she/her	'imprint/im'print
eat/ate	am/are	'dispute/dis'pute

(1) What morphological process is at work in each column?

(2) Describe in your own words the difference between the process exemplified in Column I and that in Column II.

(3) Think of at least one more English example to add to each column.

5. Each of the following words can be either a noun or a verb.

record	outline	report
journey	convict	outrage
exchange	imprint	answer
remark	contest	import
surprise	retreat	cripple

(1) For each word, determine whether stress placement can be used to make the distinction between the noun and the verb.

(2) Think of two more English examples illustrating the process of stress shift to mark a category distinction.

6. In English, the suffix -er can be added to a place name. Examine the words in the two columns below.

Column A	Column B
Londoner	Glasgower
New Yorker	Denverer
Berliner	Sydneyer
Dubkiner	Australiaer
Newfoundlander	Victoriaer
Winnipeger	Calcuttaer
New Zealander	Bristoler

(1) In general terms, what does the suffix *-er* mean in these words?

(2) How is this *-er* different in meaning from the *-er* found in the words skater and walker?

(3) State the constraint on the distribution of *-er* illustrated above in your own words.

(4) Does this constraint also apply to the type of *-er* used in the word *skater*? (Hint: What would you call "one who discovers" or "one who ploughs"?)

7. Determine whether the words in each of the following groups are related to one another by processes of inflection or derivation.

(1) go, goes, going, gone

(2) discover, discovery, discoverer, discoverable, discoverability

(3) lovely, lovelier, loveliest

(4) inventor, inventor's, inventors, inventors'

(5) democracy, democrat, democratic, democratize

参考答案

1. **Morphology**: Morphology studies the internal structure of words, and the rules by which words are formed, including inflection and word formation.

Morpheme: Morpheme is the basic unit in the study of morphology. It is the smallest unit of language that carries information about meaning or function. A morpheme is neither a meaning nor a stretch of sound, but a meaning and a stretch of sound joined together.

Free morpheme: Free morpheme is an element of meaning which takes the form of an independent word. There are two kinds of free morphemes: lexical morphemes or functional morphemes.

Bound morpheme: Bound morpheme is one that cannot occur on its own as a separated word. It must be attached to another one to form word. E. g. , -s, -er, -ed and -ing. Bound morpheme can be sorted into derivational morphemes and inflectional morphemes.

Morph: Morphs are the phonetic realizations of morphemes in general, i. e. , the minimum carrier of meaning is morph, which realize the morpheme phonologically and orthographically.

Allomorph: Depending on the context, certain morphemes can be realized by more than one morph, and all of these morphs are called allomorphs of the morpheme. Allomorphs are the variant realizations of a particular morpheme in different environments.

Derivation: Derivation refers to the process that new words are formed by the addition of affixes to other words or morphemes. Different from a compound, a derivational word consists of at least a free morpheme and a bound morpheme must be contained in a derivational word.

Clipping: Clipping is a term used to describe the process of removing parts of a word. Clipping occurs when a multi-syllabic word is simplified to a shorter form. Clipped words often seen in casual speech. E. g, gym = gymnasium, burger = hamburger.

Acronym: An acronym is a word or name formed from the initial letters of several words. They are pronounced as a single word. Words of this kind such as APEC, AIDS are called acronyms.

Initialism: Initialism are words made up of the first letters of a sequence of words and are pronounced one by one. E. g, WHO = World Health Organization, WTO = World Trade Organization.

Blending: Blending is the process of combining parts of other words to form a new word. Typically, blending is usually completed by taking just the beginning of one word and attaching it to the end of another. E. g, smog = smoke + fog, motel = motor + hotel.

Root: A word must contain a free morpheme which can constitute a word by it self, such as "talk". Root is used to refer to such this free morpheme. Root is the core of the word as it carries the major component of its meaning. A word may contain more than one root, e. g. "systematically" from "un-" + "system" + "-atic" + "-ally".

Stem: When free morphemes are combined with bound morphemes, the basic word form is known as the stem. Affixes can be added to the stem.

Prefix: Affixes added to the beginning of the root or stem are called prefixes. Prefixes can change the meaning or grammatical class of words.

Suffix: Affixes may also be attached to the end of a root or stem in which case they are referred to as suffixes. Suffixes may also alter a word's context or purpose.

2. The possible English words are (3) sproke, (5) frall, (7) fluke.

3. (1) **Simple words**: fly, suite, tree.

   Compound words: reuse, spiteful, preplan, desks, triumphed, optionality, untie, delight, fastest, prettier, justly, deform, mistreat, dislike, payment, disobey, premature.

   (2) **Bound morphemes**: re-, -ful, pre-, -s, -ed, -al, -ity, un-, de-, -est, -er, -ly, de-, mis-, dis-, -ment.

   Roots: fly, use, spite, plan, desk, triumph, suite, option, tie, light, fast, pretty, tree, just, form, treat, like, pay, obey, mature.

4. (1) Morphological process:

   column Ⅰ: Ablaut or Umlaut

   column Ⅱ: Suppletion

   column Ⅲ: Stress Modification

   (2) Ablaut and Umlaut refer to vowel alternations in morphological process. In each pair of words, the nucleus changed conditioned by different inflectional morphemes, for example: mouse/mice (number), ride/rode (tense).

   As for the case of column Ⅱ, total modification is involved. Its occurrence is by its nature idiosyncratic within inflectional categories established by regular processes. For example, the regular form for English past tense is -ed, but the past form of *go* is *went*; and the normal comparative form for adjectives is -er, but the comparative form of *good* is *better*. It is like the creation of a new word totally.

   (3) More examples:

   column Ⅰ: goose/geese draw/drew

   column Ⅱ: we/us bad/worse

   column Ⅲ: 'content/con'tent 'export/ex'port

5. (1) For all of the following words, stress placement can be used to make the distinction between the noun and the verb.

   'record n. / re'cord v. 'convict n. /con'vict v. 'contest n. /con'test v.

   While for the following words, stress placement cannot be used to make the distinction between the noun and the verb.

   outline, report, journey, outrage, exchange, imprint, answer, remark, import, surprise, retreat, cripple.

   (2) More examples: 'increase n. /in'crease v.

'protest n. /pro'test v.

6. (1) "-er" means the residents of a place.

   (2) "-er" added to a place name like "Londoner" means the residents of a place; while "-er" added to a verb such as "skater", "walker" means the doer of an action.

   (3) "-er" can be added to a place name only when the pronunciation of that place ends with a consonant like [k], [n], [d] and [g]. If it ends with a vowel, it can not be modified by an "-er".

   (4) However, such constraint sometimes applies to the type of "-er" used in the word *skater*, that is, the kind of "-ed" used after a verb, and sometimes not. For example, the verb *discover* ends with a central vowel /ə:/, but we still use "discoverer" to call one who discovers; the verb *plough* ends with a back vowel /ɔ/, and we use the word "ploughman" to call one who ploughs.

7. (1) inflection: go-goes(number & tense); go-going-gone(tense)

   (2) derivation

   (3) inflection: lovely-lovelier(comparative)-loveliest(superlative)

   (4) inflection: inventor-inventor's(case); inventor-inventors(number); inventors-inventors'(case)

   (5) derivation

3.3 考研真题与典型题详解

Ⅰ. Fill in the blanks.

1. The ________ is the minimal distinctive unit in grammar, a unit which cannot be divided without destroying or drastically altering the meaning, whether lexical or grammatical. (北二外2008研)

2. Some morphemes like *-ish*, *-ness*, *-ly*, *-dis*, *trans-*, *un-* are never words by themselves but are always parts of words. These affixes are ________ morphemes.

3. There are two fields of morphology: the study of ________ and the study of ________. (人大2006研)

4. ________ is a branch of linguistics that studies the interrelationship between phonology and morphology. (南开大学2007研)

5. ________is a relatively complex form of compounding in which a new word is formed by joining the initial part of one word and the final part of another word. For example, the English word smog is made from ________ and ________. (人大2006研)

6. An ________ is pronounced letter by letter, while an ________ is pronounced as a word.

7. Words are divided into simple, compound and derived words on the ________ level.

8. Morphology studies the ________ structure of words and the rules by which words are formed. (暨南大学2018研)

Ⅱ. Multiple Choice

1. ________ other than compounds may be divided into roots and affixes. (大连外国语学院2008研)

A. Polymorphemic words　　B. Bound morphemes

C. Free morphemes

2. ________ refers to the way in which a particular verb changes for tense, person, or number.（西安外国语学院 2006 研）

A. Affixation　　B. Inflection　　C. Derivation　　D. Conjugation

3. Compound words consist of ________ morphemes.（北二外 2003 研）

A. bound　　B. free　　C. both bound and free

4. Which of the following words is formed by the process of blending?（对外经贸 2006 研）

A. WTO　　B. Motel　　C. Bookshelf　　D. red-faced

5. Bound morphemes do not include ________.（西安交大 2008 研）

A. roots　　B. prefixes　　C. suffixes　　D. words

6. Which two terms can best describe the following pairs of words: table—tables, day + break—daybreak.（大连外国语学院 2008 研）

A. inflection and compound　　B. compound and derivation

C. inflection and derivation

7. Point out which item does not fall under the same category as the rest, and explain the reason in ONE sentence.（Focus on the type of word formation）（南京大学 2007 研）

A. burgle　　B. fridge　　C. auto　　D. math

8. There are different types of affixes or morphemes. The affix "-ed" in the word "learned" is known as a(n) ________.

A. derivational morpheme　　B. free morpheme

C. inflectional morpheme　　D. free form

9. Morphemes can be classified into ________ and ________ in terms of their capacity of occurring alone .（长沙理工大学 2019 研）

A. simple, compound morphemes　　B. single, double morphemes

C. internal, external morphemes　　D. free, bound morphemes

Ⅲ. True or False

1. Some linguists maintain that a word group is an extension of word of a particular class.（清华 2001 研）

2. Words are the most stable of all linguistic units in respect of their internal structure.（大连外国语学院 2008 研）

3. The words "loose" and "books" have a common phoneme and a common morpheme as well.（北二外 2007 研）

4. Free morpheme may constitute words by themselves.（大连外国语学院 2008 研）

5. All words contain a root morpheme.（北二外 2006 研）

6. Root also falls into two categories: free and bound.（北二外 2006 研）

7. The word of "impossibility" contains four morphemes.（对外经贸 2006 研）

8. We can always tell by the words a compound contains what it means because the meaning of a compound is always the sum of the meanings of its parts.

9. All roots are free and all affixes are bound.

Ⅳ. Explain the following terms.

1. morpheme（四川大学 2006 研；武汉大学 2008 研）
2. inflectional morpheme（南开大学 2004 研）
3. free morphemes（西安交大 2008 研）
4. bound morpheme（上海交大 2007 研）
5. bound root（四川大学 2006 研）
6. functional morpheme（上海交大 2005 研）
7. inflection（四川大学 2007 研）
8. allomorph（四川大学 2006 研；暨南大学 2018 研）
9. blending（四川大学 2008 研）
10. acronym（北航 2010 研）

Ⅴ. Short answer questions

1. Complete the words with suitable negative prefixes.（四川大学 2007 研）

   (1) rational
   (2) moral
   (3) regular
   (4) political
   (5) effective
   (6) human
   (7) relevant
   (8) legal
   (9) proportionate
   (10) resistible

2. (a) List the 'bound' morphemes to be found in the following words:

   misleads, shortened, unhappier, fearlessly

   (b) In which of the following examples should the 'a' be treated as a bound morpheme:

   a boy, apple, atypical, AWOL（上海交大 2005 研）

3. In English, the suffix "-able" as in "X + able" means "able to be X-ed." (1) Use an example to illustrate this rule. (2) What kind of words can function as "X"? (3) In words like "unthinkable," the suffix-able means more than "able to be X-ed." Think of TWO more words of this type. （南京大学 2007 研）

4. What can this rule mean in English grammar?

   {D} →(-id)/(t) —（北师大 2004 研）

5. What are phonologically conditioned and morphologically conditioned form of morphemes?

6. Analyze the morphemic structure of the English words *gentlemanliness* and *unlockable*, using a labeled tree diagram to illustrate the morphemic structure of the word under analysis.

   (1) *gentlemanliness* (2) *unlockable*

Ⅵ. Essay questions

1. What is the distinction between inflectional affixes and derivational affixes?（四川大学 2007 研）
2. How are affixes classified?（四川大学 2008 研）

3. In what way do we say English is an inflectional language?（厦门大学 2006 研）
4. Illustrate lexical change proper with the latest examples in English, covering at least four aspects.（大连外国语学院 2008 研）

参考答案及解析

Ⅰ. Fill in the blanks.

1. morpheme
（语素是最小的语言单位，不能再进一步分成更小的单位而不破坏或彻底改变词汇意义或语法意义。）
2. bound
（粘着语素指不能单独出现，必须跟至少一个其他语素共同出现的语素。）
3. inflections; word-formation
（在形态学中，有两大主要研究方面，一是词的屈折变化，一是词的派生。）
4. Morphophonology
（形态音系学是语言学的一个分支，主要研究形态学与音系学的关系。）
5. Blending
（混成构词法是指一个词由两个单词混合而成，一般把第一个单词的开头部分和第二个单词的最后部分连接起来，或者是把两个单词的开头部分连接起来。）
6. initialism; acronym
（首字母拼写词和首字母拼音词的区别在于，前者是一个一个字母读，后者是按单词读。）
7. morphemic
（从语素的角度来讲，词可以划分为简单词、合成词和派生词。）
8. internal
（形态学研究词的内部结构和构词规则。）

Ⅱ. Multiple Choice

1. A （多语素词可被分为词根和词缀，而合成词是不可以被这样分的。）
2. B （屈折变化是通过附加屈折词缀表现语法关系，如数、人称、有定性、体和格。它并不改变所附加词干的语法类别。）
3. B （合成词是由自由语素组合而成的。）
4. B （混成构词法是指一个词由两个单词混合而成，一般把第一个单词的开头部分和第二个单词的最后部分连接起来，或者是把两个单词的开头部分连接起来。Motel 是由 motor 与 hotel 二词的缩合。）
5. D （粘着语素指不能单独出现，必须跟至少一个其他语素共同出现的语素。词根与词缀都可能是粘着词素。）
6. A （屈折变化是通过附加屈折词缀表现语法关系，如 tables。合成词是由词根语素按一定的规则组合起来构成的，如 daybreak。）
7. A （是逆向构词法变来的，其他的是截短构词法变来的。）
8. C （-ed 在 learned 中改变了 learn 的时态，故为屈折变化。）
9. D （根据是否能够单独出现或独立成词，语素（morpheme）分为自由语素（free morphemes）

和粘着语素(bound morphemes)。)

Ⅲ. True or False

1. T （词组是指一组具有一定词性的词的组合扩展，且此过程并不改变词原来的词性。）
2. T （具有词汇意义(指代物质、动作和性质)的词称为词汇词，例如名词、动词、形容词和副词。）
3. F （有共同的音位，但语素[s]在两个词中的意思不一样，前者没有任何意义，后者表示复数。）
4. T （自由语素指是能够单独出现或独立成词的语素。）
5. T （所有的词都必须有词根。）
6. T （词根是构成词的基础成分，它可以是自由语素或粘着语素。）
7. F （包括三个语素："im-""possibl-""-ity"。）
8. F （合成词的词义不一定是两个单词词义的简单相加，也可能是成为惯用语的其他意思。）
9. F （词根可分为自由词根和粘着词根，所以并不是所有的词根都是自由词根。）

Ⅳ. Explain the following terms.

1. Morpheme is the smallest unit of language in terms of relationship between expression and content, a unit that cannot be divided into further smaller units without destroying or drastically altering the meaning, whether it is lexical or grammatical. For example, in *boys*, there are two morphemes: "boy" and "-s"; in *international*, there are three morphemes: "inter-" "nation" and "-al".
2. Inflectional morpheme, also called inflectional affixes, attaches to the end of words. Inflectional affixes only add a minute or delicate grammatical meaning to the stem. The plural suffix is a typical example of this kind.
3. Free morpheme is an element of meaning which takes the form of an independent word. They may occur alone, that is, they may make up words by themselves. For example, "dog", "nation" and "close" are free morphemes. And such words are called mono-morphemic words. Thus, all mono-morphemic words are free morphemes.
4. Bound morphemes refer to those morphemes that can not occur alone and must appear with at least another morpheme. For example, in the word "careless", "-less" is a bound morpheme since it could not occur by itself as a word.
5. Bound root refers to the base form of a word that cannot further be analyzed without total loss of identity, and this base form could not occur alone, such as "-ceive" in "receive".
6. This is a subtype of free morphemes, which consists largely of the functional words in language such as conjunctions, prepositions, articles and pronouns, for example, "and, about, when on, near, the" and so on.
7. Inflection is the manifestation of grammatical relationship through the addition of inflectional affixes, such as number, person, finiteness, aspect and case, which do not change the grammatical class of the stems to which they are attached. For example, the past form of the verb *work* is realized by the addition of the inflectional suffix "-ed"; the plural form of the noun *child* is realized by the inflectional suffix "-ren".

8. Allomorph: A morpheme may take various shapes or forms, and an allomorph is any of the variant forms of a morpheme as conditioned by position or adjoining sounds. For instance, the morpheme of plurality {-s} has a number of allomorphs in different sound context, as in "cats" /s/, in "bags" /z/, in "matches" /iz/.
9. Blending is a relatively complex form of compounding, in which two words are blended by joining together the initial part of the first word and the final part of the second word, or by only join the initial parts of the two words. For example, telephone + exchange→ telex; transfer + resister → transistor.
10. An acronym is a word or name formed from the initial letters of several words. They are pronounced as a single word. NATO, UNESCO, AIDS, APEC are called acronyms.

V. Short answer questions

1. (1) rational: irrational
   (2) moral: immoral
   (3) regular: irregular
   (4) political: apolitical
   (5) effective: ineffective
   (6) human: inhuman
   (7) relevant: irrelevant
   (8) legal: illegal
   (9) proportionate: disproportionate
   (10) resistible: irresistible
2. (a) misleads: mis-, -s; shortened: -en, -ed;
   unhappier: un-, -er; fearlessly: -less, -ly
   (b) Among these examples, the "a" in "atypical" should be treated as a bound morpheme.
3. (1) *applicable*, which means "able to be applied".
   (2) The words that can function as "X" are probably verbs.
   (3) *unbelievable*, *undefeatable*.
4. This rule reveals two points: First, it shows one possible allomorph of the morpheme {D}, and this allomorph has the phone (-id) as its element; second, it shows the according phonetic environment in which that allomorph can occur, that is, it will be pronounced as (-id) when it appears after the phone (t). In this rule, the arrow means the realization, and the bar indicates the environment of the target element.
5. Some phonological factors can affect the appearance of morphemes, namely, the form of a morpheme; and there could be assimilation, and dissmilation. For example, the negative morpheme could be realized as "in-" or "im-" followed by different phonological environments, as in "inefficient" and "imperfect", as a result of assimilation.

   Morphemes can also be conditioned by morphological factors; for example, the allomorphs of the plural morpheme, as could be seen in "oxen", "cows", and "feet".

6. (1)

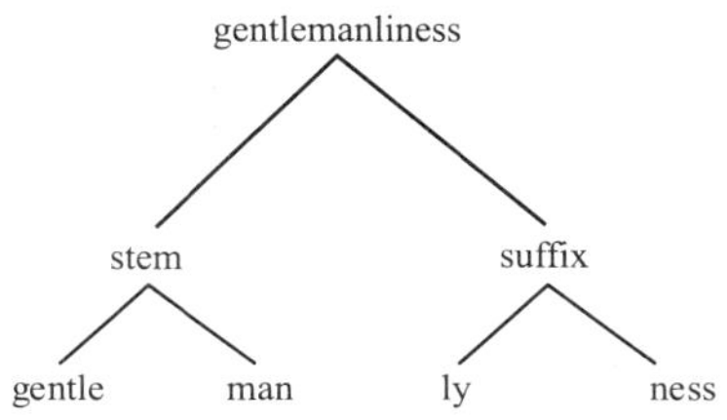

(2)

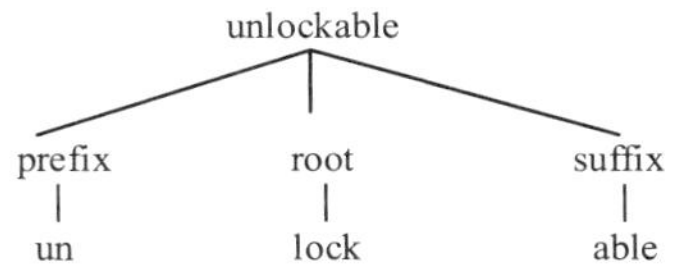

Ⅵ. Essay questions

1. The distinction between inflectional morphemes and derivational morphemes could be illustrated in the following four aspects.

   Inflectional affixes very often only add a minute or delicate grammatical meaning to the stem, for instance, those inflectional affixes in words such as *toys*, *walks*, *John's*, etc. Therefore, they serve to produce different forms of a single word. In contrast, derivational affixes often change the lexical meaning, *e. g. cite*, *citation*; *generate*, *generation.*

   Inflectional affixes do not change the word class of the word they attach to, such as *flower*, *flowers*; whereas derivational affixes might or might not, such as the relation between *small* and *smallness* for the former, and that between *brother* and *brotherhood* for the latter.

   Very often inflectional affixes are conditioned by non-semantic linguistic factors outside the word they attach to but within the phrase or sentence. Whereas derivational affixes are more often based on simple meaning distinctions.

   In English, inflectional affixes are mostly suffixes, which are always word final. But derivational affixes can be prefixes or suffixes.

2. Considering the free and bound morpheme, affix is the collective term for the type of formative that can be used only when added to another morpheme, so it is naturally bound.

   Depending on their position with reference to the root or stem of the word, affixes are generally classified into three subtypes, namely, prefix, suffix, and infix. For examples, "para-" as prefix, "-tion" as suffix, and "-bloomingly-" in word "abso-bloomingly-luty" as infix.

   Affix can also be classified depending on the distinction between inflectional affixes and derivational affixes. The former often only adds a minute grammatical function to the stem and do not change the word class of the word they attach to; while the latter are very productive in making new words and often change the lexical meaning. For instances, "-s" in words "toys", "walks" and "John's" is inflectional affixes, while "-tion" is a derivational affix in word "recitation".

   (本题考查词缀的种类。可以从两个角度对词缀进行分类：一种是前缀、中缀和后缀；另一种是屈折词缀和派生词缀。)

3. The inflectional language is a term as opposed to the isolated language, in which the morpheme has no inflected form; For exanple, in Chinese, there are only isolated characters, which can not be added to an inflectional affix. English is regarded as an inflectional language in the sense that

the inflectional affixer serves important grammatical function in the English vocabulary. In English, inflectional affixes indicating tense, numbers, case and so on. They usually manifestate the grammatical relationships between the elements of the sentences.

4. New words or expressions are created through the following processes except compound and derivation, which are called lexical change proper.

(1) Initialism

Some new words are composed of the first letters of a series of words and pronounced by saying each letter in them. Words of this kind such as VIP, WTO are called initialisms.

(2) Abbreviation

Many English words have come into being through abbreviation. This phenomenon is also called clipping: a new can be created by:

i. cutting the final part, for example, *ad* for *advertisement*.

ii. cutting the initial part, for example, *plane* for *aeroplane*.

iii. cutting both the initial and final parts accordingly, for instance, *fridge* for *refrigerator*.

(3) Blending is a relatively complex form of compounding, in which two words are blended by joining together the initial part of the first word and the final part of the second word, or by only joining the initial parts of the two words, for example, emotion + icon → emoticon; car + hijacking→carjacking.

(4) Acronym is made up from the first letters of the name of an organization, which has heavily modified headword; an example is *EU* for *European Union*. This process is also widely used in shortening extremely long words of word groups in science, technology and other special fields, for example, *SARS* is short for "Severe Acute Respiratory Syndrome". What's more, people also use this process in internet chatting or e-mail communication, such as *BTW* for "by the way", *ASAP* for "as soon as possible".

(本题考查特有的词汇变化。作答时任选四个进行描述，并举例说明。)

第4章　句法

4.1　复习笔记

本章要点：

1. Prescriptive approach and descriptive approach
   规定法和描述法
2. Immediate constituent analysis
   直接成分分析
3. Constituent structure grammar
   成分结构语法
4. The "Standard Theory"
   标准理论
5. Transformational grammar
   转化语法
6. Systemic-functional grammar
   系统功能语法

常考考点：

句法的定义；词类；乔姆斯基的经典理论；标准理论；深层结构；表层结构；成分；直接成分分析法的定义；句子成分；用实例进行分析，用直接成分分析法以及树形图分析句子的结构等。

本章内容索引：

Ⅰ. Syntax

1. Definition
2. Word Classes

Ⅱ. Two Approaches

1. The Prescriptive Approach
2. The Descriptive Approach

Ⅲ. Structural Analysis

1. The Constituent structure grammar
2. Immediate constituent analysis
   (1) Definition
   (2) Advantages
   (3) Problems

Ⅳ. The Transformational Grammar

1. Chomsky's Classical Theory
2. The "Standard Theory"

(1) Deep structure and surface structure

(2) The "standard theory"

3. Syntactic Movement

(1) NP-movement

(2) Wh-movement

(3) Aux-movement

4. Move-α rule

V. Systemic-Functional Grammar

1. General Account

2. Three General Functions of Language

Ⅰ. Syntax

【考点：名词解释】

1. Definition

Syntax is a branch of linguistics. It studies the rules that govern the ways in which words are combined to form phrases, clauses, and sentences.

2. Word Classes

The general word classes include: nouns, adjectives, verbs, adverbs, prepositions, pronouns and conjunctions.

Ⅱ. Two Approaches

1. The Prescriptive Approach

Some grammarians, mostly in eighteenth-century England, took a prescriptive approach to analyze grammar. Prescriptive linguistics attempts to establish rules defining correct usage of language. These rules may emphasize things such as spelling, pronunciation, vocabulary, syntax, and semantics.

2. The Descriptive Approach

Modern linguistics adapt the descriptive approach which objectively analyze and describe how language is actually used. It is believed that whatever occurs in the language people actually use should be described and analyzed. The descriptive approach emerged in the 20th century.

Ⅲ. Structural Analysis

【考点：名词解释】

It investigates the distribution of linguistic forms in a given language. "Test-frames," which may be sentences with empty slots, are used in structural analysis. We may produce an description of certain elements of a language's sentence structures by constructing a series of test-frames of this kind and exploring what types match the slots in the test-frames.

Ⅰ. 句法

1. 定义

句法学是语言学的一个分支，它研究词是如何被组合成词组、从句和句子的，以及支配其组合的规则。

2. 词类

常见的词类包括：名词、形容词、动词、副词、介词、代词和连词。

Ⅱ. 两种研究方法

1. 规定式

规定式指试图定义语言正确用法的研究方法。这些规则可能会强调拼写、发音、词汇、语法和语义等内容。一些语法学家，主要在18世纪的英国，采取规定式来分析语法。

2. 描写式

描写式指客观地分析和描述语言的实际使用情况的研究方法，现代语言学采用描写式。无论人们实际使用的语言中发生了什么，语言学都加以描述和分析。描述式出现于二十世纪。

Ⅲ. 结构主义研究

结构主义是研究语言的形态结构的研究。它的研究方法包括"语言框架测试"。通过语言框架测试，我们能够发现哪些形式适合哪个语言框架，并对这些句子结构的特征进行描写。

1. The Constituent structure grammar A grammar which analyzes sentences by analyzing its constituent structure, which refers to a formal representation of the grammatical structure of a sentence in terms of its individual constituents.	**1. 结构成分语法** 结构成分语法指通过分析句子的组成结构来分析句子的语法，这种语法是根据句子的各个组成部分来表示句子的语法结构。
2. Immediate constituent analysis (IC Analysis) 【考点：简答——直接成分分析法的利弊】 **(1) Definition** Immediate constituent analysis or IC analysis is a method of sentence analysis that was first mentioned by Leonard Bloomfield, and developed further by Rulon Wells. IC-analysis divides up a sentence into major parts or immediate constituents, and these constituents are in turn divided into further immediate constituents. The process continues until irreducible constituents are reached, i. e., until each constituent consists of only a word or a meaningful part of a word. The end result of IC-analysis is often presented in the form of brackets or tree diagrams.	**2. 直接成分分析法** **(1) 定义** 直接成分分析法是一种句子分析方法，由 Leonard Bloomfield 首先提出，Rulon Wells 进一步发展。直接成分分析把句子分为直接成分，这些成分又分为进一步的直接成分。这个过程会持续下去，直到达到不可还原的成分，也就是说，直到每个成分只由一个词或一个词的有意义的部分组成。分析的最终结果通常以括弧或树形图的形式表示。
(2) Advantages The internal structure of a sentence can be easily illustrated using IC analysis, and any ambiguities can be revealed.	**(2) 优点** 通过 IC 分析法，句子的内在结构可以清晰地展示出来，如果有歧义也会被揭示出来。
(3) Problems ① Supporters insisted on binary divisions at first. Any structure, at any level, would be divided into two parts. However, this isn't always feasible. ② Tree diagrams in IC analysis will have technical difficulties with structures with discontinuous constituents. In some cases, some structural ambiguities cannot be shown by IC analysis.	**(3) 问题** ① 开始的时候，一些提倡者坚持二元切分。任何结构体在任何层面都分成两个部分。但实际上并不总是如此。 ② 含有不连续成分的结构体会给 IC 分析法的树形图造成技术困难。最严重的问题是有些结构上的歧义不能用 IC 分析法来揭示和分析。
Ⅳ. The Transformational Grammar **1. Chomsky's Classical Theory** Chomsky proposed the "classical theory", a paradigm that consisted of three parts: a series of phrase structure rules, transformation rules, and morphophonemic rules in the earliest edition of transformational grammar.	**Ⅳ. 转化语法** **1. 乔姆斯基的经典理论** 乔姆斯基早期的转化语法理论包括三个部分：短语结构规则、转换规则和形态音位规则。
(1) **Phrase structure rules** are a type of rewrite rule used to describe a given language's syntax. They express the regularities of the language and make explicit a speaker's knowledge of the order of words and the grouping of words into syntactic categories.	(1) 短语结构规则是一种用于描述给定语言语法的重写规则，它们表达了语言的规律性，明确了说话者对词语顺序和词语句法类别的认识。

(2) Chomsky then proposed the idea of transformation rules which could transform these basic "kernel" sentences S →NP + VP into series of related sentences.

(3) The transformational rules' production will be subject to the morphophonemic rules. Their job is to give the different sections of the structure the right morphological form, and then to provide the correct phonological description.

2. The "Standard Theory"

(1) Deep structure and surface structure

【考点：绘制一句子的深层/表层结构树形图】

The deep structure is a level of syntactic representation with a number of properties that need not necessarily go together, i. e. , the underlying structural relationships among its constituents.

The surface structure corresponds to the final syntactic form of the sentence which results from appropriate transformations of the deep structure. It is the construction that people actually produce and receive.

(2) The "Standard Theory"

Base Component
Categorial Sub-component Lexical Sub-component
Phrase Structural Rules Lexicon + Rules

↓

DEEP STRUCTURE → to Semantics

↓

Transformational Component

↓

SURFACE STRUCTURE → to Phonology

3. Syntactic Movement

It denotes the movement of any constituent in a sentence from its original location to a new one.

(1) NP-movement

It refers to two constructions: passive sentences and raising constructions. Passive sentences are generally formed by the movement of active sentences; in the rising construction, there are two types of raising: raising verbs and raising adjectives.

(2) 基于转换规则，乔姆斯基把核心句型"S→NP + VP"转换成其他相关的句子。

(3) 形态音位规则作用于转换规则，对句子结构的形态与音系提供正确而恰当的表征。

2. 标准理论

(1)深层结构和表层结构

深层结构是一种句法抽象表示，深层结构各部分不一定要结合在一起，即句子不同成分之间的结构关系的潜在层面。

表层结构是句子的最终句法形式，它是对深层结构进行适当变换后的结果，它是人们实际产生、接收的结构组织。

(2)标准理论

3. 句法移位

句法移位是指一个句子的任意成分从原来的位置移到另一个新位置。

(1)NP 移位

NP 移位指两种结构：被动句和提升结构。一般认为，被动句是由主动句移位产生的。NP 移位不仅发生在被动句，而且发生在提升结构中。提升结构主要有两种：一类是含有提升动词的结构，另一类是含有提升形容词的结构。

(2) Wh-movement Wh-movement is the formation of syntactic dependencies involving interrogative word. It refers to the movement of a wh-phrase to the beginning of the sentence. **(3) Aux-movement** It refers to the movement of auxiliary words their original position to the beginning of the sentence. **3. Move-α rule** It's a general movement rule that explains how every constituent movement is conducted syntactically.	**(2) Wh-移位** Wh-移位是指生成疑问句句法依赖关系时形成的移位。它指的是将一个 wh-短语移到句子开头。 **(3) 助动词移位** 助动词移位是指将助动词从原来的位置移动到句首的移位。 **3. α 规则** α 规则是指任何成分皆可从句子的一个位置移至另一个位置。
V. Systemic-Functional Grammar (Halliday's approach) **1. General Account** Proposed by M. A. K. Halliday, Systemic-Functional Linguistics (SFL) is a theory of language centred around the notion of language function. While SFL accounts for the syntactic structure of language, it places the function of language as central (what language does, and how it does it), in preference to more structural approaches, which place the elements of language and their combinations as central. SFL starts at social context, and looks at how language both acts upon, and is constrained by, this social context. According to Halliday, language serves three general functions: ideational, interpersonal, and textual. They are related to three grammatical systems: transitivity, mood, and theme.	**V. 功能学派（布拉格语言学派）** **1. 概述** 系统－功能语法由韩礼德提出，它是以语言功能为中心的语言理论。虽然 SFL 解释了语言的语法结构，但它把语言的功能放在中心位置（语言做什么，如何做），而不是把语言元素和它们的组合放在中心位置。SFL 从社会语境入手，研究语言是如何受到社会语境影响和制约的。韩礼德认为语言有三种普遍的功能：概念功能、人际功能和语篇功能，而这三种功能又分别与三种语法系统相联系，即及物性、语气和主位。
2. Three General Functions of Language ① **Ideational function**: the function to organize the speaker or writer's experience of the real or imaginary world. ② **Interpersonal function**: the function to indicate, establish, or maintain social relationships between people. ③ **Textual function**: the function to organize written or spoken texts in such a manner that they are coherent within themselves and fit the particular situation in which they are used.	**2. 语言的三个功能** ① **概念功能**指组织讲话者或作者在真实或想象世界中的经历的功能。 ② **人际功能**指表达、建立或维持人与人之间社会关系的功能。 ③ **语篇功能**指将书面或口语文本组织起来，使其具有内在的连贯性，并适合特定的使用场合的功能。

4.2 课后习题详解

1. Define the following terms briefly.

syntax	word class	prescriptive approach
descriptive approach	IC analysis	structural analysis
immediate constituent		ultimate constituent

constituent structural grammar transformational grammar
ideational function interpersonal function textual function

2. Do you think that morphology and syntax should be treated as separate are as of study? Give reasons to support your views.
3. Place an asterisk next to any of the sentences that sound ungrammatical to you. Explain what makes these sentences ungrammatical.
   (1) The tutor told the students to study.
   (2) The tutor suggested the students to study.
   (3) The customer asked for a cold beer.
   (4) The customer requested for a cold beer.
   (5) He gave the Red Cross some money.
   (6) He donated the Red Cross some money.
   (7) The pilot landed the jet.
   (8) The jet landed.
   (9) A journalist wrote the article.
   (10) The article wrote very well.
   (11) Julie is bored of her job.
   (12) Julie is tired of her job.
   (13) Myself bit John.
   (14) I was surprised for you to get married.
   (15) Has the nurse slept the baby yet?
4. Explain why the following sentence is ungrammatical. Which personal pronoun in English would have the same form whether it occupied the position of "us" or "she" below?
   * Us visit she on Sundays.
5. (1) List as many examples of these constituents as you can identify in sentences (a) and (b) below: NP, PP, VP.
   (2) List as many examples of these lexical categories as you can identify in sentences (a) and (b): N, prep, V.
   a. A Guns "N" Roses concert at an arena near ST. Louis ended in disaster after some 2500 fans staged a full-fledged riot.
   b. The trouble started when Axl Rose asked venue security to confiscate a camera he saw near the front of the stage.
6. What prescriptive rules for the "proper" use of English are not obeyed in the following sentences?
   (1) That's the girl I gave my roller skates to.
   (2) He wanted to simply borrow your car for an hour.
7. In the following sentence, the phrase "in the car" could be used (i) to show where the biting took place or (ii) to specify that it was the man in the car that was bitten. How would the tree diagrams for (i) and (ii) differ?
   The dog bit the man in the car.

8. Paraphrase each of the following sentences in two different ways to show that you understand the ambiguity involved:

Example: Smoking grass can be nauseating.

a. Putting grass in a pipe and smoking it can make you sick.

b. Fumes from smoldering grass can make you sick.

(1) Terry loves his wife and so do I.

(2) They said she would go yesterday.

(3) The governor is a dirty street fighter.

(4) The design has big squares and circles.

参考答案

1. **Syntax**: Syntax is a branch of linguistics. It studies the rules that govern the ways in which words are combined to form phrases, clauses, and sentences.

Word class: Word classes are categories that are traditionally called parts of speech, including Noun (N.), Verb (V.), Adjective (Adj.), Adverb (Adv.), Preposition (Prep.), Pronoun (P.), Conjunction (Con.) and Article (Art.).

Prescriptive approach: Some grammarians, mostly in eighteenth-century England, took a prescriptive approach to analyze grammar. Prescriptive linguistics attempts to establish rules defining correct usage of language. These rules may emphasize things such as spelling, pronunciation, vocabulary, syntax, and semantics.

Descriptive approach: Linguists collects samples of the language they are interested in and attempt to describe the regular structures of the language as it is used, not according to some view of how it should be used. This is called the descriptive approach.

IC analysis: IC-analysis divides up a sentence into major parts or immediate constituents, and these constituents are in turn divided into further immediate constituents. The process continues until irreducible constituents are reached, i. e., until each constituent consists of only a word or a meaningful part of a word. The end result of IC-analysis is often presented in the form of brackets or tree diagrams.

Structural analysis: It investigates the distribution of linguistic forms in a given language. "Test-frames," which may be sentences with empty slots, are used in structural analysis. We may produce an description of certain elements of a language's sentence structures by constructing a series of test-frames of this kind and exploring what types match the slots in the test-frames.

Immediate constituent: An immediate constituent is any one of the largest grammatical units that constitute a construction. Immediate constituents are often further reducible.

Ultimate constituent: Ultimate constituent is a term used in structuralist grammatical analysis to refer to the irreducible elements which are the result of an immediate constituent analysis.

Constituent structural grammar: A grammar which analyzes sentences by analyzing its constituent structure, which refers to a formal representation of the grammatical structure of a sentence in terms of its individual constituents.

Transformational grammar: Transformational grammar, put forward by Chomsky, is a generative grammar, consisting of three parts: a set of phrase structure rules, transformation rules and morphophonemic rules.

Ideational function: The function to organize the speaker or writer's experience of the real or imaginary world.

Interpersonal function: The function to indicate, establish, or maintain social relationships between people.

Textual function: The function to organize written or spoken texts in such a manner that they are coherent within themselves and fit the particular situation in which they are used.

2. Although morphology and syntax are both concerning the study of formation, I do think there should be a division between the two. The primary difference between morphology and syntax is that the morphology is concerned with a word's internal structure, while the syntax is concerned with how words are combined to form grammatical sentences.

3. (1) Grammatical

(2) * Ungrammatical. Instead of using the form "suggest somebody to do something", we usually use "suggest + that-clause" or "suggest doing", here we'd better substitute "advise" for "suggest".

(3) Grammatical

(4) * Ungrammatical. The word "request" is a transitive verb which should take an object directly, so the word "for" should be omitted.

(5) Grammatical

(6) * Ungrammatical. The word "donate" cannot be followed by double objects as "donate somebody something". Instead we always use "donate something to somebody".

(7) * Ungrammatical. The word "land" is usually used as an intransitive verb, which can't take an object.

(8) Grammatical

(9) Grammatical

(10) * Ungrammatical. The subject of the verb "write" is usually a human; an "article" cannot write itself. In this case the passive construction is normally used: The article was very well written.

(11) * Ungrammatical. Usually we don't use "be bored of something/somebody", but "be bored with something/somebody" which means losing interest in somebody/something.

(12) Grammatical

(13) * Ungrammatical. Here "myself" is a reflexive pronoun, which can't be used as subject, and it should be replaced by "I".

(14) * Ungrammatical. The word "surprise" is usually used as a transitive verb, so the expression "...surprise for you" is ungrammatical, and it can be replaced by "surprise somebody (with something)" or "I was surprised by your getting married."

(15) * Ungrammatical. The word "sleep" is usually used as an intransitive verb, which can't take an object. The cases of "sleep" being used as a transitive verb are semantically limited, as in "to sleep a good sleep" or "the room can sleep 3 people".

4. This sentence is ungrammatical because it uses "us", an accusative in the place of a subject and a nominative "she" in the place of an object. The correct form should be "We visit her on Sundays." In English, the pronoun "you" and "it" would have the same form whether it occupied the position of subject or object.

5. (1) **NP:** a Guns "N" Roses concert, some 2500 fans, a full-fledged riot, the troubles, venue security, a camera he saw, the front of the stage.

   PP: at an arena, in disaster, near ST. Louis, after some 2500 fans staged a full-fledged riot.

   VP: ended in disaster, staged a full-fledged riot, the troubles started, confiscated a camera, near the front of the stage.

   (2) **N:** concert, fans, riot, troubles, venue, security, camera, stage, arena, ST. Louis, disaster

   Prep: at, after, near, the front of, in

   V: ended, staged, started, asked, confiscated, saw

6. (1) "I gave my roller skates to" serves as an attributive clause modifying the main clause "That is the girl", thus should be connected with an introductory word "who/whom".

   (2) Based on the meaning of the sentence, "simply" as an adverb should be used to modify verb "wanted", but was mistakenly put before "borrow", thus it fails to obey the prescriptive rules for the proper use of English.

7. （树形图略，改用括号法表示）

   1. (The (dog)) bit ((the (man)) (in (the (car)))).

   The first one is to specify that it was the man in the car that was bitten.

   2. ((The (dog)) (bit (the (man)))) (in (the (car))).

   The second one aims to show where the biting took place.

8. (1) Terry loves his wife and I love her, too.

   Terry loves his wife and I love mine, too.

   (2) Yesterday, they told us about her leaving.

   They had said that she was going to leave on yesterday.

   (3) The governor is a street fighter who is really dirty.

   The governor cannot stand the street being dirty.

   (4) The design has lots of circles and big squares.

   The design has lots of circles and squares, which are both really big.

4.3 考研真题与典型题详解

Ⅰ. Fill in the blanks

1. IC is the short form of immediate ___________ used in the study of syntax.（北二外 2003 研）
2. ___________ refers to ties and connections which exist within texts. They are also called formal links between sentences and between clauses.（人大 2007 研）
3. Syntactic movement is dictated by rules traditionally called ___________ rules, whose operation may change the syntactic representation of a sentence.

4. The level of syntactic representation that exists before movement takes place is commonly termed ________ structure.
5. A ________ is a structurally independent unit that usually comprises a number of words to form a complete statement, question or command.
6. The branch of grammar which studies the internal structure of sentences is called ________. (北二外 2010 研)

Ⅱ. Multiple Choice

1. Phrase structure rules allow us to better understand ________. (西安交大 2008 研)
   A. how people produce and recognize possible sentences
   B. what constitutes the grammaticality of strings of words
   C. how words and phrases form sentences
   D. All of the above
2. Bloomfield introduced the IC analysis, whose full name is ________ Analysis. (北二外 2010 研)
   A. Internal Component B. Innate Capacity
   C. Internal Constituent D. Immediate Constituent
3. The criterion used in IC analysis is ________
   A. transformation B. conjoining C. grouping D. substitutability
4. In Halliday's view, the ________ function of language is realized as the transitivity system in clauses as a representation of experience.
   A. ideational B. interpersonal C. textual D. social
5. The phrase "my small child's cot" is an ambiguous phrase, which can be revealed by ________ tree diagrams.
   A. one B. two C. three D. four
6. In English, ________ and ________ are often expressed by subject and predicate.
   A. theme and rheme B. theme and predicate
   C. predicate and object D. subject and predicate

Ⅲ. Explain the following terms

1. Immediate constituent(武汉大学 2008 研；武汉大学 2006 研)
2. IC analysis(人大 2006 研)
3. Concord (or: Agreement) (武汉大学 2008 研；中山大学 2008 研)
4. Government
5. Paradigmatic relations
6. Syntax
7. Constituent
8. Logical subject (中山大学 2011 研)

Ⅳ. Short answer questions

1. Distinguish between the two possible meanings of more beautiful flowers by means of IC analysis. (北二外 2006 研；北二外 2008 研)
2. What are the advantages of using tree diagrams in the analysis of sentence structures? (西安交

大 2008 研)

3. Please rephrase the following sentences, to disambiguate them.
   (1) Tom and Mary saw the mountains while they were flying over.
   (2) Old men and women are hard to live with.
   (3) They said she would go yesterday.
   (4) The governor is a dirty street fighter.
   (5) We deplore the shooting of the hunters.
4. Please disambiguate the following 5 sentences, using the tree-diagram, or any other means that you think is appropriate. (北京交通大学 2007 研)
   (1) Jane showed her baby pictures.
   (2) The old man is drinking in the air.
   (3) We need more realistic officials to handle the economy.
   (4) We are sweeping the ground cigarettes on the street.
   (5) Tom exchanged the money and fell around the corner.
5. What is Halliday's idea on the relationship between the functions performed by language and its structures?
6. What are deep and surface structures?
7. In the following three sentences, the particle "up" stays in different positions, i. e. immediately after the verb; in between the noun phrase and the relative clause; and at the end of the sentence. Can you formulate a syntactic rule to explain the position changes of the particle?
   (1) She stood up the man who offered her a diamond.
   (2) She stood the man up who offered her a diamond.
   (3) She stood the man who offered her a diamond up. (南开大学 2010 研)

V. Essay questions

1. Advantages and Disadvantages of Immediate Constituent Analysis (IC Analysis) (北京交通大学 2006 研)
2. Illustrate "Immediate Constituent Analysis". (大连外国语学院 2008 研)
3. For each of the following pairs of sentences, discuss how the two sentences are different from each other. (南京大学 2006 研)
   (1) A. His carelessness I can't bear.
       B. I can't bear his carelessness.
   (2) A. A dagger killed the tourist.
       B. The tourist was killed with a dagger.
   (3) A. A hurricane killed eight people.
       B. Eight people died in a hurricane.
4. Describe with tree diagrams the transformations involved in forming the question "Does John like the book?" (南开大学 2007 研)
5. What, in your view, makes a text a text, rather than a series of unconnected utterances? What are the implications of your answer for second language teaching? (北外 2006 研)
6. The English sentences given below are ungrammatical. You are required to give the syntactic ex-

planation to the ungrammaticality in each of the sentences.（南开大学2011研）

(1) * Jack put his ball.

(2) * I wonder Michael walked the dog.

(3) * Frank thinks himself is a superstar.

7. What are the similarities and differences between a phrase and a clause?（中山大学2011研）

参考答案及解析

Ⅰ. Fill in the blanks

1. constituent

（直接成分分析法是一种句法分析方法。它指先把句子分析为直接成分——词组（或短语），再把这些直接成分依次切分，得到各自的直接成分，层层切分，直到最终成分为止。）

2. Cohesion

（衔接不是一个句法概念，它指文本中存在的一种意义上的联系或关系，也包括句子或分句之间存在的一种形式上的联系。）

3. transformational

（句法移位是受传统上被称为转换规则的这些规则所支配的，转换规则的运用会改变句子的句法表达方式。）

4. deep

（深层结构是指一个结构体的句法属性的抽象表述，即不同成分之间的结构关系，深层结构一般指移位前的结构。）

5. sentence

（句子在结构上是一个独立的单位，通常包括许多词用以构成一个完整的陈述，提问或者命令。）

6. syntax

（句法学是研究句子内部结构的一门学科。）

Ⅱ. Multiple Choice

1. D （乔姆斯基在其经典理论中提出短语结构规则，这一规则有助于我们更好地明白句子是如何产生与被理解的，以及单词和短语是怎样根据语法规则形成句子的。）

2. D （直接成分这一术语最先是由布龙菲尔德在《语言论》中提出的。直接成分分析法，即Immediate Constituent Analysis，简称IC Analysis。）

3. D （IC分析法的标准：替换性。即看一个词语的序列是否可以被一个单词替换而结构保持不变。）

4. A （韩礼德认为概念功能就是表达说话者对现实世界的经验。）

5. C

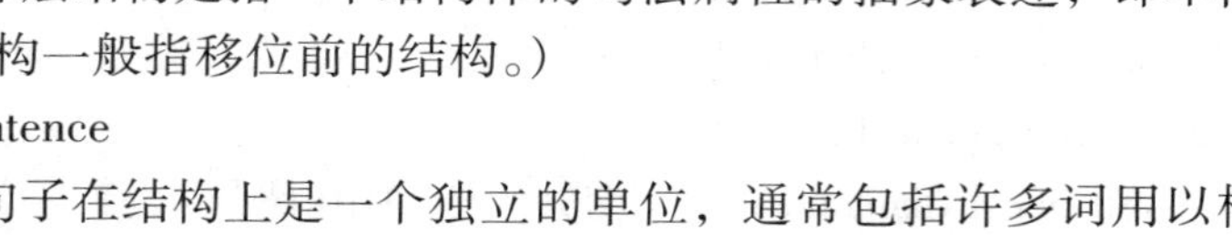

6. A （较早提出主位和述位概念的是布拉格学派创始人之一——马泰休斯。主位和述位通常指主语和谓语，但主位结构分析属于语义分析 ，而主语—谓语—补语分析属于结构分析。）

Ⅲ. Explain the following terms

1. An immediate constituent is the constituent immediately, directly, below the level of a construction. For example, in the sentence "Poor John ran away", the constituents "Poor John" and "ran away" are regarded as the immediate constituents of the sentence.
2. IC analysis (immediate constituent analysis) refers to the analysis of a sentence in terms of its immediate constituents—word groups (or phrases), which are in turn analyzed into the immediate constituents of their own, and the process goes on until the ultimate constituents are reached. In practice, for the sake of convenience, we usually stop at the level of word.
3. It may be defined as the requirement that the forms of two or more words of specific word classes that stand in specific syntactic relationship with one another shall also be characterized by the same paradigmatically marked category (or categories). For example, the syntactic relationship between *that girl* and *she* in the following dialogue: A: Who is that girl? B: Oh, she is my sister.
4. Government is another type of control over the forms of some words by other words in certain syntactic constructions. It differs from concord in that this is a relationship in which a word of a certain class determines the forms of others in terms of certain category. In English, for example, the pronoun after a verb or a preposition should be in the object form as in *She gave him a book. She gave a book to him.* In other words, the verb, or the preposition, determines, or governs, the form of the pronoun after it.
5. Paradigmatic relation, Saussure originally called associative, is a relation holding between elements replaceable with each other at a particular place in a structure, or between one element present and the others absent.
6. It is a sub-field of linguistics that studies the sentence structure of language. Specifically, it is the study of the rules governing the ways in which words, word groups and phrases are joined to form sentences in a language, or the study of the interrelationships between sentential elements.
7. Constituent is a term used in structural sentence analysis for every linguistic unit, which is a part of a larger linguistic unit. Several constituents together form a construction: for example, in the sentence "The boy ate the apple", S (A), the boy (B), ate the apple (C), each part is a constituent.
8. Logical subject is the subject of a sentence that expresses the actual agent of an expressed or implied action. In passive voice such as "John was bitten by a dog", we have two terms "grammatical subject" and "logical subject". Since the core object noun (*John* in this case) sits in the slot before the verb in the passive, it is called grammatical subject, for the original object noun phrase occupies the grammatical space before a verb, the space that a subject normally occupies; the core subject (*A dog*), now the object of a preposition (*by a dog*), is called the logical subject, since semantically the core subject still does what a subject normally does: it performs an action.

Ⅳ. Short answer questions

1. (a) ((more beautiful) flowers)　　　(b) (more (beautiful flowers))
2. The tree diagram can not only reveal a linear order, but also a hierarchical structure that groups words into structural constituents. It can, in addition, show the syntactic category of each structural constituent, thus it is believed to most truthfully illustrate the constituent relationship among

linguistic elements.

（本题考查用树形图分析句子结构的好处。）

3. (1) While Tom and Mary were flying over, they saw the mountains.

(2) It is hard to live with old men and old women.

(3) They said yesterday that she would go.

(4) The governor is a fighter against dirty streets.

(5) We deplore the hunters' shooting.

4. (1)

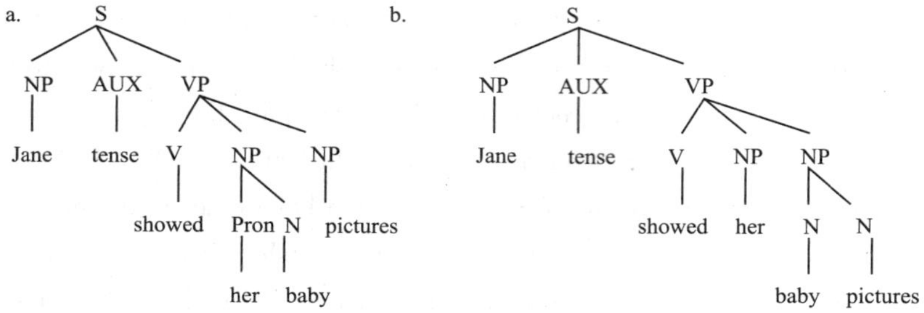

(2) a. ($_{VP}$ drinking in) ($_{NP}$ the air)

b. ($_{VP}$ drinking ($_{PP}$ in the air))

(3)

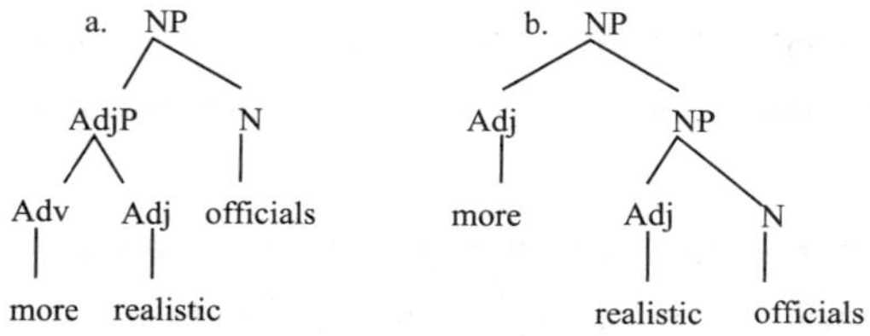

(4) a. ($_{VP}$ sweeping ($_{NP}$ the ground cigarettes ($_{PP}$ on the street)))

b. ($_{VP}$ sweeping ($_{NP}$ the ground cigarettes) ($_{PP}$ on the street))

(5) a. ($_{VP}$ exchanged the money) and ($_{VP}$ fell around the corner)

b. ($_{VP}$ exchanged the money and fell) ($_{PP}$ around the corner)

5. In Halliday's point of view, there are three general functions of language: ideational (which is subdivided into experiential and logical), interpersonal and textual. And they are related to the three grammatical systems: transitivity, mood and theme. Specifically, the ideational function is realized as the transitivity system in the clause as a representation of experience, in which there are six processes: material, mental, relational, behavioral, verbal and existential. Actor, the so-called logical subject, is an important participant in the material process. The interpersonal function is realized as the mood system in the clause as an exchange, which is divided into the two major parts of Mood and Residue. And Subject is one of the two parts of Mood, the other part being the finite verbal operator. The textual function is realized as the thematic structure of the clause as a message. The two main constituents here are theme and rheme, the former being the point of departure of the message, or the concern of the clause, while the latter is the part in which the theme is developed.

6. Deep structure is a central theoretical term in generative grammar opposed to surface structure. It

is the abstract syntactic representation of a sentence—an underlying level of structural organization which specific all the factors governing the way the sentence should be interpreted.

Surface structure is a central theoretical term in generative grammar, opposed to deep structure. It is the final stage in the syntactic representation of a sentence, which provides the input to the phonological component of the grammar, and which thus most closely corresponds to the structure we articulate and hear.

7. According to chomsky's Generative and Functional Grammar, there is an underlying representation for any sentence. Then the underlying form is transformed into the surface form through some transformational rules. The same underlyilyng form may result in different surface representation by undertaking different operation. Sometimes, the same surface form is likely to be transformed from different deep structures because of various movements.

"Stand sb. up" means that sb. fails to show up in a date though he has promised to appear, and let the other wait for him in vain. The underlying form of the above three sentences have the same underlying form, that is "She stood the man up who offered her a diamond".

The reason why they finally have the different form is that they have undertaken different operations. Because "up" is an adjunct in the three sentences, it is more convenient to put it since it will not change the property of the sentence. Therefore, finally we get the three kinds of surface forms. Sentence one, "up" is moved upward to the front of the man for the purpose of banlancing the sentence. Sentence two, "up" is moved upwards to the front of the attrubutive clause to the front of the attributive clause in order to achieve coherence. And the last sentence is the underlying form.

Consequently, we can say that it is very flexible to position the adjunct in a sentence for various purposes.

V. Essay questions

1. Through IC analysis, the internal structure of a sentence may be demonstrated clearly, and if there is any ambiguity, it could be revealed. For example, how the sentence "Leave the book on the shelf" is ambiguous could be shown after the IC analysis.

However, there are also problems in IC analysis. First, at the beginning, some advocators insisted on binary divisions, that is, any construction, at any level, will be cut into two parts. But this is not always possible. For example, in the phrase "men and women", it is not appropriate to combine "and" with only the preceding part or only the succeeding part. Second, constructions with discontinuous constituents will pose technical problems for tree diagrams in IC analysis. For example, in "make it up", the phrasal verb "make up" is separated by a pronoun. Third, which is also the most serious problem, there are structural ambiguities which cannot be revealed by IC analysis, as shown in "the love of God". In IC analysis, the different relations of "God" to the word "love" cannot be shown, which makes the expression ambiguous.

2. The relation between a sentence and its component elements is generally referred to as the relation between a construction and its constituents, in which a very important notion is immediate constituent analysis, IC Analysis for short.

The immediate constituent analysis may be defined as: the analysis of a sentence in terms of its immediate constituents—word groups (or phrases), which are in turn analyzed into the immediate constituents of their own, and the process goes on until the ultimate constituents are reached.

The immediate constituent analysis of a sentence may be carried out with brackets or with a tree diagram. The criterion for the immediate constituent analysis is substitutability: whether a sequence of words can be substituted for a single word and the structure remains the same. Through IC analysis, the internal structure of a sentence may be demonstrated clearly, and ambiguities, if any, will be revealed.

For example: the IC structure for the sentence "The boy ate the apple." is:

1) Tree diagram

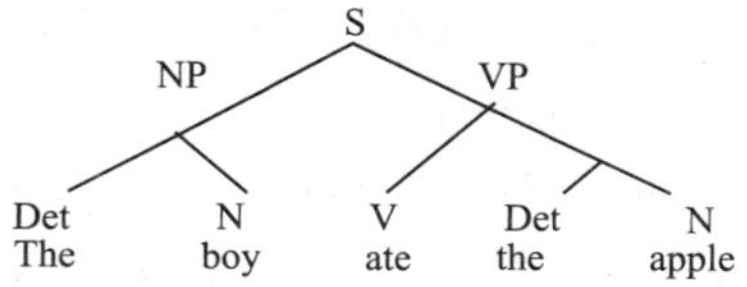

2) Bracketing

((The) (boy)) ((ate) ((the) (apple)))

(本题考查直接成分分析法。作答时给出定义、作用及其表现方法——树形图和括号，并分别举例说明。)

3. (1) These two sentences are different in the sense that the thematic structures are different. The theme of a sentence is often the known information, which the sentence is mainly about. Sentence A provides some information about "his carelessness", since "his carelessness" serves as the theme. Whereas, Sentence B is a statement about "I", and from the remainder of the sentence the recipient could know some information about "me".

(2) In sentence A, "A dagger" serves as the theme, with which the sentence could be seen as an answer of "What did the dagger do?" In sentence B, "The tourist" is treated as the given information, around which the sentence develops; thus, the corresponding question of this sentence as an answer could be "What happened to the tourist?"

(3) There are still differences of thematic structures between these two sentences, with the first one about "A hurricane" and the second one about "eight people". What's more, in sentence A, the verb "kill" emphasizes a direct relationship between the hurricane and the eight people, that is, it is the hurricane that caused the people to die. Whereas, in sentence B, a meaning like above is not entailed.

4.

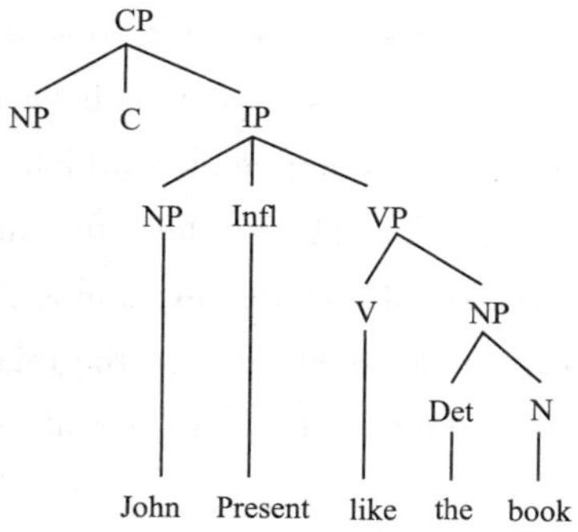

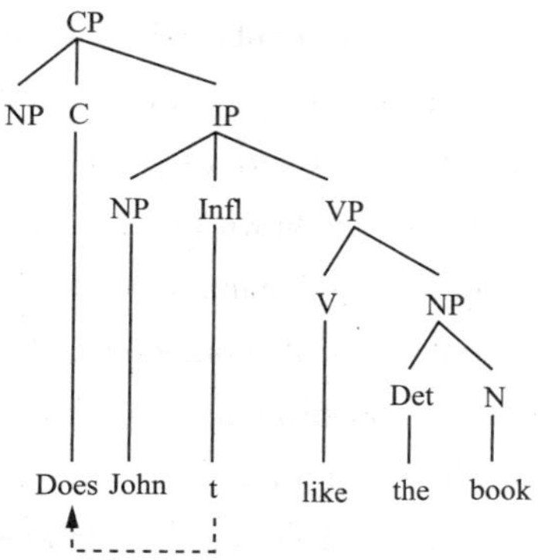

5. The factor to distinguish connected texts which make sense from those which do not is usually described as coherence. Coherence is traditionally described as the relationships that link the ideas in a text to create meaning for the readers, apart from cohesive devices. It should be noticed that cohesion by itself would not be sufficient to enable us to make sense of what read or hear; it is quite easy to create a highly cohesive text which has a lot of connections between the sentences, but which remains difficult to interpret. And coherence, as the invisible net of a text, performs a function of "connectedness" which makes the text interpretable to people.

   Regarding the importance of coherence to a whole text, it seems necessary for a teacher of SFL to help students develop coherence in writing. Research has found that in their writing, ESL/EFL students focus almost exclusively on the word and sentence levels rather than the level of the whole discourse, that is, textual coherence. A pedagogical focus on coherence can shift students' attention from sentence-level grammar to discourse features such as textual structuring and propositional unity, which are crucial to creating meaning in texts. Indeed, helping students improve the coherence of their writing ought to be a significant aspect of L2 writing instruction.

   To help students focus on coherence in writing, it is essential that teachers have a thorough understanding of what makes a text coherent. As is shown in the composition textbooks, it seems common to regard coherence simply as connectedness between sentences, use of explicit cohesive devices at the paragraph level, and use of connective devices such as pronouns, repetitive structures, and transitional markers. However, coherence should not be narrowed in terms of sentence-level connectedness and paragraph unity rather than discourse unity. Thus, to help students create coherence in their writing, it is necessary for teachers to pay more attention to the broader sense of coherence.

6. (1) *Jack put his ball. Because of the word "put", the sentence lacks a complement, which should be a PP. Therefore, it should be "Jack put his ball under the chair."

   (2) *I wonder Michael walked the dog. The sentence is ungrammatical, for what follows the word "wonder" should be a clause. The correct form is "I wonder if Michael walked the dog."

   (3) *Frank thinks himself is a superstar. In English, the pattern of the word "think" is that it pluses a clause or a complement. So the correct form should be "Frank thinks himself as a superstar." or "Frank thinks he is a superstar."

7. Phrase and clause are both grammatical units contained in the set of layers in the grammar of a language, as following: morpheme, word, phrase, clause, clause complex. They are attached to the sentences. For example, the tallest girl (nominal phrase), <u>Having finished their task</u>, they came to help us. (clause)

   Phrase is a single element of structure containing more than one word, and lacking the subject-predicate structure typical of clauses. Traditionally, it is seen as part of a structural hierarchy, positioned between clause and word. While clause is a constituent with its own subject and predicate, and it is included in a larger sentence. First, a phrase must be a group of words which form a constituent. Second, a phrase is lower on the grammatical hierarchy than clauses. More precisely, simple clauses may (and usually do) contain phrases, but simple phrases do not (in general) contain clauses.

   (考查短语与从句的异同，要分别分析其定义并举例。)

第5章　语义学

5.1　复习笔记

本章要点：

1. Semantics

   语义学

2. The referential and sense

   指称和涵义

3. Analysis of meaning

   意义分析

4. Component analysis

   成分分析

5. Sentence meaning

   句子意义

本章考点：

语义学的定义；词汇意义关系（同义、反义、上下义）；识别各种实例中词与词的意义关系、以及句与句之间的蕴涵、预设、同义、自相矛盾、含意等意义关系；用成分分析法分析同义词、反义词，句子意义的区别等；反义词的种类及举例。

本章内容索引：

Ⅰ. Definition of Semantics

Ⅱ. Some approaches to the study of meaning

1. Meaning as naming
2. Meaning as concept
3. Meaning as behavior
4. Meaning as context
5. Meaning as truth conditions

Ⅲ. Word meaning

1. Sense and reference
2. Seven types of meaning

   (1) Conceptual meaning

   (2) Connotative meaning

   (3) Social meaning

   (4) Affective meaning

   (5) Reflective meaning

   (6) Collocative meaning

   (7) Thematic meaning

3. Semantic fields
4. Componential analysis
5. Major sense relations
   (1) Homonymy
   (2) Polysemy
   (3) Homophony
   (4) Synonymy
   (5) Antonymy
   (6) Hyponymy
   (7) Meronymy

Ⅳ. Sentences meaning

1. Sentence and proposition
2. Semantic roles
3. Semantic relationships between sentences
   (1) Entailment
   (2) Presupposition
   (3) Synonymy
   (4) Inconsistency
   (5) Implicature

Ⅰ. Semantics

【考点：名词解释】

Semantics is a branch of linguistics which is concerned with the study of meaning in all its formal aspects.

Ⅱ. Some approaches to the study of meaning

1. Meaning as naming

(1) Referential theory or naming theory

Referential theory or naming theory refers to the fact that the meaning of an expression is what it refers to or names. The word *fire*, for example, names the object *fire* in the real world.

(2) Problems

An important drawback of this theory is that not all words actually refer to things existing in the real world. For example, conjunctions have no referents in the real world.

2. Meaning as concept

(1) Any particular sound image is psychologically associated with a particular concept.

Ⅰ. 语义学

语义学是语言学的一个分支，研究所有字面的意义，不考虑语境。

Ⅱ. 研究意义的几种方法

1. 命名论

(1) 指称理论或命名理论

指称理论或命名理论是指任何表达的含义是其指称或命名的事物。例如，“火”这个词的含义就是现实中存在的火。

(2) 缺点

此理论的一个重要缺点就是并不是所有的词汇在现实中存在其指称的事物。比如，连词在现实中不存在对应的事物。

2. 内涵

(1) 任何一个声音都代表着具体的内涵。

(2) Semantic triangle

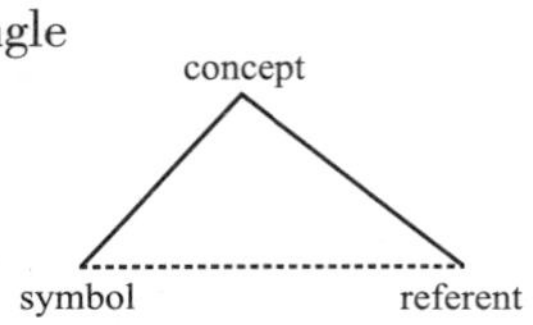

"Symbol" refers to the linguistic element like word, sentence, etc., and the "referent" refers to the object in the world of experience, while "concept" refers to human thought.

3. Meaning as behavior

Bloomfield believed that meaning exists in the relation between speech and the practical events that precede and follow it. The meaning of a linguistic form can be observed in behaviors. Such an approach to meaning refers to behaviorism, or behaviorist theory, which is clearly psychology-based.

4. Meaning as context

The meaning of the utterance can be inferred from the context. This research method is based on sociology.

5. Meaning as truth conditions

Understanding the meaning of a sentence is the same as understanding the conditions under which the sentence is true or false. Understand the meaning of a word is to see its role in the truth or falsehood of the sentence containing it. Such an approach to meaning refers to truth-conditional theory or semantics, which is clearly based on formal logic.

Ⅲ. Word meaning

1. Sense and reference

(1) Sense refers to the relationship within the linguistic elements. It is concerned with intralinguistic relations. For example, the English words bachelor and *married* have the sense relationship of *bachelor = never married*.

(2) Reference or extension refers to the relationship between linguistic elements and the non-linguistic world of experience, e. g. things, actions, events and qualities. For example, the word *tree* refers to the object *tree*.

2. Seven types of meaning

【考点：考察意义的种类】

British linguist G. Leech asserted that meaning in its broadest sense can be divided into seven types: conceptual, connotative, social, affective, reflective, collocative and thematic meanings. Among them, connotative, social, affective, reflective and collocative meanings are called associative meaning.

(2) 语义三角

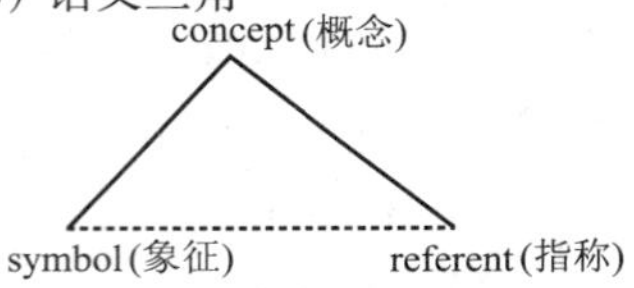

"象征"是语言学中的要素如词汇、句子等，"指称"是现实世界中的事物，"概念"是人们的思维。

3. 行为主义

布洛姆菲尔德认为意义存在于话语及话语之后的行为之间。语言形式的意义被定义为可见的行为。这种基于心理学的方法叫做行为主义，或行为理论。

4. 语境论

话语的含义可在语境中推测得出，这种研究方法建立在社会学的基础之上。

5. 真值条件论

了解句子的意义与了解此句的真值条件是一样的。了解词汇的含义就是看其在句子真值中所起的作用，这种研究方法叫做真值条件理论或真值条件语义学，这种研究方法建立在形式逻辑学的基础之上。

Ⅲ. 词汇意义

1. 涵义与指称

(1) 涵义是指语言学要素内的关系，也就是语言学内的关系。

(2) 指称或外延是指语言学要素与现实世界事物之间的关系。

2. 意义的七种类型

英国的语言学家利奇将意义大体上分为七类：概念意义、内涵意义、社会意义、感情意义、反射意义、搭配意义和主位意义，其中内涵意义、社会意义、感情意义、反射意义和搭配意义为联想意义。

(1) Conceptual meaning also known as denotative or cognitive meaning, is the most important and fundamental part of language and the central element in verbal communication. Conceptual meaning can be studied by contrasting features. For example, the word *woman* can be specified as +HUMAN, −MALE, +ADULT, as distinct from the word *boy*, which can be defined +HUMAN, +MALE and −ADULT.	**(1) 概念意义**也叫做外延或认知意义，它是语言中最重要最根本的部分，是语言交流中的中心要素。概念意义可以通过对立特征来研究，比如研究“男人”和“女人”这对词汇。
(2) Connotative meaning is the communicative value conveyed by a word or a combination of words by virtue of what it refers to, over and above its purely conceptual content. For example, the word *woman* may have such connotative meanings as “capable of speech”, “gregarious”, “frail”, “prone to tears”, “emotional”, “irrational”, and so on.	**(2) 内涵意义**是通过语言所指所传达的意义，这不仅仅是指其概念意义。比如说到“女人”这一词汇，其内涵意义就是爱交际，体质上较弱，易流泪等。
(3) Social meaning refers to the meaning conveyed about the social environment in which language is used. For example, *cast* must be used in literature, *throw* is a general word which can be used in any context, but *chuck* is slangy, which should be used in casual contexts.	**(3) 社会意义**是指所传达的关于语言使用的社会环境的意义。
(4) Affective meaning is used to express the speaker's feelings including his or her attitude or personal judgment.	**(4) 感情意义**是用来表达说话者的感情的包括其态度或个人评判。
(5) Reflective meaning arises from a variety of conceptual meanings, when one sense of a word forms part of our response to another sense. “Human language is a tool of social intercourse”. Whereas, people nowadays prefer to use communication rather than intercourse because the latter can easily remind people of something about sex.	**(5) 反射意义**是由于多种概念意义而产生的。比如人们用“communication”取代“intercourse”来表达“交流”这一含义。
(6) Collocative meaning: Collocation meaning is the meaning conveyed by association within the common collocation of words.	**(6) 搭配意义**是通过词语的常用搭配而传达的意义。
(7) Thematic meaning: Thematic meaning is the meaning conveyed by the way the speaker or writer organizes the order of information.	**(7) 主位意义**是通过说话者或写作者组织信息顺序的方式所传达的意义。
3. Semantic fields 【考点：名词解释】 **(1) Definition** Semantic field is a system that aggregates related words and expressions, in which they are interrelated. For example, kinship terms such as father, mother, brother, sister, uncle, aunt belong to a semantic field whose relevant features include generation, sex, membership of the father's or mother's side of the family.	**3. 语义场** **(1) 定义** 语义场是将相关的词汇与表达汇总到一起的系统，其中他们又是相互有关连的。比如表达亲属关系的词汇。

(2) Lexical gap In the semantic field, the absence of words at a particular place is called lexical gap. In English we have *brother* versus *sister*, *son* versus *daughter*, but no separate lexemes for "male" and "female" cousin.	**(2) 词汇差异** 在语义场中，特定位置上词汇的缺失就叫做词汇差异。
4. Componential analysis Componential analysis (CA) is the analyzing process of word meaning by breaking down the sense of a word into its minimal components, or sense components. *Woman*, for instance, can be described by following features like +HUMAN, +ADULT, +FEMALE.	**4. 成分分析法** 成分分析法(简称 CA) 是将一个词的意义分解为其最小成分或意义成分的意义分析过程。例如"woman"这个词可以认为包含下列特征：+HUMAN，+ADULT，+FEMALE
5. Major sense relations	**5. 涵义关系**
(1) Homonymy In any language there are words that have the same form but different meanings. Some examples are: *bank* (of a river)—*bank* (financial institution), *bat* (flying creature)—*bat* (used in sports), *race* (contest of speed)—*race* (ethnic group), *pupil* (at school)—*pupil* (in the eye).	**(1) 同音/同形异义关系** 任何语言中都有具有相同的形式但不同意义的词。比如"bank"(河岸)与"bank"(银行)的形式相同却有不相同的意义。
(2) Polysemy Having two or more meanings for the same word is what we call polysemy. Words with polysemy relations are called polysemic or polysemous words. For example, the word *head* can mean the object on top of your body, the part on top of a glass of beer, or the person on top of a company or department.	**(2) 多义关系** 同一个词有两种或两种以上的意义，这就是我们所说的多义关系。具有多义关系的词叫做多义词。例如"head"这个词指人的头部、杯口，还指公司或某个部门的领导者。
(3) Homophony Words that sound alike but are written differently and have different meanings are called homophones. Homophony is illustrated by such pairs as *know/no*, *threw/through*, *rode/rowed*, *bare/bear*, *meat/meet*, *flower/flour and sew/so*. Homophones are a type of homonymy, so they are sometimes called homonyms.	**(3) 同音异义关系** 发音相似但是写法不同而且有不同意义的词叫做同音异形异义词。同音异形异义词是同音异义关系中的一种，所以也叫做同音异义词。
(4) Synonymy Not only are there words that sound alike but have different meanings, but there are also words that sound different but have the same meaning. Such words are called synonyms, and the sense relation of "sameness of meaning" is called synonymy, such as answer-reply and big-large.	**(4) 同义关系** 不仅有发音相似但是意义不同的词，还有发音不同但是有相同意义的词。这样的词叫做同义词，它们之间"意义相同的"关系叫做统一关系，比如 answer-reply 以及 big-large。

(5) Antonymy Words that are opposite in meaning are often called antonyms. The oppositeness of meaning is called antonymy. ①Ungradable antonyms: a negative of one means an affirmation of the other. For example, if someone is not married, then he is unmarried; if someone is not female, he is male. There is no midway position. Such pairs of words are called ungradable antonyms. ②Gradable antonyms: a negation of one is not necessarily an affirmation of the other. For example, if someone says "The weather is not warm", this does not imply "The weather is cold". Each of these pairs represents extreme points on a scale, but there are also intermediate points. For example, the weather is may be cool. These antonyms are called gradable antonyms because degrees may be expressed.	**(5) 反义关系** 意义上相反的词叫做反义词。意义上的反义叫做反义关系。 ① 非等级反义词：一方的否定意味着对另一方的肯定。 例如：一个人没有活着，那么他就是死了；如果一个人没有睡着，那么就是醒着。这种词没有中间地带。这样的词叫做非等级反义词。 ②等级反义词：对一方的否定并不一定是对另一方的肯定。 比如：有人说"John 年纪不大"，这不一定意味着"John 是年轻的"。每一对等级反义词代表着两个极端但是存在着中间地带。这样的词叫做等级反义词。
(6) Hyponymy Hyponymy shows the relationship between a general term (hypernym) and a specific instance of it (hyponym): X is a Y, e. g. a maple is a tree, a tree is a plant.	**(6)上下义关系** 上下义关系是一种属种关系。更具体的词(下义词)包括在意义更广的词(上位词)之内。例如枫树是一种树木，而树木又是一种植物。
(7) Meronymy One word is part of another word, and this relationship is called part/whole relationship. Meronymy can be expressed by the pattern "X is a part of Y". For example, words like *second* and *minute*, *minute* and *hour*, *hour* and *day*, *day* and *week*, none of which could be described without reference to the fact that it is a subdivision of another.	**(7)整体部分关系** 一个词是另外一个词的一部分，这种关系叫做整体部分关系，可表达为"X 是 Y 的一部分"。 例如，秒与分，分钟与小时，小时与天，天与周，每个词都是构成另外一个词的一部分。
Ⅳ. Sentences meaning **1. Sentence and proposition** The same semantic content uttered by different expressions is a proposition. Generally speaking, one can find out whether the proposition is true or false. In terms of the relationship between sentence and proposition, different sentences expressing the same message are also considered to have the same proposition.	**Ⅳ. 句子意义** **1. 句子与命题** 不同的句子间共有的语义内容为命题。通常，我们能判断出命题的真值。 就句子与命题之间的关系而言，表达相同信息的不同句子也被视为具有相同的命题。

2. Semantic roles 【考点：名词解释】	**2. 语义角色**
(1) Definition Noun phrases that are described or presented within a clause are called semantic roles, for example as agent, patient, or cause.	**(1) 定义** 从句中描述或呈现的名词性指称短语叫做语义角色。
(2) Classification ① Agent&Patient ② Experiencer ③ Instrument ④ Cause ⑤ Recipient ⑥ Benefactive ⑦ Locative ⑧ Temporal	**(2) 分类** ① 施事与受事 ② 感事 ③ 工具 ④ 原因 ⑤ 领受格 ⑥ 受益格 ⑦ 处所格 ⑧ 时间
3. Semantic relationships between sentences 【考点：分析具体句子间的语义关系】	**3. 句子间的语义关系**
(1) Entailment It refers to the interdependent logical relationship between the meanings of two sentences. In terms of truth value, if A is true, then B must also be true; When B is false, A is false; When A is false, B is either true or false; When B is true, A is either true or false. For example: a. That person is a bachelor. b. ENTAILS: That person is a man.	**(1) 蕴含** 它是指两个句子的意义具有相互依赖的逻辑关系。如果 a 蕴含 b，那么它们存在着如下的真值关系：当 a 为真时，b 也一定为真；当 b 为假时，a 为假；当 a 为假时，b 或真或假；当 b 为真时，a 或真或假。
(2) Presupposition In terms of truth value, the following relationships exist between two sentences: When a is true, b is necessarily true; when a is false, b is still true; when b is true, a can either be true or false; when b is false, no truth value can be said about a. For example: a. The king of France is bald. b. PRESUPPOSES: There is a king of France.	**(2) 预设** 在真值方面，它们存在着如下关系：当 a 为真时，b 也一定为真；当 a 为假时，b 仍为真；当 b 为真时，a 或真或假；当 b 为假时，无真假值可言。
(3) Synonymy Both sentences have the same meaning, that is, in terms of truth value, A and B have the same truth value. If A is true, B is also true; If A is false, B is false; And vice versa. a. I am an orphan. b. I am a child and have no father or mother.	**(3) 同义关系** 两个句子拥有同样的意义，即在真值方面，a 与 b 真值相同。若 a 为真，b 亦为真；若 a 为假，b 亦为假；反之亦然。

(4) **Inconsistency or contradiction**	(4) **自相矛盾**
A is inconsistent with b: if a is true, b is false; also, if b is true, a is false. For example: a. I am an orphan. b. I have a father.	a与b自相矛盾，即若a为真，b为假；同样当b为真，a亦为假。这种关系就叫做不一致或自相矛盾，因为两个句子之间的真值互相矛盾。
(5) **Implicature**	(5) **含意**
Implicature is also a kind of semantic relationship between sentences. For example, if we can derive the conclusion b from sentence a, then b is the implicature of a. a. Few girls are coming. b. Some girls are coming.	含意也是一种句子之间的语义关系。例如，如果我们能从句子a中得到结论b，那b就是a的含意，通常是一种语用含义的关系。

5.2 课后习题详解

1. Define the following terms briefly.

semantics	truth-conditional semantics	naming theory
behaviorist theory	use theory	sense
reference	conceptual meaning	connotative meaning
semantic field	lexical gap	componential analysis
semantic feature	synonymy	antonymy
hyponymy	meronymy	semantic role
entailment	presupposition	

2. Explain the semantic ambiguity of the following sentences by providing two or more sentences that paraphrase the multiple meanings. Example: *She can't bear children* can mean either *She can't give birth to children* or *She can't tolerate children.*

(1) He waited by the bank.

(2) Is he really that kind?

(3) We bought her dog biscuits.

(4) He saw that gasoline can explode.

(5) Fifty soldiers shot three wild foxes.

(6) He saw her drawing pencils.

3. Two relations involving word meaning are antonymy and synonymy. Which relation is illustrated in each of the pairs of words below?

(1) flourish-thrive	(2) intelligent-stupid	(3) casual-informal
(4) young-old	(5) uncle-aunt	(6) intelligent-able
(7) flog-whip	(8) drunk-sober	

4. What connotations or connotative meanings do you think the following nouns have in English?

charity iron mole snow street

5. Some of the sets of terms below form semantic fields. For each set:

(1) Identify the words that do not belong to the same semantic field as the others in the set.

(2) Identify the superordinate term of the remaining semantic field, if there is one (it may be a word in the set).

(3) Determine whether some terms are less marked than others, and justify your claim.

a. acquire, buy, collect, hoard, win, inherit, steal

b. whisper, talk, narrate, report, tell, harangue, scribble, instruct, brief

c. road, path, barn, way, street, freeway, avenue, thoroughfare, interstate, method

d. stench, smell, reek, aroma, bouquet, odoriferous, perfume, fragrance, scent, olfactory

6. Identify which of the following may be considered to have or to be homographs, homophones, homonyms or polysemy:

sea break line ear prayer mature trace house

7. What are the differences between less marked and more marked terms in the same semantic field?

8. For each group of words given below, state what semantic feature or features distinguish between the classes of (a) words and (b) words. If asked, also indicate a semantic feature shared by both the (a) words and the (b) words.

Example: a. widow, mother, sister, aunt, maid

b. widower, father, brother uncle, valet

The (a) and (b) words are "human".

The (a) words are "female" and the (b) words are "male".

(1) a. bachelor, man, son, paperboy, pope, chief

b. bull, rooster, drake, ram

The (a) and (b) words are ____________________

The (a) words are ____________________

The (b) words are ____________________

(2) a. ask, tell, say, talk, converse

b. shout, whisper, mutter, drawl, holler

The (a) and (b) words are ____________________

The (a) words are ____________________

The (b) words are ____________________

(3) a. walk, run, skip, jump, hop, swim

b. fly, skate, ski, ride, cycle, canoe, hang-glide

The (a) and (b) words are ____________________

The (a) words are ____________________

The (b) words are ____________________

参考答案

1. **Semantics**: Semantics is a branch of linguistics which is concerned with the study of meaning in all its formal aspects. A sentence needs to be well formed both syntactically and semantically. The sentence "Mary married the Mickey Mouse", for example, is syntactically well formed but semantically ill formed; for we know that a lady cannot marry the Mickey Mouse. Semantics is concerned with such information.

Truth-conditional semantics: Understanding the meaning of a sentence is the same as understanding the conditions under which the sentence is true or false. Understand the meaning of a word is to see its role in the truth or falsehood of the sentence containing it. Such an approach to meaning refers to truth-conditional theory or semantics, which is clearly based on formal logic.

Naming theory: Referential theory or naming theory refers to the fact that the meaning of an expression is what it refers to or names. The word fire, for example, names the object fire in the real world.

Behaviorist theory: Bloomfield believed that meaning exists in the relation between speech and the practical events that precede and follow it. The meaning of a linguistic form can be observed in behaviors. Such an approach to meaning refers to behaviorism, or behaviorist theory, which is clearly psychology-based.

Use theory: The semantic theory according to which the meaning of a word is determined by its use in communication and more generally, in social interaction.

Sense: Sense refers to the relationship within the linguistic elements. It is concerned with intra-linguistic relations. For example, the English words bachelor and married have the sense relationship of bachelor = never married.

Reference: Reference or extension refers to the relationship between linguistic elements and the non-linguistic world of experience, e. g. things, actions, events and qualities. For example, the word tree refers to the object tree.

Conceptual meaning: Conceptual meaning, also known as denotative or cognitive meaning, is the most important and fundamental part of language and the central element in verbal communication. It means that the meaning of words may be discussed in terms of what they denote or refer to.

Connotative meaning: Connotative meaning is the communicative value conveyed by a word or a combination of words by virtue of what it refers to, over and above its purely conceptual content.

Semantic field: Semantic field is a system that aggregates related words and expressions, in which they are interrelated. For example, kinship terms such as father, mother, brother, sister, uncle, aunt belong to a semantic field whose relevant features include generation, sex, membership of the father's or mother's side of the family.

Lexical gap: In the semantic field, the absence of words at a particular place is called lexical gap. In English we have *brother* versus *sister*, *son* versus *daughter*, but no separate lexemes for "male" and "female" cousin.

Componential Analysis: Componential analysis(CA) is the analyzing process of word meaning by breaking down the sense of a word into its minimal components, or sense components.

Semantic feature: Semantic feature, which is also called semantic component, is a universal set of components which can be used to describe meaning in each and every language in the world.

Synonymy: Not only are there words that sound alike but have different meanings, but there are also words that sound different but have the same meaning. Such words are called synonyms, and the sense relation of "sameness of meaning" is called synonymy.

Antonymy: Antonymy refers to the sense relation of various kinds of opposing meaning between lexical items, e. g. *big/small*, *alive/dead* and *father/daughter*.

Hyponymy: Hyponymy shows the relationship between a general term(hypernym) and a specific instance of it (hyponym).

Meronymy: One word is part of another word, and this relationship is called part/whole relationship. For example, words like *second* and *minute*, *minute* and *hour*, *hour* and *day*, *day* and *week*, none of which could be described without reference to the fact that it is a subdivision of another.

Semantic role: By semantic role we mean such things as *who* did *what* to *whom*, with *whom*, and for *whom*. Noun phrases that are described or presented within a clause are called semantic roles, for example as agent, patient, or cause.

Entailment: It refers to the interdependent logical relationship between the meanings of two sentences. In terms of truth value, if A is true, then B must also be true; When B is false, A is false; When A is false, B is either true or false; When B is true, A is either true or false.

Presupposition: In terms of truth value, the following relationships exist between two sentences: When a is true, b is necessarily true; when a is false, b is still true; when b is true, a can either be true or false; when b is false, no truth value can be said about a.

2. (1) He waited by the bank of a river.

   He waited by the bank where people can save or deposit money.

   (2) Does he really belong to that kind of man?

   Is he really a kind-hearted man as we have imagined?

   (3) We brought some biscuits for her dog.

   We brought some dog biscuits for her.

   (4) The explosion of that gasoline can was seen by him.

   He saw the fact that gasoline is able to explode.

   (5) Fifty soldiers shot three wild foxes with guns.

   Fifty soldiers shot three wild foxes with cameras.

   (6) Her drawing pencils were seen by him.

   Her drawing pencils were cut off by him with a saw.

3. **Antonymy**: (2), (4), (5), (8)

   Synonymy: (1), (3), (6), (7)

4. **Charity**: social responsibility, kind-heartedness, consciousness

   Iron: strong, perseverance, firmness

   Mole: stealthiness, blindness (as blind as a mole)

   Snow: white, pure, beautiful

   Street: broad, straight, plain

5. (1) a. hoard (all other words are indicating "the way one gets sth.")

   b. scribble (all other words concern about "manner in talking" while scribble is a "manner of writing")

c. barn (all other words relates to "way".)

d. olfactory (all other words are a kind of "smell", while olfactory is the organ of smelling)

(2) a. "acquire/get"; b. "tell/say"; c. "way"; d. "smell".

(3) Yes, there are words which are less marked than other words. Let's take a group of words for example: words like *road*, *path*, *way*, *street* and *method* are less marked than words like *freeway*, *avenue*, *thoroughfare*, and *interstate*. The less marked members of a semantic field will usually be easier to learn and remember than more marked members. Typically, a less marked word consists of only one morpheme, in contrast to more marked words. The less marked member of a semantic field cannot be described by using the name of another member of the same field, for instance, *method* cannot be replaced by *street*.

6. **Homographs**: break n. /break v. line n. /line v. ear n. /ear v.

Homophones: sea/see prayer/preyer

Homonyms: break n. /break v. line n. /line v. ear n. /ear v.

Polysemy: sea, mature, trace, house.

7. The differences between less marked words and marked words in a semantic field are:

The less marked members of a semantic field will usually be easier to learn and remember than more marked members. Typically, a less marked word consists of only one morpheme, in contrast to more marked words. The less marked member of a semantic field cannot be described by using the name of another member of the same field; while more marked words can be thus described. Less marked words also tend to be used more frequently in conversation and writing. Besides, less marked words are also often broader in meaning than more marked terms. Finally, less marked words are not the result of the metaphorical usage of the name of another object or concept, whereas more marked words often are.

8. (1) a. bachelor, man, son, paperboy, pope, chief

b. bull, rooster, drake, ram

The (a) and (b) words are "male living/animate things"

The (a) words are "human beings"

The (b) words are "animals"

(2) a. ask, tell, say, talk, converse

b. shout, whisper, mutter, drawl, holler

The (a) and (b) words are "speaking"

The (a) words are "reciprocal"

The (b) words are "alone"

(3) a. walk, run, skip, jump, hop, swim

b. fly, skate, ski, ride, cycle, canoe, hang-glide

The (a) and (b) words are "sports"

The (a) words are "done with one's body"

The (b) words are "done with instruments"

5.3 考研真题与典型题详解

Ⅰ. Fill in the blanks.

1. According to G Leech, __________ meaning is the communicative value an expression has by virtue of what it refers to, over and above its purely conceptual content.（北二外 2006 研）
2. According to G Leech, __________ meaning refers to logic, cognitive, or denotative content.（北二外 2005 研）
3. According to G. Leech, __________ meaning refers to what is communicated of the feelings and attitudes of the speaker/writer.（北二外 2007 研）
4. Terms like "apple", "banana" and "pear" are __________ of the term "fruit".（北二外 2007 研）
5. "X buys something from Y" and "Y sells something to X" are in a relation of __________.（北二外 2006 研）
6. "Mary gave a book to Jack" is synonymous with "Jack __________ a book from Mary."（北二外 2005 研）
7. __________ = PARENT(x, y) & MALE(x).（北二外 2005 研）
8. __________ = CHILD (x, y) & MALE (x).（北二外 2006 研）
9. Sentence meaning is the combination of the meanings of the component words and ________.
10. The hyponyms under the same superordinate are called ________.

Ⅱ. Multiple Choice

1. Point out which item does not fall under the same category as the rest. (Focus on connotation)（南京大学 2007 研）

   A. corpulent　　B. statesman　　C. slim　　D. decease

2. __________ deals with the relationship between the linguistic element and the non-linguistic world experience.（西安交大 2008 研）

   A. Reference　　B. Concept　　C. Semantics　　D. Sense

3. Which of the following is NOT included in G. Leech's seven types of meaning?（大连外国语学院 2008 研）

   A. Connotative meaning.

   B. Denotative meaning.

   C. Conceptual meaning.

4. Point out which item does not fall under the same category as the rest. (Focus on the type of semantic relation)（南京大学 2007 研）

   A. school/college　　B. move/run　　C. furniture/table　　D. mature/ripe

5. Point out which item does not fall under the same category as the rest. (Focus on the type of semantic opposition)（南京大学 2008 研）

   A. wake-asleep　　B. inside-outside

   C. teacher-student　　D. right-left

6. There are generally three kinds of sense relations recognized, sameness relation, oppositeness relation and inclusiveness relation. They are represented by __________ respectively.（大连外国

语学院 2008 研）

A. synonymy, antonymy, and hyponymy

B. synonymy, hyponymy, and antonymy

C. antonymy, synonymy, and hyponymy

7. By componential analysis, BECOME(x, (~ALIVE(x))) is an explanation of ________. （西安外国语学院 2006 研）

A. die　　B. dead　　C. kill　　D. killed

8. The sense relationship between "John plays the piano" and "John plays a musical instrument" is ________.（北二外 2004 研）

A. synonymy　　B. antonymy　　C. entailment

9. Conceptual meaning is not ________

A. affective　　B. cognitive　　C. logic　　D. denotative

10. The semantic triangle holds that the meaning of a word ________

A. is interpreted through the mediation of concept.

B. is related to the thing it refers to.

C. is the idea associated with that word "in the minds of speakers".

D. is the image it is represented in the mind.

11. Lexical ambiguity arises from polysemy or ________ which can not be determined by the context.

A. homonymy　　B. antonymy　　C. meronymy　　D. synonymy

Ⅲ. True or False

1. In the sentence "Money is often said to be the root of all evil", "root" is used in its conceptual meaning.（北二外 2007 研）

2. After comparing "They stopped at the end of the corridor." with "At the end of the corridor, they stopped.", you may find some difference in meaning, and the difference can be interpreted in terms of collocative meaning.（北二外 2006 研）

3. Conceptual meaning overlaps to a large extent with the notion of "reference".（北二外 2005 研）

4. When you use your own sentence with a meaning other than the conceptual, the meaning is sometimes referred to as speaker's meaning, or contextual meaning.（大连外国语学院 2008 研）

5. Reference is one of the rarely used cohesive devices.（南开大学 2005 研）

6. Ogden and Richards argue that the relation between a word and a thing it refers to is not direct.（南开大学 2004 研）

7. "Tulip", "rose" and "violet" are all included in the notion of "flower". Therefore they are superordinates of "flower".（北二外 2006 研）

8. Sense is regarded as a kind of intralinguistic relationship.（北二外 2010 研）

9. All the words in a language can be used to refer, but only some have senses.（北二外 2010 研）

Ⅳ. Explain the following terms.

1. Semantic Triangle（大连外国语学院 2008 研）

2. Gradable antonym（人大 2006 研）

3. Semantic feature（四川大学 2006 研）

4. Componential analysis（浙江大学 2005 研；北航 2008 研）
5. Entailment（武汉大学 2006 研）
6. Presupposition （武汉大学 2004 研）

Ⅴ. Short answer questions

1. What is conceptual meaning? Try to distinguish it from any other types of meaning classified by Leech?（北二外 2008 研）
2. Explain the notion of hyponym.（北二外 2008 研）
3. How would you describe the oddness of the following sentences, using semantic features?（浙江大学 2004 研）
   (a) The television drank my water. (b) His dog writes poetry.
4. What is one obvious presupposition of the speaker who says:
   (a) Where did he buy the beer?
   (b) Your watch is broken.（上海交大 2006 研）
5. Tell the sense relation between a and b in each pair:（北二外 2007 研）
   (1) a. He no longer likes coffee. b. He liked coffee.
   (2) a. Mary is working in China. b. Mary is working in Beijing.
6. In what way is componential analysis similar to the analysis of phonemes into distinctive features?
7. Are utterances, sentences, and propositions the same?
8. Do you think there are true synonyms in English? Why?（厦门大学 2010 研）
9. Words are in different sense relations with each other. What sense relation is illustrated in each of the pairs of words below? Add one more example to each pair.（北航 2008 研）
   (a) *casual-informal*
   (b) *intelligent-stupid*
   (c) *steal-steel*
   (d) *animal-dog*

Ⅵ. Essay questions

1. Explain the seven types of meaning and use examples to illustrate your ideas.（人大 2007 研；南开大学 2004 研）
2. Discuss *sense*, *denotation and reference*, using Chinese examples to illustrate your points.（北外 2008 研）
3. For each of the following pairs of words, state the principal reason why they may not be considered to be synonyms:（浙江大学 2005 研）
   a. man boy b. toilet loo c. determined stubborn
   d. pavement sidewalk e. slim skinny f. move run
4. Put the following words in a hierarchical order (you can use a tree diagram if need be) and try to define at least two of them:（北师大 2003 研）
   crocodile, mammal, reptile, rabbit, primate, animal
5. Study the following exchange and then answer the questions that follow.（南京大学 2006 研）
   "Take some more tea." the March Hare said to Alice, very earnestly.
   "I've had nothing yet," Alice replied in an offended tone, "so I can't take more."

(1) Why was Alice offended?

(2) What is the problem with the March Hare's remark? What is the linguistic issue involved here?

6. Consider the following statements. When do we say Statement A entails Statement B? When do we say Statement A presupposes Statement B? Does Statement A necessarily entail Statement C? Why? Do Statements A and D both presuppose Statement B? Why? (南京大学 2008 研)

A. *Jack's brother has gone bankrupt.*

B. *Jack has a brother.*

C. *Jack's sibling has gone bankrupt.*

D. *Jack's brother has not gone bankrupt.*

7. In each of the following sentences, the second part cancels some information given by the first part. However, this seems to result in quite acceptable utterances in group(1) and in very awkward utterances in group(2). Explain why. (北外 2002 研)

Group(1)

a. 老张有三个小孩子，其实还不止三个。

b. 我只喜欢黄色和蓝色，不过试试红色也未尝不可。

c. 约翰的普通话说得还可以，确切地说是非常棒。

Group(2)

*d. 我特后悔选修了这门课，其实我没有选修这门课。

*e. 她这次考试又不及格，不过她上次及格了。

*f. 我在乡下日子过得很苦，说真的我没在乡下呆过。

8. The following four sentences present four different usages of the word *不过*. Please discuss the distinctions and connections among the four usages, illustrating your points with your own examples where necessary.

1)*不过*二年，君必无患。

2)他十七岁就结婚，一年后当了爸爸*不过*十八岁。

3)这是个乖巧*不过*的孩子。

4)我也没有长策，*不过*这种事情，其事已迫，不能计出万全的。

9. Comment on the following observation in about 150 words. (武汉大学 2010 研)

"The meaning of a word is not an unanalysable whole."

参考答案及解析

Ⅰ. Fill in the blanks.

1. connotative

(利奇认为内涵意义是指通过语言所指传达的意义，是位于纯粹的概念意义之上的。)

2. conceptual

(利奇认为概念意义是指逻辑的、认知的、外延的内容。)

3. affective

(利奇认为感情意义是指所传达的关于说话人/作者感情、态度方面的意义。)

4. hyponyms

（在上下义关系中，一个坐标词通常有很多下义词。同类中的成员叫做同下义词。题中“苹果”和“香蕉”都是“水果”的下义词。）

5. synonymy
（“X 从 Y 那里买东西”与“Y 卖给 X 东西”的意思相同，所以两句话的关系是同义关系。）

6. received
（同义关系句的表达，“Mary 给 Jack 书”即“Jack 从 Mary 那得到一本书”。）

7. father
（同时满足“父母亲”和“男性”的条件的只能是“父亲”。）

8. son
（同时满足“孩子”和“男性”的条件的只能是“儿子”。）

9. the meaning of its structure
（句子的意义是由词汇意义与句子结构两者决定的。）

10. co-hyponyms
（同类中的成员叫做同下义词。）

Ⅱ. Multiple Choice

1. A （从内涵意义来看，corpulent 有些贬义的意思，而其他词则是褒义的且表意委婉。）
2. A （指称指拥有某些属性的具体实体，它处理的是语言元素与非语言世界的关系。）
3. B （利奇提出的 7 种意义分别为概念意义、内涵意义、社会意义、感情意义、反射意义、搭配意义和主位意义。）
4. C （C 中的词为上下义关系，其他组的词为近义关系。）
5. C （A、B、D 为互补反义词，而 C 为反向反义词。）
6. A （词汇之间存在三种涵义关系，分别为同义关系，反义关系和上下义关系。）
7. A （表达式的意思是“X 变成无生命的”，所以选项 A 是正确的。）
8. C （如果知道一个句子的真假能够判断另一个句子的真假，那么第一个句子就蕴含了第二个句子。题中如果第一个句子为真，则第二句为真；第一句为假，第二句或真或假。所以第一句蕴含第二句。）
9. A （概念意义是逻辑的、认知的、外延的内容，而不是感情的。）
10. A （语义三角学说认为词汇的意义是通过概念表现出来的。）
11. A （当语境无法决定多义词或同音异义词的具体含义时，就会产生分歧。）

Ⅲ. True or False

1. F （这里的“root”是用了它的联想意义中的内涵意义，不是概念意义。）
2. F （搭配意义是通过词语的常用搭配而传达的意义；主位意义是通过顺序和重音这种信息的方式所传达的意义。显然这里用的是主位意义。）
3. T （概念意义是逻辑的、认知的、外延的内容。指称理论指把词语意义跟它所指称或所代表的事物联系起来，二者有其相似之处。）
4. T （句意有时要根据说话人想表达的意思而定，这也可称为语境意义。）
5. F （指称是一种常用的衔接手段。）
6. T （奥格登和理查兹在《意义的意义》一书中提出了语义三角的理论。他们认为词与所指事物之间没有直接的关系，它们是以概念为中介的。）
7. F （位于上下义这种意义关系上位的词语，即类名，叫做上坐标词；居于下位的是成员，叫做下义词。这里的上标词应该是"flower"。)

8. T （涵义是可看作是它和其他词之间的涵义关系网络，我们可以把涵义界定为词语之间的语义关系，更概括地说，是语言单位之间的语义关系。它体现的是语言内关系。)

9. F （一种语言中的所有词都有涵义(sense)，但并不是每个词都有指称(reference)。)

Ⅳ. Explain the following terms.

1. Ogden and Richards presented the classic "Semantic Triangle" as manifested in the following diagram, in which the "symbol" or "form" refers to the linguistic elements (word, sentence, etc.), the "referent" refers to the object in the world of experience, and "thought" or "reference" refers to concept or notion. According to this view, there is no direct link between symbol and referent, that is, between language and the world. The link is via thought, the concept in our minds.

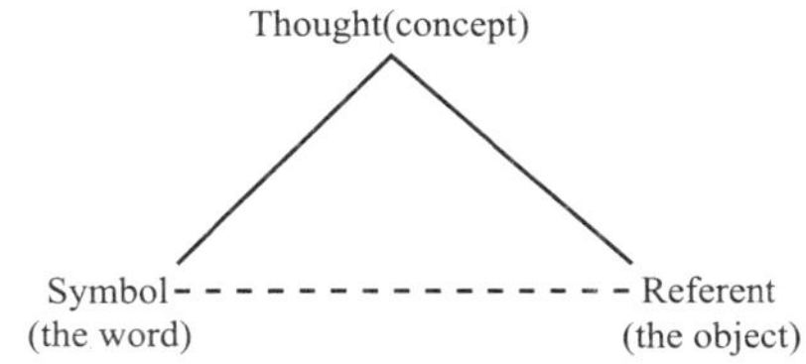

2. Gradable antonyms are antonyms that are gradable because there are often intermediate forms between the two members of a pair. For example, *cold* and *warm* constitute a pair of gradable antonyms.
3. The meaning of a word can be dissected into meaning components which are called semantic features. For example, the word "man" is analyzed as comprising the features of +HUAMN, +ADULT, +ANIMATE, +MALE.
4. Componential analysis (CA) is the analyzing process of word meaning by breaking down the sense of a word into its minimal components, or sense components. *Woman*, for instance, can be described by following features like +HUMAN, +ADULT, +FEMALE.
5. It refers to the interdependent logical relationship between the meanings of two sentences. In terms of truth value, if A is true, then B must also be true; When B is false, A is false; When A is false, B is either true or false; When B is true, A is either true or false. For example, the sentence "He has been to France" entails "He has been to Europe".
6. In terms of truth value, the following relationships exist between two sentences: When a is true, b is necessarily true; when a is false, b is still true; when b is true, a can either be true or false; when b is false, no truth value can be said about a. For example, *John didn't pass chemistry* presupposes that *John took chemistry*.

Ⅴ. Short answer questions

1. According to Leech, conceptual meaning refers to the logical, cognitive or denotative content of the meaning of a word. It is concerned with the relationship between a word and the thing it refers to.

   Conceptual meaning overlaps to a large extent with the notion of reference. But the term "connotative" is used in daily conversation, refers to some additional, especially emotive, meaning. This type of meaning and the following four types, namely, social meaning, affective meaning, reflected meaning and collocative meaning, are collectively known as associative meaning in the sense that an elementary associationist theory of mental connections is enough to explain their use. The last type, thematic meaning, is more peripheral since it is only determined by the order of the words in a sentence and the different prominence they each receive.

2. A term which is subordinate to another in that its extension is contained in the extension of another, e. g. "lion" or "tiger" is a hyponym of "animal".
3. (a) The verb *drink* represents a behavior of the animate beings, therefore, it is required that the subject of this verb should have a semantic feature as (+ ANIMATE), however, the word *television*, which is in position of subject, has an opposite feature: (– ANIMATE). That's why such a collocation results in oddness.

   (b) The action of writing poetry is normally one which only human beings could do, therefore, the subject is required to have a semantic feature as (+ HUMAN); however, the word *dog* in the subject position is featured as (– HUMAN). Therefore, the sentence is odd.
4. (a) One obvious presupposition of the sentence "Where did he buy the beer" should be "He has some beer".

   (b) One obvious presupposition of the sentence "Your watch is broken" should be "You have a watch".
5. (1) a entails b (2) b presupposes a
6. In the light of componential analysis, the meaning of a word consists of a number of distinctive meaning features; the analysis breaks down the meaning of the word into these features, and it is these different features that distinguish word meaning similarly. A phoneme is considered a collection of distinctive sound features; a phoneme can be broken down into these distinctive sound features and it is these sound features that distinguish different sounds.
7. No. These three terms are used to describe different levels of language. The most concrete is utterance which is created by speaking (or writing) a piece of language. Sentences, on the other hand, are abstract grammatical elements obtained from utterances. For example, an utterance has a tone, or perhaps some accent due to regional or social variation, and phonetic details which identify individual speakers, etc. But at the level of sentence, these kinds of information are ignored. Propositions are the result of a further abstraction of sentences, which are descriptions of states of affairs and which some writers see as a basic element of sentence meaning. For example, the two sentences "Caesar invaded Gaul" and "Gaul was invaded by Caesar" hold the same preposition.
8. Synonymy is the technical name for the sameness relation. It is used to mean sameness or close similarity of meaning. Total synonymy is rare. The so-called synonyms are all context dependent. They all differ in one way or another. When you consider the meaning of a word, you need to consider both its denotation and its connotation. The denotation is the primary, literal meaning of a word. The connotation is the suggested or implied meaning of a word. Connotations usually come from experience or associations. Seeing a word used repeatedly in certain contexts gives the word a different color than it gets in the dictionary.

   There are no real synonyms, because two or more words named synonyms are expected without exception to differ from one another in one of the following aspects:

(1) in shade of meaning (finish, complete, close, conclude);

(2) in stylistic meaning(father, dad);

(3) in emotive(or affective) meaning(smart, crafty);

(4) in range of use or collocative meaning (accuse, charge);

(5) in British and American English usages(autumn, fall).

For example, they may differ in style. In the context "Little Tom __________ a toy bear", here *buy* is more appropriate than *purchase*. Because *purchase* is more formal than *buy*.

9. (a) Synonymy; see-watch

(b) Antonymy; pretty-ugly

(c) Homophone; die-dye

(d) Hyponymy; fruit-apple

Ⅵ. Essay questions

1. The seven types of meaning were first postulated by G. Leech. They are respectively illustrated as follows:

(1) Conceptual meaning, which refers to logical, cognitive, or denotative content. This type of meaning is "denotative" in that it is concerned with the relationship between a word and the thing it denotes, or refers to.

(2) Connotative meaning, what is communicated by virtue of what language refers to. It refers to some additional, especially emotive, meaning.

(3) Social meaning, referring to what is communicated of the social circumstances of language use.

(4) Affective meaning, which refers to what is communicated of the feelings and attitudes of the speaker/writer.

(5) Reflected meaning, which refers to what is communicated through association with another sense of the same expression.

(6) Collocative meaning, what is communicated through association with words which tend to occur in the environment of another word.

The five types of meanings from (2) to (6) are collectively known as associative meaning in the sense that an elementary associationist theory of mental connections is enough to explain their use.

(7) Thematic meaning, what is communicated by the way in which the message is organized in terms of order and emphasis. It is more peripheral since it is only determined by the order of the words in a sentence and the different prominence they each receive.

2. Sense is concerned with the inherent meaning of the linguistic expression. It is the collection of all the features of the linguistic form; it is abstract and de-contextualized. It is the aspect of meaning dictionary compilers are interested in. For example, the word "狗" in Chinese is given the definition of "哺乳动物，种类很多，听觉嗅觉都很敏锐，善于看守门户，有的可以训练成军犬、警犬". This does not refer to any particular dog that exists in the real world, but applies to any animal that meets the features described in the definition. So this is the sense of

the word *dog*.

Reference means what a linguistic expression refers to in the real, physical world; it deals with the relationship between the linguistic element and the non-linguistic world of experience. If we say "这只狗真可爱", we must be talking about a certain dog existing in the situation; the word "狗" here refers to a dog known to both the speaker and the hearer. This is the reference of the word "狗" in this particular situation.

Denotation refers to the relationship between an expression and its extension. The term extension of an expression is the set of things which could be possibly be the referent of that expression. So the extension of the word "狗" is "所有种类的狗". Thus, the relationship between the word "狗" and "所有种类的狗" is denotation, that is, the word "狗" denotes "所有种类的狗".

Furthermore, the differences between the three terms are discussed as follows.

Sense and reference are two different but related aspects of meaning. Two expressions may refer to the same referent but have different senses. For example, in sentences "1949 年 10 月 1 日，毛泽东在天安门城楼上宣布：今天，中华人民共和国成立了!" and "1949 年 10 月 1 日，那位伟大的领袖在天安门城楼上宣布：今天，中华人民共和国成立了!", expressions "毛泽东" and "那位伟大的领袖" refer to the same person (have the same referent) but with different senses. There is also another difference between sense and reference. To some extent, all words have senses, but not every word has a referent. Some words like "和", "但是", "假如", "的" do not refer to anything. Therefore, the meaning if an expression will arise both from its sense and its reference.

Both reference and denotation refer to the relationship between a linguistic expression and the world, but there are also differences. Denotation refers to the relationship between a linguistic expression and a set of possible referents of that expression in the world; while reference is used for the relationship between a linguistic expression and a particular entity in the world. For example, in the sentence "一只云鹊飞进了房间", the expression "一只云鹊" refers to the lark in that particular situation, while denotes to the whole class "鸟". Another difference is that denotation is a stable relationship in a language which is not dependent on any one use of a word. Reference, on the other hand is a moment by moment relationship: what entity somebody refers to by using the word "云雀" depends on the situation.

3. a. The reason for not regarding *man* and *boy* as synonyms could be seen from the semantic components they include respectively. *Man*: +HUMAN, +MALE, +ADULT; while *boy*: +HUMAN, +MALE, -ADULT. Since they do not have the same semantic components, they are not considered as synonyms.

   b. The principal reason for not regarding *toilet* and *loo* as synonyms could be attributed to the different styles where they are used. *Toilet* is a more standard expression, while *loo* is a slang, which is more informal, compared to *toilet*.

   c. The two words *determined* and *stubborn* are quite different in their emotive or evaluative meaning. The word *stubborn* is usually used by the speaker to express a negative attitude, while the other word is not.

d. *Pavement* and *sidewalk* are dialectally different. *Pavement* is more often used by British people, while in America, people will be more likely to use *sidewalk*.

e. Although both *slim* and *skinny* could refer to the thinness of a person, they are different in that *skinny* emphasizes more on the excessive thinness, while *slim* has no connotation of the excessiveness.

f. These two words, *move* and *run*, are semantically different: *run* means to move swiftly, so comparatively speaking, *move* is more general.

4.

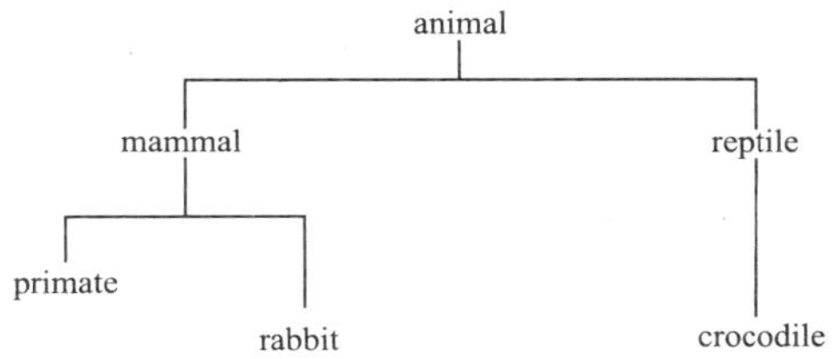

animal: A multi-cellular organism of the kingdom Animalia, differing from plants in certain typical characteristics such as capacity for locomotion, non-photosynthetic metabolism, pronounced response to stimuli, restricted growth, and fixed bodily structure.

reptile: Any of various cold-blooded, usually egg-laying vertebrates of the class Reptilia, such as a snake, lizard, crocodile, turtle, or dinosaur, having an external covering of scales or horny plates and breathing by means of lungs.

5. (1) Alice was offended because she felt that she seemed to be accused of something she hadn't done. The March Hare's remark could be interpreted in a way that he presupposed Alice had already had some tea, which was not true.

(2) The March Hare ignored the possible presuppositive relations among sentences. Presupposition is the relation between propositions by which A presupposes B if, for A to have a truth-value, B must be true. In his utterance, the word "more" functions as the presupposition triggers. It presupposes that there is already something existing. In this specific utterance, it presupposes "You have already had some tea", which is not true according to the reality.

6. A truth-based approach is a good way to characterize the semantic relations of entailment and presupposition. In a truth-based definition of entailment, a sentence p entails a sentence q when the truth of the first (p) guarantees the truth of the second (q), and the falsity of the second guarantees the falsity of the first. Thus, when we examine Statement A and Statement B here, suppose the result is like this: if A is true, B is also true; if B is false, A is also false, then we can say A entails B. However, the result is the opposite. The true result we find is: if A (Jack's brother has gone bankrupt.) is true, B (Jack has a brother.) is true; if B (Jack has a brother.) is false, A (Jack's brother has gone bankrupt.) fails, that is, if Jack has no brother, how can A (Jack's brother has gone bankrupt.) be judged? Is it false? Is it in grey area, neither true nor false? If A is false, then A entails B; but if we can not judge, we can not say A entails B.

If we view presupposition as a truth relation, then: if p is true, q is also true; if p is false, q is still true; if q is true, p could be either true or false; if q is false, no truth value can be said about p. Adopting this approach, we find the relation between Statement A and Statement B here is: if A (Jack's brother has gone bankrupt.) is true, B (Jack has a brother.) is true; if A (Jack's brother has gone bankrupt.) is false, B (Jack has a brother.) is still true; if B (Jack has a brother.) is true, A (Jack's brother has gone bankrupt.) can be either true or false; if B (Jack has a brother.) is false, we can not say anything true or false about A (Jack's brother has gone bankrupt.). Therefore, from the above analysis, the conclusion we get here is A presupposes B.

No, Statement A not necessarily entails Statement C here, because the word "sibling" does not necessarily have all the semantic components of "brother". Entailment is concerned with the meaning of the sentence itself. It does not depend on the context in which a sentence is used. Therefore, the context whether Jack has a brother or sister is not necessarily taken into consideration. Just in terms of semantic meaning, the word "sibling" means "a brother or sister". A brother? Or a sister? If it refers to a brother, we can say that Statement A entails Statement B; but if it refers to a sister, the semantic relation between A and B will fail to be an entailment.

Yes, statements A and D both presuppose Statement B. Statement D is the negation of Statement A. According the above analysis about presupposition, we have already drawn the conclusion that Statement A presupposes Statement B, so both the truth and falsity of Statement A can prove the truth of Statement B, that is to say, both Statement A and D can prove the truth of Statement B. Therefore, it is undoubtedly that Statement D also presupposes Statement B.

7. In group (1), the second parts of the three sentences all cancel the implied meaning of the first part by adding some extra contents. This is a character of cancellation of conversational implicature. The presence of a conversational implicature relies on a number of factors: the conventional meaning of words used, the CP, the linguistic and situational context, etc., if any of them changes, the implicature will also change. This can be done simply by adding more information, like the examples in group (1). When the second parts are added, the original implicatures are no longer there.

   In group (2), the case is very different because the two parts of those sentences are self-contradictory. While in group (1), even the second part's function of cancellation of implicature is based on the truth-value of the first part. So each second part in group (1)'s sentences will not change the truth-value of its corresponding first part. But in group (2), the sentences' second part actually deny the truth value of the first part, thus the two parts are inconsistent with each other and can not exist simultaneously. The sentences examples in group (2) are considered self-contradictory and then not acceptable.

8. In any language there are words which have the same linguistic form but are different in meanings. These words are called polysemic or polysemous words. There are also lots of polysemants in Chinese. for instance, the Chinese word "不过" embodies different meanings in actual usage. Take the examples provided above for example.

   In (1), the word "不过" expresses the meaning of "no more than". Hence, this sentence can be rewritten as "you will have nothing to be worried about after no more than two years."

   In (2), the meaning is a little bit different and it means "only, just". The example can be interpreted as "one year later he became a father who was only 18 years old."

In (3), it has used another meaning of this word, namely "very, extremely". Therefore, this sentence can be interpreted like this: this is a very cute kid.

However, the most commonly-used meaning of "不过" can be identified in the last example (4). In Chinese, more often than not, we use this word to indicate the change or transition of meaning. It has the same meaning with the English conjunctions "however", "but", "nevertheless", etc. Therefore, the sentence in the example can be paraphrased as "I have no good suggestions, either. However, this is very urgent; there is no way that we can make sure it is perfect". Through these four examples we can observe that the meaning of the specific words is context-dependent. The meanings may vary due to the change of the context. "不过" in most cases is used as an adverb, indicating the degree, such as the example (1)—(3). It is used as a conjunction in (4) indicating transition or change of ideas.

（本题考查汉语中一词多义的现象，通过分析例句指出同一词语不同意义之间的联系与区别，具有较强的灵活性。）

9. (1) On the analogy of distinctive features in phonology, some linguists suggest that there are semantic features or semantic components. Componential analysis is a way proposed by the structural semanticists to analyze word meaning. This is based on the belief that there are semantic units smaller than the meaning of a word, that is to say the meaning of a word can be dissected into meaning components, called semantic features or properties. The analysis breaks down the meaning of the word into these features, and it is these features that distinguish word meaning. Since it is economical, componential analysis gives a better account for sense relations and those between sentences.

(2) Plus and minus signs are used to indicate whether a certain semantic feature is present or absent in the meaning of a word, and these feature symbols are written in capitalized letters. For example, the meaning of the word "boy" can may be analyzed into + HUAMN, − ADULT, + MALE.

第 6 章　语用学

6.1　复习笔记

本章要点：

1. Speech act theory
   言语行为理论
2. Cooperative principle and its maxims
   合作原则及其准则
3. Politeness principle
   礼貌原则

常考考点：

语用学的定义；语法分析与语用学的区别；微观语用学中的基本概念；宏观语用学中言语行为理论(言内行为、言外行为和言后行为)；合作原则；实例分析言语行为、合作原则的违反和会话含意；礼貌原则。

本章内容索引：

Ⅰ. Pragmatics

1. Definition of pragmatics
2. Difference between pragmatics analysis and grammatical analysis
3. Definition of micropragmatics and macropragmatics

Ⅱ. Micropragmatics

1. Reference
2. Deixis
3. Anaphora
4. Presupposition

Ⅲ. Macropragmatics

1. Speech Act Theory
   (1) Theory of the Illocutionary Act
   ① Locutionary act
   ② Illocutionary act
   ③ Perlocutionary act
   (2) Classification of Illocutionary Act
   ① Representatives
   ② Directives
   ③ Commissives
   ④ Expressives
   ⑤ Declarations

(3) Indirect speech acts

2. The Cooperative Principle (CP)

(1) Cooperative Principle and Its Maxims

(2) Violation of the Maxims

3. Politeness Principle (PP)

Ⅰ. Pragmatics 【考点：名词解释】 **1. Definition of pragmatics** Pragmatics is the study of the use of natural language in communication, focusing on speakers' meaning, discourse meaning or contextual meaning.	**Ⅰ. 语用学** **1. 定义** 语用学是研究语言实际运用的学科，集中研究说话人意义、话语意义或语境意义。
2. Difference between pragmatics analysis and grammatical analysis First of all, grammatical studies focus on rules while pragmatic studies focus on principles. Secondly, in grammar studies, we pay attention to products while in pragmatics we focus on processes.	**2. 语用分析与语法分析的区别** 首先，语法研究注重规则而语用研究注重原则。 其次，语法研究重视最终的话语结果，而语用学重视其过程。
3. Definition of micropragmatics and macropragmatics 【考点：名词解释】 (1) The study of the meaning of utterances in smaller contexts is called micropragmatics. For example, reference, deixis, anaphora and presupposition are the topics in this field. (2) The study of the larger chunks of language and more in-depth exploration of the discourse mechanisms is called macropragmatics.	**3. 微观语用学与宏观语用学的定义** (1) 在较小的语境中研究话语的含义的研究叫做微观语用学。例如指称、指示、回指及预设现象都是这一领域的研究内容。 (2)在更广范围内研究并且更深入探究话语机制。这种研究方法是宏观语用学。
Ⅱ. Micropragmatics **1. Reference** An inference the act of connecting what the hearer has heard with what must be meant. In pragmatics, the act of the speaker or writer using language to make the hearer or reader identify something is called reference.	**Ⅱ. 微观语用学** **1. 指称** 推理是指听话者将所听到的与其必要的话语含义联系起来的行为。 在语用学中，说话者或写作者用语言使听者或读者辨认实际事物的行为，叫做指称。
2. Deixis 【考点：名词解释】 **(1) Definition** Deixis refers to the pointing or specifying function of some words (such as definite articles and demonstrative pronouns) whose denotation changes from one discourse to another.	**2. 指示** **(1) 定义** 指示指某些词(如定冠词和指示代词)的指向或指定功能，这些词的指称会随着语篇的改变而改变。

(2) Types ① Person deixis: me, you, him and them ② Time deixis: now, tonight, last week and this year ③ Space/spatial/place deixis: here, there and yonder ④ Discourse deixis: in the previous/next paragraph ⑤ Social deixis: forms to show respect e. g. Professor Li	**(2) 类型** ① 人称指示:我,你,他,他们 ② 时间指示:现在,今晚,上周,今年 ③ 空间指示:这里,那里,那边 ④ 篇章指示:前一段中,后一段中 ⑤ 社交指示:尊称,如李教授
3. Anaphora 【考点:名词解释】 Anaphora is the use of a pronoun or other linguistic unit to refer back to another word or phrase used earlier in a text or conversation.	**3. 回指** 文章中的一个单词或短语指前文中所提到的内容,叫做回指。
4. Presupposition **(1) Definition** A presupposition is something that you assume to be true, especially something which you must assume is true in order to continue with what you are saying or thinking.	**4. 预设** **(1) 定义** 预设是指你认为是正确的东西,特别是为了继续你所说或所想而必须假设为正确的东西。
(2) Presupposition triggers In any language, there are expressions and structures that can serve as the sources of presuppositions. Such expressions and structures are called presupposition triggers.	**(2) 预设触发语** 任何一种语言中,都有可以作为预设语源的表达与结构。这种表达与结构叫做预设触发语。
Ⅲ. Macropragmatics **1. Speech Act Theory** **(1) Theory of the Illocutionary Act** ① **Locutionary act**: the act of saying words, phrases and clauses, the literal meaning of the utterance; ② **Illocutionary act**: the act of expressing the speaker's attention. The utterance is produced on the basis of its literal meaning; ③ **Perlocutionary act**: a perlocutionary act is an action or state of mind brought about by saying something.	**Ⅲ. 宏观语用学** **1. 言语行为理论** **(1) 行事行为理论** ①言内行为是说出词、短语、分句的行为,是通过句法、词汇和音位手段表达字面意义的行为。 ②言外行为是表达说话人意图的行为,是在说话过程中所完成的行为。 ③言后行为是通过说话完成或通过说话所产生的行为,是由话语所带来的结果和变化。
(2) Classification of Illocutionary Act ① Representatives: those kinds of speech acts state that the speaker makes a statement or description, saying what he believes to be true. ② Directives: those kinds of speech acts that the speaker tries to get the hearer to do something. ③ Commissives: those kinds of speech acts that the speaker commits himself to a certain future action.	**(2) 言语行为的分类** ① 阐述类:说话人进行陈述或描写,说自己相信是真的话。 ② 指令类:说话人试图让听话人做某一件事。 ③ 承诺类:说话人使自己对某一未来的行为做出许诺。

④ Expressives: those utterances stating that the speaker expresses his feelings or attitude towards the current state of affairs.

⑤ Declarations: those utterances that the speaker makes an immediate change in an existing situation by speaking.

(3) Indirect speech acts

It is an utterance that the literal meaning (locution) is different from the intended meaning (illocution). For example, "*Can you help me close the window?*" is literally a yes/no question but is usually uttered as a request or polite directive for action.

2. The Cooperative Principle (CP)

【考点：合作原则及其准则】

(1) Cooperative Principle and Its Maxims

Make your conversational contribution such as is required, at the stage at which it occurs, by the accepted purpose or direction of the talk exchange.

① The Maxim of Quality

Try to make your contribution true, i. e.

a. Do not say what you believe to be false;

b. Do not say that for which you lack adequate evidence.

② The Maxim of Quantity

a. Make your contribution as informative as is required;

b. Do not make your contribution more informative than is required.

③ The Maxim of Relation

Be relevant.

④ The Maxim of Manner

Be perspicuous, i. e.

a. Avoid obscurity of expression;

b. Avoid ambiguity;

c. Be brief;

d. Be orderly.

(2) Violation of the Maxims and conversational implicature

According to Grice, people do not always adhere to the Cooperative Principle and its four maxims. When people deliberately and openly flouting the maxims, conversational implicatures arise. The following are a few cases in which the maxims of the Cooperative Principle are violated.

④ 表达类：说话人对现存事态表明自己的感受或态度。

⑤ 宣告类：说话人通过说话使现有的事态马上发生变化。

(3) 间接言语行为

表面意思(发话行为)与其实际含义(施事行为)不同的话语。例，“能帮忙关下窗户吗?”表面上这是个回答能不能的问题，实际上是委婉地请对方做某事。

2. 合作原则

(1) 合作原则及其准则

使你所说的话，在其所发生的阶段，符合你所参与的交谈的公认目标或方向。

① 质量准则

设法使你的话语真实。

a. 不要讲明知是虚假的话；

b. 不要说没证据的话。

② 数量准则

a. 使你的话语如(交谈的当前目的)所要求的那样信息充分；

b. 不要使你的话语比要求的信息更充分。

③ 关系准则

所谈内容要密切相关。

④ 方式准则

要清晰。

a. 避免含糊不清；

b. 避免歧义；

c. 要简练(避免冗长)；

d. 要有序。

(2) 违反会话原则与会话含意

使用原则和准则这两个术语，并不是说每个人一直遵守合作原则及其四条准则。人们会违反准则，会撒谎。也因为如此而产生了会话含意。以下是违反合作原则具体准则的几种情况。

① **Violation of the Maxim of Quantity**; —Man: Does your dog bite? —Woman: No. (the man reaches down to pet the dog. The dog bites the man's hand.) —Man: Hey! You said your dog doesn't bite. —Woman: He dosen't. But that's not my dog.	①违反数量准则;
② **Violation of the Maxim of Quality**; (tell lies; rhetoric device) a: Tom is a brave soilder, isn't he? b: yes, he is a lion in battle.	②违反质量准则;
③ **Violation of the Maxim of Relation**; —How do you like this performance? —It's a nice theatre.	③违反关系准则;
④ **Violation of the Maxim of Manner.** —Where are you going? —s-u-p-e-r-m-a-r-k-e-t.	④违反方式准则。
3. Politeness Principle (PP) 【考点：礼貌原则的六条准则】	**3. 礼貌原则**
Based on Grice's description of the Cooperative Principle, Leech also proposed the following six principles of the Politeness Principle:	基于格赖斯对合作原则的描述，利奇也提出了礼貌原则的如下六条准则：
Minimize (other things being equal) the expression of impolite beliefs and maximize (other things being equal) the expression of polite beliefs.	如果其他情况相同，尽量少表达不礼貌的信念，尽量多表达有礼貌的信念。
(1) Tact Maxim: Minimize cost to other; maximize cost to self.	(1) 得体准则：使他人受损最小；使他人受惠最大。
(2) Generosity Maxim: Minimize benefit to self; maximize benefit to other.	(2) 慷慨准则：使自身受惠最小；使自身受损最大。
(3) Approbation Maxim: Minimize dispraise of other; maximize dispraise of self.	(3) 赞誉准则：尽量少贬低别人；尽量多赞誉别人。
(4) Modesty Maxim: Minimize praise of self; maximize praise of other.	(4) 谦虚准则：尽量少赞誉自己；尽量多贬低自己。
(5) Agreement Maxim: Minimize disagreement between self and other; maximize agreement between self and other.	(5) 一致准则：尽量减少双方的分歧；尽量增加双方的一致。
(6) Sympathy Maxim: Minimize antipathy between self and other; maximize sympathy between self and other.	(6) 同情准则：尽量减少对别人的反感，尽量增大双方的同情。

6.2 课后习题详解

1. Define the following terms briefly.

pragmatics	deixis	reference
anaphora	presupposition	Speech Act Theory
indirect speech act	the Cooperative Principle	
the Politeness Principle	conversational implicature	

2. What are the deictic expressions in the following utterance?
   I'm busy now so you can't do that here. Come back tomorrow.
3. What are the anaphoric expressions in the following utterance?
   Dr. Dang gave Jane some medicine after she asked him for it.
4. What is one obvious presupposition of a speaker who says:
   (1) Where did he buy the beer?
   (2) Your watch is broken.
   (3) We regret buying that car.
5. Someone stands between you and the TV set you were watching, so you decide to say one of the following. Identify which would be direct and which would be indirect speech acts.
   (1) Move!
   (2) You're in the way.
   (3) Could you sit down?
   (4) I can't see anything.
   (5) Please get out of the way.
6. What are the four maxims of the Cooperative Principle?
7. Which maxim does this speaker seem to be particularly careful about:
   Well, to be quite honest, I don't think she is ill today.
8. How would you describe this short exchange in terms of the actions performed by the speakers?
   Carol: Are you coming to the party tonight?
   Lara: I've got an exam tomorrow.

参考答案

1. **Pragmatics**: Pragmatics is the study of the use of natural language in communication, focusing on speakers' meaning, discourse meaning or contextual meaning.
   Deixis: Deixis refers to the pointing or specifying function of some words (such as definite articles and demonstrative pronouns) whose denotation changes from one discourse to another.
   Reference: An inference the act of connecting what the hearer has heard with what must be meant. In pragmatics, the act of the speaker or writer using language to make the hearer or reader identify something is called reference.
   Anaphora: Anaphora is the use of a pronoun or other linguistic unit to refer back to another word or phrase used earlier in a text or conversation.
   Presupposition: A presupposition is something that you assume to be true, especially something

which you must assume is true in order to continue with what you are saying or thinking.

Speech Act Theory: Speech Act Theory was proposed by J. L. Austin and has been developed by J. R. Searle. Basically, they believe that language is not only used to inform or to describe things, it is often used to "do things", and to perform acts.

Indirect speech act: It is an utterance that the literal meaning (locution) is different from the intended meaning (illocution). For example, "*Can you help me close the window*?" is literally a yes/no question but is usually uttered as a request or polite directive for action.

The Cooperative Principle: the Cooperative Principle is the assumption that participants in a conversation normally attempt to be informative, truthful, relevant, and clear. It has four maxims: the maxim of quality, quantity, relation and manner.

The Politeness Principle: The politeness principle (PP) is introduced by Geoffrey Leech. PP is Minimizing (other things being equal) the expression of impolite beliefs. The PP contains six maxims: the maxim of tact, generosity, approbation, modesty, agreement and sympathy.

Conversational implicature: According to Grice, people do not always adhere to the Cooperative Principle and its four maxims. When people deliberately and openly flouting the maxims, conversational implicatures arise

2. **Deictic expressions**: I, now, you, that, here, tomorrow.
3. **Anaphoric expressions**: She, him, it.
4. (1) He bought some beer.
   (2) You have a watch.
   (3) We have already bought that car.
5. **Direct speech act**: (1), (5)
   Indirect speech act: (2), (3), (4)
6. The Cooperative Principle(CP) contains four maxims:

   The Maxim of Quantity

   Make your contribution as informative as is required (for the current purposes of the exchange).
   Do not make your contribution more informative than is required.

   The Maxim of Quality

   Try to make your contribution one that is true.
   Do not say what you believe to be false.
   Do not say that for which you lack adequate evidence.

   The Maxim of Relation Be relevant.

   The Maxim of Manner Be perspicuous.

   Avoid obscurity of expression.
   Avoid ambiguity.
   Be brief (avoid prolixity).
   Be orderly.
7. This speaker is particularly careful about the maxim of quality, because he/ she said, "to be quite honest", which means he/ she does not want to say what he/ she believes to be false.
8. It is an indirect speech act. Carol invites Lara to a party, but Lara wants to decline the invita-

tion. To be polite, she doesn't choose a direct refusal, instead she says "I've got an exam tomorrow" as a reasonable excuse to decline the invitation. In this way, she minimizes the expression of impolite beliefs, thus the utterance conforms to PP. Obviously Lara breaks the maxim of relation of CP by talking about something totally irrelevant with Carol's question. However, we can understand her meaning perfectly. Lara is conveying an indirect meaning by giving out an utterance containing a conversational implicative. Her aim is to refuse Carol's invitation in an polite and less harsh manner.

6.3 考研真题与典型题详解

Ⅰ. Fill in the blanks.

1. A perlocutionary act is the act performed by or resulting from saying something; it is the __________ of, or the __________ the utterance.（人大 2004 研）
2. When a teacher says "The exam this year is going to be really difficult", the sentence would have an __________ force.（清华 2001 研）
3. There has been a maxim in __________ which claims that "You are what you say."（中山大学 2008 研）
4. The theory of conversational implicature was proposed by __________.（中山大学 2008 研）
5. Y's utterance in the following conversation exchange violates the maxim of __________.
   X: Who was that you were with last night?
   Y: Did you know that you were wearing odd socks?
6. Promising, undertaking, vowing are the most typical of the __________.

Ⅱ. Multiple Choice

1. The speech act theory was developed by __________.（对外经贸 2006 研）
   A. John Searle　B. John Austin　C. Levinson　D. G. Leech
2. Point out which item does not fall under the same category as the rest. (Focus on the type of illocutionary act)（南京大学 2007 研）
   A. threaten　B. advise　C. beseech　D. urge
3. __________ is using a sentence to perform a function.（西安外国语学院 2006 研）
   A. A perlocutionary act　B. An illocutionary act
   C. A locutionary act　D. Speech act
4. By saying "You have left the door wide open," a speaker might be performing the three acts: locutionary, illocutionary and perlocutionary __________.（西安交大 2008 研）
   A. at the same time　B. one after another
   C. two first and then the other　D. one first and then the other two
5. The Illocutionary Act was developed by __________.（西安交大 2008 研）
   A. John Austin　B. Levinson　C. John Lyons　D. John Searle
6. According to the conversation maxim of __________ suggested by Grice, one should speak truthfully.（西安外国语学院 2006 研）
   A. quantity　B. quality　C. relevance　D. manner
7. Which of the following is NOT one of the four maxims of the Cooperative Principle?（对外经贸

2006 研)

A. the maxim of quantity
B. the maxim of quality
C. the maxim of manner
D. the maxim of strength

Ⅲ. True or False

1. A speaker flouts the Maxim of Quantity when his contributions to the conversation are not truthful. (对外经贸 2005 研)
2. The co-operative principle was proposed by Grice. (南开大学 2004 研)
3. When performing an illocutionary act of representative, the speaker is making a statement or giving a description which he himself believes to be true.
4. As the process of communication is essentially a process of conveying meaning in a certain context, pragmatics can also be considered as a kind of meaning study.
5. Inviting, suggesting, warning, ordering are instances of commissives.

Ⅳ. Explain the following terms.

1. Locutionary Act, Illocutionary Act and Perlocutionary Act (北京交通大学 2005 研；武汉大学 2005 研)
2. Conversational Implicature (武汉大学 2004 研；北京交通大学 2007 研)
3. Cooperative principle (北师大 2003 研；长沙理工大学 2019 研)
4. Violation of maxims (北京交通大学 2006 研)

Ⅴ. Short answer questions

1. What are the major concerns of pragmatics? (人大 2006 研)
2. How would you describe this short exchange in terms of the ardors performed by the speakers? (浙江大学 2005 研)

   Motorist: My car needs new exhaust system.

   Mechanic: I'll be busy with this other car all day.
3. Conversational implicature is comparable to illocutionary force in speech act theory in that they are both concerned with the contextual side of meaning, or "言外之意" in Chinese. (中山大学 2005 研)
4. Decide which maxim of the cooperative principle has been flouted in the following utterances and what implicature can be drawn. (厦门大学 2006 研)

   (1) A: Can you tell me the secret?

   B: But John is there.

   (2) A: Let's go to the movies.

   B: I'll bring the Kleenex.

   (3) A: Would you drive a Mercedes?

   B: I wouldn't drive ANY expensive car.
5. Do you think B is cooperative in the following dialogue? Support your argument with Cooperative Principle. (南开大学 2004 研)

   A: When is the bus coming?

   B: There has been an accident further up the road.
6. Analyze the following dialogue with reference to Grice's Cooperative Principle. (北二外 2005

研)

A: Oh I like this popular song so much. How about you?

B: I often hear classical music, especially, the symphonies composed by Beethoven His Symphony No. 9 is my favorite.

7. In what ways do people cooperate in their conversations? (人大 2006 研)

Ⅵ. Essay questions

1. When a teacher says "it's so hot in here" during a class, what does she probably mean? Refer to the theory of pragmatics when you analyze the situation. (人大 2002 研)
2. A speech act consists of three related acts according to J. L. Austin's Speech Act theory. What are they? Analyze the following conversation in the light of Speech Act theory. (北航 2008 研)

   Customer: *Waiter! There's a fly in my soup.*

   Waiter: *Don't worry, there's no extra charge.*
3. Explain speech act theory and list the different kinds of speech acts with examples for each. (浙江大学 2004 研)
4. Discuss the following sentences in terms of violation of maxims in the cooperative principle. (浙江大学 2007 研)

   a. I think he was married and had a lioness at home.

   b. A: What do you intend to do?

   B: I have a terrible headache.

   c. A: Where've you been?

   B: Out.
5. Discuss the following advertisement extensively: "你不理财，财不理你". (浙江大学 2007 研)
6. Imagine you were at a bus stop and two people approached you one after the other. The first said

   "哎，几点了?"

   and the second said

   "不好意思，打搅一下，请问您戴表了吗?"

   What assumptions would you make if you were addressed in these two ways and why would you make them? (北外 2007 研)
7. What kind of linguistic phenomenon can you identify in the following dialogue? Define, analyse and explain the phenomenon. (北外 2010 研)

   甲：上车请买票。

   乙：三张天安门。

   甲：您拿好。

参考答案及解析

Ⅰ. Fill in the blanks.

1. consequence; change brought about by

   (根据言后行为的定义，这一话语行为指由话语所带来的结果和变化。)
2. illocutionary

（言外行为是表达说话人意图的行为，老师所说的话表明了让学生努力学习的意图。）

3. quantity

（格莱斯的数量准则指：使你的话语如（交谈的当前目的）所要求的那样信息充分；不要使你的话语比要求的信息更充分。即说你该说的。）

4. Grice

（格赖斯认为一定存在一些管理话语产生和理解的机制，他把这种机制称为合作原则。合作原则包含四条准则，即数量、质量、关系和方式准则。）

5. relation

（很显然 Y 的回答与 X 的问题“你昨晚跟谁在一起?”无关。）

6. commissives

（承诺类指说话人使自己对某一未来的行为做出许诺。）

Ⅱ. Multiple Choice

1. A （言语行为理论最初由英国哲学家约翰·奥斯汀于 1905 年在美国哈佛大学做 William James 系列演讲时将该理论作为一种哲学分析工具提出，后经他的学生——语言学家约翰·舍尔等众多语言学家不断总结、创新和规范后形成一个系统。）
2. A （A 为命令性言语行为，而其他三项为指示性言语行为。）
3. D （约翰·奥斯丁在他《如何以言行事》一文中提出言语行为理论，此理论对语言交际的本质进行解释，即指出言语行为是指用一句话来发挥去完成某些事情的作用。）
4. A （奥斯汀认为说话人说话时可以完成三种行为：发话行为，行事行为和取效行为。）
5. D （美国的哲学语言学家约翰·舍尔对言语行为理论的发展做出了巨大的贡献，尤其是他对行事行为的分类。）
6. B （格莱斯的合作原则有四条准则，它们分别为数量、质量、关系和方式准则。其中质量准则指：设法使你的话语真实——不要讲明知是虚假的话；不要说没证据的话。）
7. D （格莱斯的合作原则有四条准则，它们分别为数量、质量、关系和方式准则。）

Ⅲ. True or False

1. F （说假话违反的是质量准则而不是数量准则。）
2. T （合作原则是由格莱斯提出的。）
3. T （阐述类是指说话人进行陈述或描写，说自己相信是真的话。）
4. T （语用学是研究语言在某种语境下所传达的意义，也是研究语言意义的。）
5. F （题中所描述的是指令性话语，是指说话人试图让听话人做某一件事。）

Ⅳ. Explain the following terms.

1. According to Austin, a speaker might be performing three acts simultaneously when speaking. A locutionary act is the act of saying, the literal meaning of the utterance. Therefore, when somebody says “Morning”, we can ask a question like “What did he do?”, and the answer could be “He offered a greeting.”

   An illocutionary act is the extra meaning of the utterance produced on the basis of the literal meaning. Therefore, for the same example, we can say “He meant it as a greeting”.

   A perlocutionary act is the effect of the utterance on the hearer. Thus, by saying “Morning!” the speaker has made it clear that he wants to keep friendly relations with the hearer.

2. Conversational implicature refers to a type of implied meaning, which is deduced on the basis of

the conventional meaning of words together with the context, under the guidance of the CP and its maxims. For example, the implicature of *He is a tiger* could probably be *he has some characteristics of a tiger*.

3. Cooperative principle was proposed and formulated by Grice. It expresses that in making a conversation, the participants must first of all be willing to cooperate; otherwise, it would not be possible for them to carry on the talk. It goes like this: "make your conversational contribution such as is required, at the stage at which it occurs, by the accepted purpose or direction of the talk exchange in which you are engaged". This principle can be further specified as the four following maxims: Quantity, Quality, Relation, Manner.
4. There are circumstances where speakers may not follow the maxims of the cooperative principle. For example, in conversation, a speaker may violate the maxim expectations by using an expression like "No comment" in response to a question. Although it is typically not "as informative as is required" in the context, it is naturally interpreted as communicating more than is said (i. e. the speaker knows the answer). This typical reaction to any apparent violation of the maxims is actually the key to the notion of conversational implicature. When we violate any of these maxims, our language becomes indirect. In this way, we can convey more than is literally said. For example, there is violation of the first maxim of Quantity, and sometimes the first Quantity maxim can be in conflict with the Quality maxim.

V. Short answer questions

1. Pragmatics is the study of the language in use. It is mainly about how speakers use language appropriately and effectively in accordance with a given context. It is concerned with the study of meaning as communicated by a speaker (or writer) and interpreted by a listener (or reader). It has more to do with participants of communication and context in which communication takes place. Hence the study of speaker meaning, that of contextual meaning, of what is unsaid but communicated.
2. In the motorist's utterance, there are two types of speech acts performed, namely representative and directive, and as to the latter one, it is recognized as an indirect speech act, which is performed through the performance of the former one. Thus, by stating that his car needs new exhaust system, the motorist has in fact asked the mechanic to equip a new exhaust system for him.

   Similarly, in the mechanic's utterance, there are two types of speech acts performed; one is representative, the other commissive. The commissive speech act in fact is an indirect one since it is recognized through the performance of representative action. That is to say, by stating that he will be busy with another car all day, the mechanic has in fact told the motorist that he could not repair his car right away.
3. We may summarize conversational implicature as a type of implied meaning. It could be inferred only by the dependence on the context of the utterance and shared knowledge between the speaker and listener. Illocutionary force, on the other hand, refers to speaker's meaning, contextual meaning, or extra meaning, that is, the meaning the speaker wants to convey in a specific context. By an illocutionary force, we can say "What does he mean by saying that?" In this sense, implicature is comparable to illocutionary force in speech act theory in that they are both con-

cerned with the contextual side of meaning, or "言外之意" in Chinese.

4. In the exchanges, the maxim of relation has been flouted. As to instance (1), A will assume that if B is cooperative, his reply must be relevant in a different sense: I will not talk about my secret now because I do not want to let John know. In (2), the answer of B seems irrelevant to A's utterance. By doing so, A will likely derive the implicature that B has accepted his suggestion, and is going to get prepared. In (3), by violating the maxim of relation, B intends to implicate that Mercedes is an expensive car and he would not drive a Mercedes.
5. On the face of it, B violated the maxim of relation since he did not provide a direct answer to A's question. But A would assume that B is cooperative in the conversation, and would try to explore the link between the seemingly irrelevant response to something relevant. Thus, A would interpret B's utterance in such a way that because there had been as accident further up the road, it was quite possible that the road was blocked; in a consequence, the bus would not be able to come.
6. B has obviously violated Maxim of Relation: A was asking B's opinion about a particular popular song, but B's response was actually about classical music. By such a violation, B probably wanted to imply that he did not like that popular song.
7. In daily conversations people do not usually say things directly but tend to imply them, and according to Grice, they seem to observe willingly or unwillingly certain principle, which is called "cooperative principle": "Make your conversational contribution such as is required, at the stage at which it occurs, by the accepted purpose or direction of the talk exchange in which you are engaged". Under this principle, there are four maxims, namely, Quantity, Quality, Relation, and Manner.

Ⅵ. Essay questions

1. This utterance would be semantically ambiguous if it was seen isolated without any context of situation. Its interpretation has to rely on the context in which it was uttered.

   There could be generally two types of situation in which this utterance could happen. One may be that it is summer; the teacher just came into the class and was sweating heavily. The other may be that in class the students are quite active towards the questions or problems the teacher has posed, for example, discussing in group, or debating in a large scale.

   According to the cooperative principle, in our conversation, in order to be cooperative, that is, to make his intentions to be known by the hearer, the speaker will try to make his conversational contribution such as is required, at the stage at which it occurs.

   Therefore, according to the third maxim of cooperative principle, RELATION, which says "be relevant", the utterance could be interpreted differently as follows:

   In the first situation, when the students hear the teacher saying "it's so hot in here", they would probably assume that the teacher is obeying the cooperative principle, and what he says is relevant to the context, which is that the teacher is sweating, and maybe accompanied by fanning herself with his hand. Therefore, what the teacher means is probably that the temperature is high. What's more, if the windows in the classroom are closed, this utterance will go further to be an implication of an request for opening the windows.

In the second situation, the students would assume that the teacher should have observed the maxim of relation, since it is under normal circumstances. Given the context in which the students are discussing or debating about certain questions furiously, the hearer would tend to interpret the teacher's utterance as: "you are discussing (or debating) so actively", which implies a praise for the active participation of the students in class activity.

2. A speech act consists of three related acts according to J. L. Austin's Speech Act theory, namely, locutionary act, illocutionary act and perlocutionary act. The locutionary act is the ordinary act we perform when we speak. It is the act of saying. The illocutionary act is the act performed in the performing of a locutionary act, that may said to be the extra meaning of the utterance; while perlocutionary act concerns the consequential effects of a locution upon the hearer, depending on specific circumstances. Austin suggests that the three kinds of acts are performed simultaneously when a speaker saying something.

   In this conversation, by saying "Waiter! There's a fly in my soup", the locutionary act of this utterance is that the customer produces a number of sounds with the literal meaning that there is a fly in his/ her soup. The illocutionary act is that the customer intends not to just review the information to the waiter, but might express his feelings and expect the waiter to do something. It might be a complaint, a warn, a criticism, or a threat, but whatever it might be, it is no doubt a force, making the waiter to change soup or give some compensation. The perlocutionary act of the utterance here is the waiter's doing nothing but giving a strange respond.

   As to the waiter's responding, by saying that he not only produces a number of sounds to state that there is no extra charge, but also shows his possible misinterpretation or his sense of humor or his indirect refusal.

3. The speech act theory was proposed by John Austin. According to this theory, we are performing various kinds of acts when we are speaking. Actions performed through utterances are generally called speech acts. An utterance can perform different speech acts depending on the context and that one speech act can be performed by more than one utterances.

   According to Searle, speech acts fall into five general categories. Specific acts that fall into each type share the same illocutionary point, but differ in their strength.

   (1) Representatives: acts of saying what the speaker believes to be true; they include stating, describing, asserting, and so on; such as "It's raining", "They won the game".

   (2) Directives: acts of trying to get the hearer to do something. Commands, orders, requests, warnings, suggestions, and on so are of this type, as illustrated in "Be quiet!", "Don't touch that!"

   (3) Commissives: acts of committing the speaker himself to some future course of action. They include promising, vowing, offering, threatening, and so on. Examples are "I'll take her to the vet." and "We won't do that."

   (4) Expressives: acts of expressing feelings or attitude towards an existing state. They can be statements of pleasure, pain, likes, sorrow, and so on. For example, "I'm sorry to hear that".

   (5) Declarations: acts of bringing about immediate changes by saying something. They include

resigning, dismissing, naming, appointing, and so on. For example, the priest may say in a wedding "I now pronounce you husband and wife".

4. In sentence *a*, the speaker has violated the first Quality maxim, which says "do not say what you believe to be false". In the literal sense, no human being would marry a lioness, and therefore at this level, it is a false statement. However, the deliberate violation of the maxim will lead us to interpret it as a metaphor, meaning that his wife had a bad temper.

   In sequence b, B has flouted the maxim of Relation, since he did not answer A's question directly. However, assuming that B was co-operative, A was likely to derive the implicature that since B had a terrible headache, he would probably just lie in bed and do nothing.

   In exchange *c*, a violation of the first Quantity maxim was recognized, which says "make your contribution as informative as is required for the current purposes of the exchange". B was supposed to provide the specific information of the place he had been to; however, he didn't. By such a violation, B probably implied that "I do not want to tell you where I have been".

5. This advertisement is an interesting one, for its witty use of pun words. There are two places of punning. First, "理财" could be interpreted in two different ways: one is "to manage one's money", the other is "not to ignore money". Second, in the second part of the sentence, "财" is punned through homophony: it could be interpreted as "财", therefore, the whole part "财不理你" could mean "fortune will ignore you", or rather, "fortune will pass you away". This character could also be interpreted as "才", therefore, the whole part "财不理你" could mean "I will ignore you", or rather, "I will show you my cold shoulder" (Here "I" refers to the company which put out this advertisement).

   Therefore, this utterance could be possibly interpreted in the following ways. 1) If you do not handle your money in a proper way, then money will pass you by. 2) If you do not handle your money properly, then I won't take care of any of your business. 3) If you ignore money, and do not pay any attention to it, then money will pass you by. 4) If you ignore money, then I will ignore you, too, and I won't take care of any of your business. In these four interpretations, it is clear to see that in 1 and 4, the advertiser conveyed the messages to the readers as if he was having a face-to-face talk to a friend. This has in some way made the piece of ad interesting to read.

   It is known the punning is by nature ambiguous. Therefore, according to Grice, the advertisement has violated the principle of avoiding ambiguity under Manner Maxim. By such a violation, the advertiser has possibly intended to make the potential consumers pay more attention to it, and spend more time on it, since it is known that ambiguity will increase the time for processing the sentence; and by interpreting it in additional ways, the readers are also expected to get another interesting message from this ad. All of these could eventually come to a higher memorability of the advertisement.

6. As to the first one, an immediate assumption coming to our mind would be the person is asking for the time. The assumption that the hearer gets arises out of the conventional meaning of the expression. The conventional meaning is related to the existing knowledge of the world, and is the meaning that is achieved by the conventions, and is generally accepted by the society. It can be

accessed to when we turn to the knowledge towards the world that we have. The expression "几点了" is such an conventional meaning that when it is spoken out, everyone will unexceptionally accept it as a way of asking for the time.

As to the explanation of the second one, Levinson's M-principle could come into use. Considering the context, which is in the bus stop, what it expresses is no longer a conventional one, but rather a conversational implicature. According to M-principle, the speaker normally will not use a prolix, obscure or marked expression without reason; on the hearer's side, if the speaker used a prolix or marked expression, he did not mean the same as was conveyed by means of the unmarked expression. That is to say, in the normal situation, as shown by the example above, the reason why the speaker asks others such questions is not merely to care about whether the recipient has a watch or not, but to get the exact time. And it would be bizarre to ask a stranger in the bus stop about such a personal staff. Therefore, the hearer has to assume that the expression is related to the situation, and this expression is not what it literally means. Following this, the hearer reaches a connection between the bus stop and the watch, that is the time. As a consequence, he knows what the speaker intends is the inquiring of the time.

7. This conversation consists of the linguistic phenomenon which is called the "Cooperative Principle", proposed and formulated by P. Grice, based on such a pragmatic hypothesis that the participants must first of all be willing to cooperate; otherwise, it would not be possible to carry on the talk. It goes as follows:

Make your conversational contribution such as required at the stage at which it occurs by the accepted purpose or direction of the talk exchange in which you are engaged. To be more specific, there are four maxims under this general principle:

The maxim of quantity:

(a) Make your contribution as informative as is required (for the current purposes of the exchange).

(b) Do not make your contribution more informative than is required.

The maxim of quality:

(a) Do not say what you believe to be false.

(b) Do not say that for which you lack adequate evidence.

The maxim of relation:

Be relevant.

The maxim of manner:

(a) Avoid obscurity of expression.

(b) Avoid ambiguity.

(c) Be brief (avoid unnecessary prolixity).

(d) Be orderly.

There are circumstances where speakers may not follow the maxims of the cooperative principle. For example, in this conversation, the speaker may violate the maxim expectations by using an expression like "三张天安门" in response to a question. Although it is typically "more informative than is required" in the context, it is naturally interpreted as communicating more than is said (i. e. the speaker knows the answer). This typical reaction (i. e. there must be something "special" here) of listeners to any apparent violation of the maxims is actually the key to the notion of conversational implicature. When we violate any of these maxims, our language becomes indirect. In this way, we can convey more than is literally said.

第 7 章　语篇分析

7.1　复习笔记

本章要点：

1. Discourse and discourse analysis
   话语及话语分析
2. Given and new information
   已知信息与新信息
3. Cohesion and coherence
   衔接与连贯
4. Conversational analysis
   会话分析

常考考点：

话语及话语分析的定义；已知信息与新信息的异同；衔接手段包括指称、替代、省略、连词与词汇衔接；话语标记语的定义与特征；会话分析中的配组会话、首选结构及前序列；批判性话语分析。

本章内容索引：

Ⅰ. Definition of discourse and discourse analysis

Ⅱ. Information structure

1. Given and new information
2. Topic and comment
3. Contrast

Ⅲ. Cohesion and coherence

1. Cohesion.
   (1) Reference
   (2) Substitution
   (3) Ellipsis
   (4) Conjunction
   (5) Lexical cohesion
2. Coherence

Ⅳ. Discourse markers

1. Definition
2. Functional-pragmatic nature
3. Features of discourse markers

Ⅴ. Conversational analysis

1. Adjacency pairs

2. Preference structure

3. Presequences

Ⅵ. Critical discourse analysis

Ⅰ. Definition of discourse and discourse analysis

1. Discourse

Discourse refers to the use of language, that is to say, discourse is the product of people's communication. It refers to larger units of language, such as paragraphs, dialogues, interviews, etc.

2. Discourse analysis

Discourse analysis aims to study how sentences form larger meaningful linguistic units in spoken and written language, such as paragraphs, dialogues, interviews, etc.

Ⅱ. Information structure

1. Given and new information

Given information is the information that the speaker thinks the hearer already knows, while new information is the information that the speaker thinks the hearer doesn't know.

New information is usually presented in an elaborate way, for example, using a full noun phrase instead of a pronoun. In contrast, given information is presented in a more concise form—that is, in a short or condensed form. Typical attenuating expressions include pronouns and unstressed noun phrases.

2. Topic and comment

【考点：名词解释】

(1) Definition

Topic is the subject of a conversation, and comment is what is said about the subject.

(2) Differences with given-new information

The difference between given information and new information lies in the hearer, while the difference between topic and comment lies in the speaker.

3. Contrast

In the discourse, when a noun phrase has the opposite meaning to another noun phrase, they are called contrasts. For example, the noun phrase Susan in Speaker B's answer is contrasted with the noun phrase Amy.

A: Did Amy eat the cake?

B: No, Susan did.

Ⅰ. 话语及话语分析的定义

1. 语篇

泛指语言的运用，也就是说，话语是人们进行交流的产物。它指更大的语言单位，比如段落、对话、采访等。

2. 话语分析

研究句子在口语及书面语中如何构成有意义的语言单位比如段落、对话、采访等。

Ⅱ. 信息结构

1. 已知信息与新信息

已知信息是指说话者认为听话者已经知道的信息，而新信息是指说话者认为听话者不知道的信息。

新信息通常以详尽的方式表述，例如，用完整的名词短语而不是代词。相比较而言，已知信息以更加简洁的方式表达——即简短或精简的方式。典型的简洁表达包括代词和非强调性的名词短语。

2. 话题与述题

(1) 定义

话题是谈话的主题，述题是围绕主题所谈论的内容。

(2) 话题与述题的区别

已知信息与新信息的区别在于听话者一方，而话题与述题的区别在于说话者一方。

3. 对比

在话语中，当一个名词短语与另一个名词短语意义正好相反时，则他们被叫做对比。例如，B 的回答就与 Amy 这个名词短语形成对比。

A：Amy 吃了蛋糕吗？

B：没有，Susan 吃了。

Ⅲ. Cohesion and coherence	**Ⅲ. 衔接与连贯**
【考点：衔接与连贯的区别】	
1. Definition of cohesion.	**1. 衔接的定义**
Cohesion is an important research field in discourse analysis. It refers to relations of meaning that exist within the text, and that define it as a text.	衔接是话语分析中的一个重要研究领域。衔接概念是一个语义概念，它指形成语篇的意义关系。
2. Cohesive devices	**2. 衔接手段**
(1) Reference	**(1) 指称**
The most common cohesive devices are the use of referential words, including pronouns(it, they, he, it), demonstratives (this, that, these, those), the article (the), and phrases like *such as*.	最常用的衔接手段就是指称词汇的运用，包括代词(如它、他们、他、它等)，指示代词(这个、那个、这些、那些)，定冠词 *the*，还有像 *such as* 这样的短语。
There are two types of reference: One is endophoric reference (endophora), which refers to the interpretive source lying in the co-text; the other is exophoric reference (exophora), which refers to the interpretive source lying in the context.	指称包括两种类型：一种是内参照，其所指在上文中；另一种是外参照，其所指在其下文中。
(2) Substitution	**(2) 替代**
The process or result of replacing one word by another at a particular position in a structure is called substitution.	用一个词代替另一个词在结构中的位置的过程或结果叫做替代。
There are three types of substitution, that is, nominal (to replace a noun or noun phrase), verbal (to replace a verb phrase) and clausal (to replace a clause) substitution.	替代有三种类型：名词替代(替代名词或名词性短语)、动词替代(替代一个动词短语)、从句替代(替代一个从句)。
(3) Ellipsis	**(3) 省略**
Ellipsis is the omission of a word or phrase of a sentence for brevity, emphasis or style, and the omitted parts can be found by the reader from the previous discourse.	省略是指为了简洁，强调或风格而省去句子中的词或短语，并且读者可以在前文中找到省略的部分。
There are three types of ellipsis: nominal, verbal and clausal.	省略有三种类型：名词省略、动词省略、从句省略。
(4) Conjunction	**(4) 连词**
Conjunctions are words that have the function of connecting words or other constructions. In the example, "I was late for school because I got up late", the two clauses are connected by the cohesive conjunction because.	连词是指具有连接词汇或其他结构的功能的词。
There are three types of conjunctions: coordinating conjunctions (and, or, but), subordinating conjunctions (because, when, unless) and adverbial words (however, moreover, indeed, nevertheless).	连词有三种类型：并列连词(和、或、但)、从属连词(因为、当……时、除非)、作状语的词(然而、另外、确实、不过)。

(5) Lexical cohesion Lexical cohesion is the lexical device that can cross short or large pieces of the discourse. There are following three types: ① Repetition ② Synonym ③ Superordinate	**(5) 词汇衔接** 词汇衔接是指用词汇将话语中的不同部分连接起来。有以下三种类型: ① 重复 ② 同义词替代 ③ 上义词替代
3. Coherence Coherence is a state or situation in which all the parts or ideas fit together well so that they form a united whole.	**3. 连贯** 连贯是一种状态或情况，在这种状态或情况下，话语中话段的含义或篇章中句子的意义很好地结合在一起形成一个整体。
Ⅳ. Discourse markers **1. Definition** Discourse markers are words or phrases that are used at the beginning of sentences and are syntactically detachable from a sentence.	**Ⅳ. 话语标记语** **1. 定义** 话语标记语是指通常用在句首或与句子结构联系不紧密的词汇表达。
2. Functional-pragmatic nature (1) In narratives In narratives, discourse markers can be found as the temporal terms, that is, of the presentation of new events as occurring later in time.	**2. 语用功能的特质** (1) 记叙文中 在记叙文中，话语标记语经常以时间性的词汇出现，即用在陈述即将发生的事情之后。
(2) In non-narratives In non-narrative texts, discourse markers can connect the discourse together.	(2) 非记叙文中 在非记叙文中，话语标记语可以把整个话语连接在一起。
3. Features of discourse markers (1) They do not belong to the sentence elements proper (subject, verb, complement);	**3. 话语标记语的特征** (1) 话语标记语不属于句子本身结构划分中的成分(主语、谓语、补语);
(2) They usually appear at the beginning of a sentence or at a transitional position in the whole text. (beginning and end of units);	(2) 话语标记语通常出现在句首或在整篇中的过渡性的位置(句首或句末);
(3) They don't always have explicit propositional (semantic) meaning, and their propositional meaning is replaced by their discourse functions;	(3) 话语标记语通常没有明确的命题(语义)意义，其意义被他们的话语功能所取代;
(4) There are multiple roles in signaling relations (ideational, textual, and interpersonal) between units at different levels.	(4) 话语标记语在不同层次单位间的标记关系存在多种角色(概念、语篇及人际)。
Ⅴ. Conversational analysis **1. Adjacency pairs** 【考点：名词解释】	**Ⅴ. 会话分析** **1. 配组会话**

(1) Definition An adjacency pair is composed of two turns produced by different speakers which are placed adjacently and where the second utterance is identified as related to the first. **(2) Properties** ① Adjacency pairs include two utterances, a first part and a second part. ② The two parts are spoken by different speakers. ③ The two sentences belong to a specific type. ④ The content and form of the second part depend on the first part. ⑤ After the speaker says the first part, the other speaker's response is related to the first part. **2. Preference structure** The answers to many of these questions are not the exact answers but are meant to be the second part of the conversation. Basically, a first part that includes a request or an offer is typically expected to receive an acceptance in the second part. An acceptance is structurally more likely than a refusal. This structural likelihood is called preference. Preference structure divides second parts into preferred and dispreferred. The preferred leads to the next act, while the dispreferred does not lead to the next act. In the second part, the preferred is more common. **3. Presequence** 【考点：名词解释】 Presequence refers to the opening sequences or utterances used to introduce specific potential actions. **Ⅵ. Critical discourse analysis** Critical discourse analysis studies discourse from the perspective of sociopolitical and cultural factors and their interrelationships, focusing on how discourse is ideologically influenced by social power relations and how it affects social power relations.	**(1) 定义** 两个说话者之间相联系的两句对话。其中第二句是对第一句的回应。 **(2) 特征** ① 配组会话包括两句对话，第一部分与第二部分。 ② 两部分由不同的说话者说出。 ③ 两句话分别属于一种具体的类型。 ④ 第二部分的内容与构成取决于第一部分。 ⑤ 说话者说出第一部分后，由另一位说话者进行相关的回应。 **2. 首选结构** 很多问题的回答并不是确切的答案而只是作为对话的第二部分。 通常来说，包含请求或者提议的第一部分都期待着能够接受该请求或者提议的第二部分。从结构上讲，接受比拒绝更有可能让会话继续。这种可能的结构叫做首选。首选结构把第二部分分成了首选与非首选。首选结构上引出下一个动作，而非首选结构上不会引出下一个动作。首选结构的第二部分更加常见。 **3. 前序列** 前序列是指开篇话，即用来引出具体的潜在行为的话语。 **Ⅵ. 批判性话语分析** 批判性话语分析从社会政治、文化因素及其相互关系的视角研究话语，重点研究话语是如何在意识形态上受社会权力关系的影响，以及它自身又是怎样影响社会权力关系的。

7.2 课后习题详解

1. Define the following terms briefly.

discourse	discourse analysis	given information
new information	topic	cohesion
coherence	discourse marker	adjacency pair
preference structure	presequence	critical discourse analysis

2. What is meant by the term "cohesion" in the study of discourses?
3. Say what *one* is replacing in the following text.

   A group of people marching on the road should keep to the left. There should be look-outs in front and at the back wearing reflective clothing at night and fluorescent clothing by day. At night the look-out in front should carry a white light and the *one* at the back should carry a bright red light visible from the rear.
4. Pick out all the instances of discourse reference in the following text.

   At one point the Brundtland report states that "The loss of plant and animal species can greatly limit the options of future generations; so sustainable development requires the conservation of plant and animal species". What, all of them? At what price? . . . At another point the Brundtland report says that economic growth and development obviously involve changes in the physical ecosystem. "Every ecosystem everywhere cannot be preserved intact." Well, that's a relief. But how can it be made consistent with the earlier objective? Does it mean that it is all right to deprive some people in some parts of the world of a piece of their ecosystem but not others? What justification is there for this discrimination?
5. Do you think that the following passage is a coherent discourse? Why or why not?

   I bought a Ford. A car in which President Wilson rode down the Champs Elysees was black. Black English has been widely discussed. The discussions between the presidents ended last week. A week has seven days. Every day I feed my cat. Cats have four legs. The cat is on the mat. Mat has three letters.
6. Find the general words which contribute to the coherence of the following extract, and discuss how each of these words is used.

   And what about interviewing, because you interview a number of politicians like, well, the Prime Minister or the Chancellor or the Exchequer. Is that an easy thing to do and how difficult is it when you're interviewing people that you don't particularly agree with or who get difficult with you during an interview?

参考答案

1. **Discourse**: Discourse refers to the use of language, that is to say, discourse is the product of people's communication. It refers to larger units of language, such as paragraphs, dialogues, interviews, etc.

   Discourse analysis: Discourse analysis aims to study how sentences form larger meaningful linguistic units in spoken and written language, such as paragraphs, dialogues, interviews, etc.

Given information: Given information is the information that the speaker thinks the hearer already knows.

New information: New information is the information that the speaker thinks the hearer doesn't know.

Topic: Topic is the subject of a conversation, and comment is what is said about the subject.

Cohesion: Cohesion is an important research field in discourse analysis. It refers to relations of meaning that exist within the text, and that define it as a text.

Coherence: Coherence is a state or situation in which all the parts or ideas fit together well so that they form a united whole.

Discourse marker: Discourse markers (DM) are words or phrases that are used at the beginning of sentences and are syntactically detachable from a sentence. These expressions comprise a subset of linguistic expressions though not to affect the propositional content of utterances in which they occur.

Adjacency pair: An adjacency pair is composed of two turns produced by different speakers which are placed adjacently and where the second utterance is identified as related to the first.

Preference structure: There can be several second parts to one first part, but they are not of equal status. The structural likelihood is called preference. Preference structure divides second parts into preferred and dispreferred.

Presequence: Presequence refers to the opening sequences or utterances used to introduce specific potential actions.

Critical discourse analysis: Critical discourse analysis (CDA) studies discourse from the perspective of sociopolitical and cultural factors and their interrelationships, focusing on how discourse is ideologically influenced by social power relations and how it affects social power relations.

2. Cohesion is an important field of study in discourse analysis. It refers to the grammatical and/or lexical relationships between the different elements of a discourse. This may be the relationship between different sentences or between different parts of a sentence. Actually, cohesion concerns the question of how sentences are explicitly linked together in a discourse by different kinds of overt devices. Such cohesive devices include reference, substitution, ellipsis, conjunction and lexical cohesion.
3. "One" is used to replace "look-out".
4. Pronouns: them, it;

   What, all of *them*?

   But how can *it* be made consistent with the earlier objective?

   Demonstratives: that, this;

   Well, *that's* a relief.

   What justification is there for *this* discrimination?

   Article: the;

   The loss of plants and animal species....

   Others

"Does it mean...a piece of their ecosystem but not *others*?"

5. The following passage is obviously not a coherent discourse. Although the writer uses lots of cohesive devices like lexical cohesion through the repetition of the last word of the previous sentence at the beginning of the second one, the meaning of the whole discourse is unclear. The sentences are irrelevant to each other. A coherent discourse is not simply based on connections between the words. The fact we have to know is that by itself, cohesion would not be sufficient to enable us to make sense of what we read or hear. It is easy to create a highly cohesive discourse but which remains difficult to interpret.

6. Words that contribute to the coherence of the extract are: *and*, *because*, *that*, *it*, *or*.

   Conjunction is one important cohesive device as we study the notion of cohesion. Conjunction involves those short linguistic forms that connect clauses and establish various kinds of relations in between, such as *and*, *or*, *because*.

   Another cohesive device used here is the reference words i. e. , *that* and *it*. These words do not have a self-evident meaning. To work out what they mean on particular occasion, we have to refer to something else. In this extract, both *that* and *it* refer to "interviewing politicians".

7.3 考研真题与典型题详解

Ⅰ. Fill in the blanks

1. __________ refers to ties and connections which exist within texts. They are also called formal links between sentences and between clauses.（人大 2007 研）
2. __________ is the information that the addresser believes is known to the addressee, while __________ is the information that the addresser believes is not known to the addressee.
3. __________ represents what the utterance is about; __________ is what is said about it.

Ⅱ. True or False

1. All languages have some differences in verb forms which are used to produce cohesion.（南开大学 2005 研）
2. One of properties of the adjacency pairs is that the form and content of the first part depends on the type of the second part.
3. The topic-comment distinction depends on the point of view of the listener.

Ⅲ. Explain the following terms

1. coherence /cohesion（浙江大学 2004 研）
2. adjacency pairs
3. preference structure

Ⅳ. Essay questions

1. What is meant by the term "cohesion" in the study of texts? What is "cohesion" is different from the term "coherence"?（上海交大 2007 研；浙江大学 2005 研）
2. In interpreting utterances such as (1) and (2), the hearer generally treats the events described in the two sentences in each group as causally related even though such relationship is not encoded in the meanings of the sentences. That is, the hearer tends to think that Helen fell on the ground because of Tom's pushing and that the vase broke because it was dropped. Explain why.

(1) Tom pushed Helen. Helen fell on the ground.

(2) Peter dropped the vase. It broke.（北外 2005 研）

3. In a coherent piece of writing, words and clauses are tied together in some ways. Use the following text to discuss what are some of the ways of tying together words and clauses to make a coherent piece of writing.

With the careful dress of a bank manager and a fiat, classless accent, John Major is impossible to pigeonhole on either right or left of the Conservative Party. He has made remarkably few enemies in his rapid rise, although his easygoing charm reputedly conceals "a bit of a temper", and he can be caustic. Nevertheless, he numbers Labour MPs among his long-standing friends.

4. What kind of implicature do the following exchanges of conversation possibly make?

A: The skirt she is wearing is beautiful, isn't it?

B: Oh, the pattern is nice.

(The conversation is made when Speaker B knows for sure the obvious beauty of the skirt.)（南开大学 2010 研）

参考答案及解析

Ⅰ. Fill in the blanks

1. Cohesion

（衔接不是一个句法概念，它指文本中存在的一种意义上的联系或关系，也包括句子或分句之间存在的一种形式上的联系。）

2. Given information; new information

（已知信息是指说话者认为听话者已经知道的信息，而新信息是指说话者认为听话者不知道的信息。）

3. The topic; the comment

（话题是谈话的主题，述题是围绕主题所谈论的内容。）

Ⅱ. True or False

1. T （语言中的动词会有不同的形式来连接上下文。）

2. F （配组对话的其中一个特征是第二部分的内容与构成取决于第一部分。）

3. F （已知信息与新信息的区别在于听话者一方，而话题与述题的区别在于说话者一方。）

Ⅲ. Explain the following terms

1. Cohesion refers to the grammatical and/or lexical relationships between the different elements of a discourse. This may be relationship between different sentences or between different parts of a sentence. It can be achieved by cohesive devices include reference, substitution, ellipsis, conjunction and lexical cohesion. Coherence, on the other hand, refers to the quality of a discourse which makes it a connected text coherent to the context, not a series of juxtaposed sentences.

2. An adjacency pair is composed of two turns produced by different speakers which are placed adjacently and where the second utterance is identified as related to the first.

It has five properties:

① Adjacency pairs include two utterances, a first part and a second part.

② The two parts are spoken by different speakers.

③ The two sentences belong to a specific type.

④ The content and form of the second part depend on the first part.

⑤ After the speaker says the first part, the other speaker's response is related to the first part.

3. The answers to many of these questions are not the exact answers but are meant to be the second part of the conversation.

Basically, a first part that includes a request or an offer is typically expected to receive an acceptance in the second part. An acceptance is structurally more likely than a refusal. This structural likelihood is called preference. Preference structure divides second parts into preferred and dispreferred. The preferred leads to the next act, while the dispreferred does not lead to the next act. In the second part, the preferred is more common.

Ⅳ. Essay questions

1. Cohesion refers to the grammatical and/or lexical relationships between the different elements of a discourse. This may be relationship between different sentences or between different parts of a sentence. What it is concerned with is the question of how sentences are explicitly linked together in a discourse by different kinds of overt devices. Such cohesive devices include reference, substitution, ellipsis, conjunction and lexical cohesion.

However, cohesion by itself would not be sufficient to create a highly cohesive discourse which has a lot of connections between the sentences, but which remains difficult to interpret. The connectedness which we experience in our interpretation of normal texts is not simply based on connections between words. There is some other factor which leads us to distinguish connected texts which make sense from those which do not. This factor is usually described as coherence. Therefore, if cohesion is the visible net of a discourse, then coherence is the invisible one.

2. The phenomenon described can be illustrated by the theory of cohesion and coherence in discourse analysis, especially the conjunctive kind of cohesive relation. Text processing requires inferences for establishing coherence between successive sentences. The achievement of coherence partly relies on the cohesive relationships within and between the sentences. Cohesion occurs where the interpretation of some element in the discourse is dependent on that of another. It is realized partly through grammatical device and partly through lexical cohesion.

Conjunction is one of the grammatically cohesive relations. It is based on the assumption that there are forms of systematic relationships between sentences in the linguistic system. Conjunction can be realized by some conjunctive words and some adverbs, such as *so*, *but*, *furthermore*, and so on. But in fact, the conjunctive relation between the discourses need not be realized by conjunctive words, as can be seen in these two examples.

Yet it is not enough for the text to have connections between elements, there is also the coherence which distinguishes connected texts which make sense from those which do not. It enables people to make sense of what they read and hear, and then try to arrive at an interpretation which is in line with their experience of the way the world is. In fact, our ability to make sense of what we read is probably only a small part of that general ability we have to make sense of what we experience or perceive in the world.

Therefore, by the coherence which helps us to connect the discourse with the world we experience, we, the hearers, will tend to make the discourse fit some situation which could accommodate all the details, and just as in the two examples, the causal conjunctive relations are established.

3. Coherence means that one sentence moves into the next logically and smoothly within paragraphs and from paragraph to paragraph. It refers to the unity created between the ideas, sentences, paragraphs and sections of a piece of writing. Coherence is what gives a piece of writing its flow. It also gives the reader a sense of what to expect and, therefore, makes the reading easier to follow as the ideas appear to be presented in a natural, almost automatic way. When a writing lacks coherence, the reader is forced to stop and reread. Generally speaking, the coherence can be achieved via four different ways, 1) using appropriate transition words/phrases and conjunctions, 2) using referents, words or phrases that stand for previously mentioned words/ideas, 3) the repetition of key words, 4) arranging sentence and paragraphs in a logical order.

The coherence of this piece of writing can be also achieved through these four different aspects:

Firstly, the employment of conjunctions. Many different types of conjunctions can be detected in this short passage, namely, "although", "and", "or", and "nevertheless". "Although" is employed to express the meaning of concession, "and" serves as the addition, and "nevertheless" is used to show the change or transition of the meaning.

Secondly, the reference. In this short passage, we can identify the anaphoric pronouns serve as the reference. For example, "He" can refer to "John Major", "his" can refer to "John Major's" in this text, which has contributed to the smooth transition of the plot.

Thirdly, the repetition of key words. The hero of the text, the pronoun "he", is constantly emphasized.

Last but not the least, the arrangement of sentences and paragraphs in a logical order. The logic of this passage is actualized through the development of plot and the employment of conjunctions.

In a word, the employment of these four different ways has greatly contributed to the coherence of the short text, without which we would have great difficulty in understanding what the text is about.

(本题考查话语分析中如何使文章连贯的问题，答案中共给出四个方面，答题时可以围绕这几个方面展开论述。)

4. There could be generally two types of implicature in which this utterance is made. One may be that speaker B wants to emphasize it is the pattern that makes the skirt beautiful. The other may be that speaker B doesn't like the woman who wears the skirt.

According to the cooperative principle, in our conversation, in order to be cooperative, that is, to make his intentions to be known by the hearer, the speaker will try to make his conversational contribution such as is required, at the stage at which it occurs. Therefore, according to the third maxim of cooperative principle, RELATION, which says "be relevant", the utterance could be interpreted differently as follows:

In the first situation, when speaker B hear speaker A saying "The skirt she is wearing is beautiful", he/she wants to add that the pattern is especially good. The utterance is actually relevant to the context and further stress the beauty of the dress.

In the second situation, speaker B doesn't like the woman who wear the skirt, but according to the Politeness Principle, in order to be polite, speaker B would violate the maxim of relation, thus to make the utterance euphemistic. By emphasizing it is the pattern that makes the skirt beautiful, speaker B gives an implication that the woman who wears the skirt is not so nice.

第 8 章　社会语言学

8.1　复习笔记

本章要点：

1. Sociolinguistics
   社会语言学的概念
2. Language varieties
   语言变体
3. Linguistic taboos and euphemisms
   禁忌语与委婉语
4. Language and gender
   语言与性别

常考考点：

社会语言学的定义；语言的各种变体；禁忌语与委婉语；语言和性别的关系。

本章内容索引：

Ⅰ. Definition

Ⅱ. Language varieties

1. Standard language
2. Dialects
3. Registers
4. Pidgins and creoles

Ⅲ. Choosing a code

1. Diglossia
2. Bilingualism and multilingualism
3. Code-switching

Ⅳ. Linguistic taboos and euphemisms

Ⅴ. Language and gender

1. Two focuses
2. The correlation between sex and style of speech

Ⅰ. Definition Sociolinguistics is the descriptive study of the effect of any and all aspects of society, including cultural norms, expectations, and context, on the way language is used, and society's effect on language.	**Ⅰ. 定义** 社会语言学是对文化规范，文化期望和语境，对语言的使用方式，以及社会对语言的影响的描述性研究。

【考点：区分"研究社会的社会语言学"与"研究语言的社会语言学"】 **Ⅱ. Language varieties** language variety is a general term for any distinctive form of a language or linguistic expression. Language evolves in accordance with social development. Language varieties are used to refer to such language changes. Language varieties are related to social status, educational background, regions, ethnicity and so on. Language varieties include standard language, dialects, registers, pidgins, creoles, and so on.	**Ⅱ. 语言变体** 语言变体是任何一种语言或语言表达的独特形式的通称。语言是随着社会的发展而发展的，而语言变体则指这种语言变化。语言变体与社会地位、教育背景、地域、种族等有关。这些语言的变体包括标准语言、方言、语域、皮钦语、克里奥尔语等。
1. Standard language A standard language is a language variety that has undergone substantial codification of grammar and usage and is employed by a population for public communication.	**1. 标准语言** 标准语言指一种经过大量语法和用法编纂的语言变体，被人们用于公共交流。
2. Dialects 【考点：名词解释】 A dialect is a variety of a language that is spoken in a particular part of the country or by a particular group of people. A dialect isn't really less complete, logical, or linguistic than a language. It is a variety that is distinct enough to be categorized as a separate entity, but not distinct enough to be another language. A dialect can beselected as the standard. The study of dialects is called dialectology. Dialects can be categorized into following types: (1) **Regional/geographical dialects**: language varieties used by people living in the same geographical region. (2) **Temporal dialects**: varieties of a language that were used at specific times in its historical developments. (3) **Social dialects or sociolects**: language varieties characteristic of a particular social class. (4) **Idiolects**: varieties of a language used by individuals that combine elemets regarding regional, social, gender, and age variations.	**2. 方言** 方言是指在一个特定的区域或一个特定的社会阶层内所使用的语言变体。方言不一定不如语言完整、逻辑更强以及更具语言特征。它是语言的一个变体，由于其不同之处能够划分为一个单独的实体，但是还不足以划分成为一门语言。有时候方言的地位也会得到提升成为一个国家的标准语言。对方言的研究称作方言学，方言可以细分为以下几类： (1) **地域方言**：生活在同一地理区域的人们使用的语言变体。 (2) **时间方言**：在历史发展的特定阶段的语言变体。 (3) **社会方言**：特定社会阶层所使用的语言变体。 (4) **个人方言**：个体所使用的语言变体，结合了地区、社会、性别和年龄等因素的差异。
3. Registers In the narrow sense, register refers to the variety of language shared by people of the same occupation or the same interests. In the broad sense, register refers to a variety of language used for a particular purpose or in a particular communicative situation. 【考点：Register 与 Dialect 的区别】	**3. 语域** 狭义上，语域是指具有相同职业或兴趣爱好的人所共有的语言变体。广义上，语域是指为了特定目的或特定交际场合使用的语言变体。

4. **Pidgins and creoles**

A pidgin is a grammatically simplified language variety that develops between two or more groups that do not have a language in common as a result of communication such as trading. A pidgin becomes a creole as it evolves from trading language and into the primary language of a speech community. Creolization is the process by which a pidgin becomes a creole.

【考点：名词解释 & 辨析—Pidgin 和 Creole 的区别】

Ⅲ. Choosing a code

1. Diglossia

【考点：名词解释】

Diglossia is the use of language varieties existing side by side throughout a community and each has a different role to play. The high variety, also known as H-variety, is the more standard variety, and it is used by government, the media, schooling. The other is a low variety or L-variety, which is used in the home, with relatives, while shopping, and so on.

2. Bilingualism and multilingualism

Bilingualism is the use of two languages side by side by an individual or a speech community, e. g. in Canada, both French and English are official languages. Multilingualism is the use of three or more languages by an individual or a speech community, such as residents of a certain region or country.

【考点：名词解释 & 辨析—Diglossia 和 Bilingualism 的区别】

3. Code-switching

【考点：名词解释】

Code-switching is a process that speaker or writer switching from one language or language variety to another. Situational code-switching and metaphorical code-switching are the two main types of code-switching. Situational code-switching takes place when the speakers find the situations in which they are in are changed. Metaphorical code-switching takes place when topic requires a change in the language used.

Ⅳ. Linguistic taboos and euphemisms

Taboo is a term that involves restricting the use of words or other parts of language due to social constraints. Taboo words are commonly avoided with euphemisms. E. g. , *pass away* for *die*.

4. **皮钦语和克里奥尔语**

皮钦语是一种语法简化的语言变体，在两个或两个以上没有共同语言的群体之间发展而成，这是交流的结果。当皮钦语得到发展，不再是作为交易的语言而成为一个社会群体的第一语言时，它就成为克里奥尔语。由皮钦语转变成为克里奥尔语的过程就称作克里奥尔语化。

Ⅲ. 选择语码

1. 双言现象

双言现象指当两种语言变体同时存在于一个语言社区，并且每一种语言都有不同的使用目的的语言现象。通常情况下，更标准的语言变体被称作高标准语言，用于政府、新闻媒介、教育。另一种是低标准语言，用于家里、亲戚之间、购物时等。

2. 双语和多语

双语指的是个人或群体使用两种语言的情况，例如在加拿大英语法语都是官方语言。多语则是指个人或群体使用至少两种语言的情况。

3. 语码转换

语码转换是指说话者或写作者从一种语言或语言变体转用另一种语言或语言变体的现象。语码转换又可以分为情景语码转换和隐喻语码转换。当参与者自身认识的境况发生改变，其所使用的语言随着情境的变化而变化时就叫做情景语码转换。当话题的转变要求语言也随之变化时就叫做隐喻语码转换。

Ⅳ. 禁忌语和委婉语

禁忌语是由于社会的限制而限制词语或语言的其他部分的使用。禁忌语通常用委婉语来避免，例如用 *pass away* 来代替 *die*。

Euphemism is a term that refers to innocuous word or expression used in place of one that may be found offensive or suggest something unpleasant.	**委婉语**指的是一个无害的词或表达，用来代替一个可能冒犯或不愉快词语。
V. Language and gender	**V. 语言和性别**
1. Two focuses	**1. 两个关注点**
The study of language in relation to gender has two main focuses: ① the different way men and women speak. ② the discriminatory language against women.	和性别有关的语言研究包括两个主要方面：①男女不同的说话方式。②对女性的歧视在语言中的体现。
2. The correlation between sex and style of speech	**2. 性别与语言风格的关系**
(1) Language reflects discrimination towards women in society.	(1) 语言反映社会中的性别歧视现象。
(2) Nonlinguistic aspects of society may have effect on our interpretation of the word sense.	(2) 社会中的非语言因素会影响我们对词汇意义的理解。
(3) There lacks equivalence between terms of male and female in many languages. many languages.	(3) 语言中存在男性和女性词汇不对等的现象。

8.2 课后习题详解

1. Define the following words briefly.

sociolinguistics	standard language	dialect
register	pidgin	creole
language planning	diglossia	bilingualism
code-switching	taboo	euphemism

2. What is meant by the term *idiolect*?
3. During the 1976 presidential campaign, a Georgia state official was hoping that Governor Carter would be the next president, saying that it would be nice to have a president who did not have an accent. What do you think the state official meant by his remark?
4. What is *language planning*, and how might it be carried out effectively?
5. What is a *pidgin*, and how may it be distinguished from a *creole*?
6. Euphemisms abound for "toilet" (which is itself a euphemism). What are some of them? Can you judge them in terms of acceptability for various kinds of social functions and interactions?
7. There are various suggestions why women tend to approximate more closely to the standard language than men do. What do you consider to be relevant factors? Why?
8. Below are given some words used in British English for which different words are usually used in American English. See if you can match the British and American equivalents.

British	American
a. clothes peg	A. candy
b. braces	B. truck
c. lift	C. line

d. pram	D. main street
e. waistcoat	E. crackers
f. shop assistant	F. suspenders
g. sweets	G. wrench
h. boot (of a car)	H. flashlight
i. bobby	I. potato chips
j. spanne	J. vacation
k. biscuits	K. baby buggy
l. queue	L. elevator
m. torch	M. can
n. underground	N. cop
o. high street	O. wake up
p. crisps	P. trunk
q. lorry	Q. vest
r. holiday	R. subway
s. tin	S. clothes pin
t. knock up	T. clerk

参考答案

1. **Sociolinguistics**: Sociolinguistics is the descriptive study of the effect of any and all aspects of society, including cultural norms, expectations, and context, on the way language is used, and society's effect on language.

Standard language: A standard language is a language variety that has undergone substantial codification of grammar and usage and is employed by a population for public communication.

Dialect: A dialect is a variety of a language that is spoken in a particular part of the country or by a particular group of people.

Register: In the narrow sense, register refers to the variety of language shared by people of the same occupation or the same interests. In the broad sense, register refers to a variety of language used for a particular purpose or in a particular communicative situation.

Pidgin: A pidgin is a grammatically simplified language variety that develops between two or more groups that do not have a language in common as a result of communication such as trading. A pidgin becomes a creole as it evolves from trading language and into the primary language of a speech community. Creolization is the process by which a pidgin becomes a creole.

Creole: A pidgin becomes a creole as it evolves from trading language and into the primary language of a speech community. Creolization is the process by which a pidgin becomes a creole.

Language planning: Governments and citizens closely study all of the country's languages and dialects to determine which is the standard language or languages, as well as the extent of their use. They also arrange for the use and/or growth of other languages and dialects in the area. This process is known as language planning.

Diglossia: Diglossia is the use of language varieties existing side by side throughout a community and each one have a different role to play. The high variety, also known as H-variety, is the more standard variety, and it is used by government, the media, schooling. The other is a low variety or L-variety, which is used in the home, with relatives, while shopping, and so on.

Bilingualism: Bilingualism is the use of two languages side by side by an individual or a speech community, e. g. in Canada, both French and English are official languages. Multilingualism is described as the use of three or more languages by an individual or a speech community, such as residents of a certain region or country.

Code-switching: Code-switching refers to a process that speaker or writer switching from one language or language variety to another. Situational code-switching and metaphorical code-switching are the two main types of code-switching. Situa tional code-switching takes place when the speakers find the situations in which they are in are changed. Metaphorical code-switching takes place when topic requires a change in the language used.

Taboo: Taboo is a term that involves restricting the use of words or other parts of language due to social constraints. Taboo words are commonly avoided with euphemisms. E. g., *pass away* for *die*.

Euphemism: Euphemism is a term that refers to innocuous word or expression used in place of one that may be found offensive or suggest something unpleasant.

2. Idiolect are varieties of a language used by individuals that combines elemets regarding regional, social, gender, and age variations. Each member of a speech community expresses his or her thoughts in a distinctively personal manner and with carefully chosen words. Idiolects emphasize individual differences, since no two speakers speak the same dialect. In his or her manner of communicating, each speaker has distinct characteristics. When we talk about "Shakespeare's language" or "Lu Xun's language," we're talking about their idiolects.
3. The state official means the existence of the language phenomenon as diglossia. Diglossia is described as the use of language varieties existing side by side throughout a community and each one have a different role to play. Both varieties are standardized to some extent, native speakers consider them to be alternatives, and they typically have unique names. The high variety, also known as H-variety, is the more standard variety, and it is used by government, the media, schooling. The other is a low variety or L-variety, which is used in the home, with relatives, while shopping, and so on. However, there is no such a difference between the status of languages or language varieties; no one is superior or inferior to others, as long as it can serve its users well.
4. Governments and citizens closely study all of the country's languages and dialects to determine which is the standard language or languages, as well as the extent of their use. They also arrange for the use and/or growth of other languages and dialects in the area. This process is known as language planning. An official language policy is developed and enforced by language planning. The official effort can focus on the status of a language in relation to other languages or varieties, or on its internal state in order to modify it. Any of these aspects of language planning may be involved; the first is known as status planning, and the second is known as corpus planning.
5. A pidgin is a grammatically simplified language variety that develops between two or more groups

that do not have a language in common as a result of communication such as trading. A pidgin arose from a blending of several languages such as Chinese dialects and English. A pidgin is normally built on a single language, but it quickly absorbs elements from other languages. It typically has a limited vocabulary and a simplified grammatical structure, which can extend over time or for a variety of purposes.

A pidgin becomes a creole as it evolves from trading language and into the primary language of a speech community. Creolization is the process by which a pidgin becomes a creole. The structure of the original pidgin is expanded to enable it to fulfill its new functions. The vocabulary is mostly enriched, and new syntactic-semantic concepts developed.

6. Euphemism for toilet: Men's room, Lady's room, Restroom, Powder room, Lavatory, and so on.

When we are together with intimate people such as friends or family members, we can ask them about the position of toilet or lavatory. However, if we are in public places, together with people we are not so familiar, such as business partners, fresh acquaintances, especially people of the other sex, we seldom use *toilet*, *lavatory* and *WC*. We prefer to use more polite words like *gentlemen's/ lady's room*, *restroom* instead. Sometimes, ladies use *powder room* as if they are going to powder their face, and then comes the expression "I have to powder my nose." which actually means that she is going to answer the call of nature.

7. In my opinion, the fact that women tend to approximate more closely to the standard language than men do is related to their social positions.

Women, from a historical perspective, were in an inferior position to men. To obtain the same right, women are constantly in struggling with discriminations. A sense of social role leads to a language consciousness inevitably. So they do their best to use more of a standard and prestigious speech patterns in their community. From the point of culture, girls are taught to be gentle and quiet. There are more taboo words for women than men, swearwords and four-letter-words are considered to be unbearable for women. Besides, men's and women's different social roles and field of activities are important factors. Men are rated socially by their occupations, incomes and other abilities, while for the most of the time women's ability and potentiality are underrated or even denied. Therefore, women have to find other ways to maintain and raise their social status, one of which is through language.

8.

a – S	b – F
c – L	d – K
e – Q	f – T
g – A	h – P
i – N	j – G
k – E	l – C
m – H	n – R
o – D	p – I
q – B	r – J
s – M	t – O

8.3 考研真题与典型题详解

Ⅰ. Fill in the blanks.

1. Language varieties other than the standard are called nonstandard, ________ language.
2. A speech ________ is a group of people who share the same language or a particular variety of language.
3. A ________ language is originally a pidgin that has become established as a native language in some speech community.
4. A linguistic ________ refers to a word or expression that is prohibited by the "polite" society from general use.
5. Language itself is not sexist, but its use may reflect the ________ attitude connoted in the language that is sexist.
6. In terms of sociolinguistics, ________ is sometimes used to refer to the whole of a person's language.
7. In many societies of the world, we find a large number of people who speak more than one language. As a characteristic of societies, ________ inevitably results from the coming into contact of people with different cultures and different languages.

Ⅱ. Multiple Choice

1. ________ variation of language is the most discernible and definable in speech variation.
   A. Regional B. Social C. Stylistic D. Idiolectal
2. The most recognizable differences between American English and British English are in ________ and vocabulary.
   A. diglossia B. bilingualism C. pidginization D. blending
3. ________ are language varieties appropriate for use in particular speech situations.
   A. Slang B. Address terms C. Registers D. Education varieties
4. Probably the most widespread and familiar ethnic variety of the English language is ________.
   A. British English B. American English
   C. Black English D. Australian English
5. ________ refers to a marginal language of few lexical items and straight forward grammatical rules, used as a medium of communication.
   A. Lingua franca B. Creole
   C. Pidgin D. Standard language

Ⅲ. True or False

1. Regional dialect is a variety of language related to the use of language.（东南大学 2003 年研）
2. Sociolinguists are interested in "terms of address" because they offer some socio-cultural information about the type of relationship between the speaker and the hearer.（上外 2000 年研）
3. Micro-sociolinguistics is sociolinguistics proper.（东南大学 2003 年研）
4. The most distinguishable linguistic feature of a regional dialect is its grammar and uses of vocabulary.（暨南大学 2018 研）

Ⅳ. Explain the following terms.

1. Intercultural communication（南开大学 2006 研）
2. Diglossia（南开大学 2010 研）
3. Speech community（北外 2010 研）
4. Sociolect（中山大学 2000 年；南开大学 2003 年研）
5. Linguistic variable（北外 2011 研）

Ⅴ. Short answer questions

1. What is sociolinguistics?（北航 2008 研）
2. The following is a statement by a Japanese businessman: "You buy in your own language, but you sell in your customer's language." How do you understand it?（人大 2005 研）
3. What is language variation?
4. What distinction, if any, can you draw between bilingualism and diglossia?
5. How do the speech of women and the speech of men differ from each other?
6. The following statements are examples of excessive use of euphemism. How to improve them? Examples of excessive use of euphemism:
   (1) The employees who had been notified of an interruption in their employment were referred to their outplacement manager.
   (2) The official acknowledged that he had misspoken when he said the troops had not engaged in any protective-reaction missions.
   (3) The prisoner's life will be terminated at dawn.
   (4) The non-essential personnel in this division will be vacationed by next week.
   (5) Reaching the top of the ladder of success must be a moving experience.
   (6) I was told that he did away with himself.
   (7) It is a widespread but unproven hypothesis that the parameters of significant personal change for persons in mid-life are extremely narrow.
   (8) I purchased a residential property that was in need of substantial upgrading.
7. It is claimed in sociolinguistics that you are what you say. How would you comment on this theoretical claim?（武汉大学 2011 研）

Ⅵ. Essay questions

1. Why do you think that, all other things being equal, women use more standard variants of stable sociolinguistic variables than men?（北外 2006 研）
2. How do you understand the role of linguistic research in social and economic development?（南开大学 2004 研）
3. What are sociolinguistics of society and sociolinguistics of language?（武汉大学 2007 研）
4. How much does our language influence the way we think? How deeply do language and culture interpenetrate and influence one another? These questions about language have fascinated thinkers throughout the ages. For example, Johann Gottfried Herder and Wilhelm yon Humboldt in the German Romantic tradition regarded language as a prisma or grid spread over things in the world so that each language reflects a different worldview. Write a short essay to explain your position on this view.（北外 2004 研）

参考答案及解析

Ⅰ. Fill in the blanks.

1. vernacular
（凡属标准语之外的那些语言变体都被叫做非标准语或本地语。）
2. community
（语言社区指的是说同一种语言或语言变体的一群人。）
3. creole
（克里奥尔语最初也是在一些言语社区中作为本族语发展起来的一种皮钦语。）
4. taboo
（禁忌语是由于宗教、政治或性别原因而避免使用的词汇，通常被委婉语所代替。）
5. social
（语言本身是不存在性别歧视的，但当语言被不同的人使用时，则会反映出社会中存在的性别歧视现象。）
6. idiolect
（从社会语言学的角度讲，个人习语指个人语言风格。）
7. bilingualism
（双语现象源于不同文化和不同语言相互交流的结果。双语是对于两种或更多语言的了解及经常使用的能力。）

Ⅱ. Multiple Choice

1. A （地域变异是指由于言语使用者们地区的不同而呈现出来的言语变异现象。语言的地域变异是最明显的，也是最容易界定的。）
2. C （美国英语和英国英语最大的不同在于词语的皮钦语化。）
3. C （语域是特殊人群使用的言语变体，通常指具有相同职业或具有同样爱好的人。某一语域通常具有自己一些独特的词汇或使用词或短语的特殊方式，而使其与其他语域区分开来。）
4. C （黑人英语很可能是分布范围最广的、英语语言中人们最熟悉的少数民族语言变体。）
5. C （皮钦语不是任何人的母语，是在交往联系的情况下（例如交易）学习的语言变体。）

Ⅲ. True or False

1. F （语言的变体可从使用者和使用两个角度划分为方言变体和类型变体，前者称为方言，后者为语域。地域方言应该与语言的使用者相关。）
2. T （称谓语中包含社会文化意义。）
3. T （“微观社会语言学”又被称为“严格意义上的社会语言学（sociolinguistics proper）”，主要研究微观的语言现象，如语言结构变异、称呼形式、性别差异、话语分析、禁忌和委婉，以及其他一些具体的语言问题。“宏观社会语言学”研究社会中的语言问题，如双语、语言接触、双方言、语言规范化问题等。）
4. F （区域方言最显著的特点是其语音语调。）

Ⅳ. Explain the following terms.

1. Intercultural communication, also known as cross-cultural communication, is communication between people whose cultural perceptions and symbols systems are distinct enough to alter the

communication event. It is frequently used to refer to communication between people from different cultures, which implies a comparison between cultures.

2. Diglossia is the use of language varieties existing side by side throughout a community and each has a different role to play. The high variety, also known as H-variety, is the more standard variety, and it is used by government, the media, schooling. The other is a low variety or L-variety, which is used in the home, with relatives, while shopping, and so on.
3. Speech community is a group of people who share a set of norms and expectations regarding the use of language. Speech communities can be members of a profession with a specialized jargon, distinct social groups like high school students or hip-pop fans. In addition, online and other mediated communities, such as many internet forums, often constitute speech communities. Members of speech communities will often develop *slang* or *jargon* to serve the group's special purposes and priorities.
4. Dialects which identify where a person is in terms of a social scale are called "social dialects" or "class dialects" or "sociolects" for short.
5. Linguistic variables are those where the meaning remains constant but form varies like *cat* and *pussy* have the same social meaning but different forms. So far as pronunciation is concerned *house* [h] and *with* [h] has same social meaning with different pronunciations. Here variables are just the tools to analyze the language to set social dimensional society.

Ⅴ. Short answer questions

1. Sociolinguistics is an umbrella term which covers a variety of different interests in language and society, including the social functions of language and the social characteristics of its users. It studies the characteristics of language varieties, the characteristics of their functions, and the characteristics of their speakers as these three constantly interact and change within a speech community.

   (本题考查社会语言学的定义。)
2. This reflects some features of pidgin which is a special language variety that mixes or blends languages and it is used by people who speak different languages for restricted purposes such as trading. And also, it reflects the tendency of intercultural communication from the aspect of language.
3. It is differences in pronunciation, grammar, or word choice within a language. Variation in a language may be related to region, to social class and/or educational background or to the degree of formality of a situation in which language is used.

   For sociolinguists, the most important verity is that a language—any language—is full of systematic variation, variation that can be only accounted for by appealing, outside language, to socially relevant forces and facts.

   Sociolinguistics takes as its primary task to map linguistic variation on to social conditions. This mapping helps understand not just synchronic variation (variation at a single point of time), but also diachronic variation (variation over time) or language change.
4. Bilingualism refers to a linguistic situation in which two standard languages are used in a speech community; whereas in a diglossia community, two varieties of language are used for different sit-

uations, one being more standard and higher, and used for more formal matters, and the other less prestigious, and used for colloquial situations.

5. Women tend to use more prestigious forms, more polite and indirect language, more tag questions, less powerful curse words, more statement questions, and more specific color terms than their male counterparts.

   In mixed-gender groups, at public gatherings, and in many informal conversations, men spend more time talking than do women. For example, in one experiment, the men with expertise talked longer than the women with expertise. Men initiate more interaction than do women.

6. Improved versions:

   (1) The laid-off employees were told to speak to the person who would try to help them find new jobs.

   (2) The official admitted that he had lied when he claimed the troops had not engaged in any offensive missions.

   (3) The prisoner will be executed at dawn.

   (4) The unnecessary people in this division will be laid off by next week.

   (5) Being successful must be a pleasant experience.

   (6) I was told that he had committed suicide.

   (7) It is a widely held myth that middle-aged people can't change.

   (8) I bought a house in need of repair.

   (9) It is a language that is used for communication between different groups of people, each speaking a different language. The lingua franca could be an internationally used language of communication (e. g. English), or it could be the native language of one of the groups, or it could be a language which is not spoken natively by any of the groups but has a simplified sentence structure and vocabulary and is often a mixture of two or more languages.

7. Everyone speaks differently. A personal dialect of an individual speaker combines elements regarding regional, social, gender, and age variations. In other words, an individual speaker's regional and social background, his/her gender and age jointly determine the way he/she talks. From this point, we can claim that "You are what you say".

   Following this claim, we may expand the scope of our observation by introducing some social factors that are believed to influence our language behavior in a social context. Among these factors, some major ones include a) class; b) gender; c) age; d) ethnic identity; e) education background; f) occupation and g) religious belief. In our daily speaking, the potential selection of linguistic forms can reflect the above factors, which determine our identities.

   For example, women use more "fancy" color terms such as "mauve" and "beige"; use less powerful curse words; use more intensifiers such as "terrible" and "awful"; use more tag questions. On the other hand, your way of speaking, to some extent, reflect your identity.

   (本题为开放式题目，围绕自语言与社会及文化之间的关系简要阐述自己对这句话的观点即可。)

Ⅵ. Essay questions

1. Language is a social, *value-loaded* practice, which reflects an intricate network of social, politi-

cal, cultural, and age relationships within a society.

Women's speech closely approaches the standard variety than the speech of men, which has been explained in terms of a greater consciousness of status on the part of women. Women are more usually more status-conscious than men in the English-speaking world, they are aware of their low status in society and, as a result, use more standard speech forms in their attempt to claim equality or achieve high social status. In a sense, they are up in arms against men's society. The status of men has been traditionally defined by their occupation and wealth, while women have had to find other ways of establishing their position and one of these has been their speech.

A second explanation relates to the ways in which society treats women. Women are expected to behave better than men, traditionally, just as society has been harsher on women with regard to such vices as promiscuity and drunkenness, a better standard of language may have been required.

A third explanation is that, by using standard or polite forms, a woman is trying to protect her face. In other words, a woman claims more status in society. Her greater use of standard forms may also imply that she does not attend solely to her own face needs but also to those of the people she is interacting with, thus avoiding disagreement and seeking agreement and rapport.

2. To see the role linguistics plays in social and economic development, we could specifically consider the integration of linguistic research with other fields of social life, such as computational linguistics, psycholinguistics, applied linguistics and anthropological linguistics.

As to the applied linguistics, it is undeniable that linguistic research has greatly influenced the language teaching and learning. For example, various linguistic schools have shed insight into the methodology of language teaching, especially foreign language teaching. Those different models of language teaching are all aimed at a more successful and effective language teaching.

As is known, for a human being in the society, communication is very important. In the social communication, linguistic research has also made some important interpretations and explanations. Such as Grice's Cooperative Principle, Brown& Levinson's face and politeness theory, etc. Those theories generate good inspirations as to how to create a successful communication, and how to avoid and deal with miscommunication.

In a word, although without linguistic research, society and economics could still develop in their own way, yet linguistics with its effort to explain what is the nature of the activities concerning language, and how these activities works, has undoubtedly made it easier for the social and economic development.

3. If we want to know more about a given society or community by examining the linguistic behavior of its members, we are doing a sociolinguistic study of society. That is, we are doing sociolinguistics at a macro level of investigation. At this level of discussion, things that we are interested in include bilingualism or multilingualism, language attitudes, language choice, language maintenance and shift, language planning and standardization, vernacular language education, and so on.

On the other hand, if we want to know more about some linguistic variations in language use by turning to potential socio-cultural factors for a description and explanation, we are doing a sociolinguistic study of language. Consequently, we are more interested in examining micro linguistic phenomena such as structural variants, address forms, gender differences, discourse analysis,

Pidgin and Creole languages, and other more language related issues.

4. Humans have a unique linguistic system for communication that serves as the primary vehicle for expressing thoughts. Language and thought may be viewed as two independent circles that develop along two different routes but overlap in some parts, where language and thought are consistent with each other. But language is not the only means of expressing thought. As for the relationship between language and the thought, we think that language does not determine the way we think but influences the way we perceive the world and recall things, and affects the ease with which we perform mental tasks. That is, language may be used to provide new ideas, bring about a change in beliefs and values, solve problems, and keep track of things in memory. For example, a well-developed vocabulary may well assist us in learning the concepts the lexis covers. We recall things more easily when they correspond to readily available words or phrases. It is certainly easier for us to make a conceptual distinction if it neatly corresponds to a particular lexical item available in our language. When we label our experience with linguistic symbols, our language will influence how we remember and think about those experiences; otherwise the relationship between language and perception, memory or thinking will be greatly reduced.

In terms of relationship between language and culture, we can infer that a language not only expresses facts, ideas, or events that represent similar world knowledge by its people, but also reflects the people's attitudes, beliefs, world outlooks, and etc. Language expresses cultural reality. On the other hand, as people's language uses express their culture represented by its social conventions, norms and social appropriateness, the culture both emancipates and constrains people socially, historically and metaphorically. Sharing a same community culture, people have acquired common ways of viewing the world through their speech interactions with other members of the same group. Although language and culture are inextricably intertwined, culture is a wider system that completely includes language as a subsystem. The knowledge and beliefs that constitute a people's culture are habitually encoded and transmitted in the language of the people. Language, as an integral part of human beings, permeates his thinking and way of viewing the world, and both expresses and embodies cultural reality.

As for the relationship between language and world views, the language system does not necessarily provide specifics of one's worldview. All humans share a general conceptualizing capacity; Speakers of different languages are capable of distinguishing and recognizing experiences according to their respectively different linguistic coding systems for the same objective world. On the one hand, people speaking the same language may have different worldviews, including political, social, religious, scientific and philosophical views. On the other hand, people speaking different languages may share similar worldviews on the above aspects. Moreover, one language can describe many different worldviews, as is evident in the case of successful translation.

According to the theories shown above, we can infer that Johann Gottfried Herder and Wilhelm yon Humboldt's view has both merits and limitations. First, they see clearly that there exists a relationship between language and thoughts. Second, they assume that language influences so much the way people think that people who think in different ways will have different world views. Based on the theoretical views above we think this view is not rational in this aspect.

第 9 章　心理语言学

9.1　复习笔记

本章要点：

1. Psycholinguistics
   心理语言学
2. Language acquisition
   语言习得
3. Language production
   语言的产生
4. Language comprehension
   语言的理解
5. The relation between language and thought
   语言和思维的关系

常考考点：

语言习得；语言的理解和产生；萨丕尔假说；Berlin 和 P. Kay 的光谱试验。

本章内容索引：

Ⅰ. Definition of Psycholinguistics

Ⅱ. Language Acquisition

1. Definition
2. Four Stages of Language Acquisition

Ⅲ. Language Production

1. Definition
2. Four Stages of Language Acquisition
   (1) Conceptualization
   (2) Formulation
   (3) Articulation
   (4) Self-regulation

Ⅳ. Language comprehension

1. Sound Comprehension
2. Word Comprehension
3. Sentences Comprehension
4. Text Comprehension

Ⅴ. Language and Thought

1. Language determines thought
2. Thought determines language

Ⅰ. Definition of Psycholinguistics

【考点：名词解释】

Psycholinguistics, the psychology of language, is the study of the mechanisms that process language. It explores the relationship between language and human mind. And it is a discipline thatcombines psychology and linguistics.

Ⅱ. Language Acquisition

【考点：名词解释】

Language acquisition refers to the process a human learns and develops his language. First language acquisition refers to the learning of a native or first language and second language acquisition is that of one's second or foreign language.

Ⅲ. Language Production

1. Definition

Language production is the process where language creates and expresses meaning.

2. Four Stages of Language Production

【考点：语言产生的四个过程】

(1) Conceptualization

Conceptualization refers to that before being translated into linguistic forms thoughts exist in the form of mentalese.

(2) Formulation

As the second phase of speech production, formulation mainly analyzes the final output of the process. For example, analyzing choice of words or sentence structures and speech errors would facilitate understanding speech production. The main types of slips of the tongue include addition, deletion, shift, exchange, substitution, blend, anticipation and perseveration.

(3) Articulation

Articulationis the third and a significant phase of speech production. When we have translated our thoughts into a linguistic plan, our brains must convey the information to the muscles in the speech system for them to perform the needed and vocalize the desired sounds.

(4) Self-regulation

The final phase of speech production is self-regulation. Since everyone can make mistakes, we would often conduct self-repairs while expressing.

Ⅰ. 心理语言学的定义

心理语言学是对语言心理方面的研究，通常研究的是语言过程中的运行机制。它更关心语言和思维之间的关系，是把心理学和语言学连接起来的一个学科。

Ⅱ. 语言习得

语言习得指人们语言的学习和发展。第一语言或母语的学习称为母语习得，第二语言或外语的学习称为二语习得。

Ⅲ. 语言的产生

1. 定义

语言的产生是指通过语言来创造和表达意义的过程。

2. 语言生成的四个阶段

(1) 概念化

概念化指在言语形成前，思想以某种元语言的形式存在。

(2) 形式化

形式化是言语产生的第二个阶段，它主要分析这个过程的最终结果，如语言错误，词汇或句子结构的选择对理解语言的产生有很大帮助。

口误的主要类型：增加、减少、转移、倒置、代替、混合、提前和延缓。

(3) 发音

发音是语言产生过程的第三个阶段，也是很重要的阶段。当我们把自己的想法组织成语言时，这些信息要从大脑传递到话语系统，然后由器官运动来得到我们想发出的声音。

(4) 自我监控

自我监控是语言产生的最后阶段。人们总会犯错，所以每个人在表达时都会一遍遍地进行自我修正。

Ⅳ. Language comprehension

【考点：语言理解的四个过程】

1. Sound Comprehension

Sound comprehension is not a passive process, the success of which often hinges on the context that listeners are in. People figure out the meaning in its entirety instead of in isolation. Particularly, they do not listen to individual words. To successfully comprehend speech sounds requires people to have the innate ability to differentiate between the subtle differences of speech sounds, and to be adapted to the acoustic categories of the language they are listening to.

2. Word recognition

Understanding words is quite a complex psychological process and is way more complex than processing speech sounds. Because of its vital role in conveying meaning, word is placed at the center of language comprehension. Word recognition refers to the recognition of the spoken and written forms of words.

3. Comprehension of sentences

In addition to the comprehension of sounds and words, the comprehension of language also involves understanding sentences. There are several factors which may influence the understanding of sentences. Firstly, the ambiguous meaning of word causes difficulties in understanding sentences. Secondly, the complex linguistic structure of a sentence may greatly lengthen the processing time.

4. Comprehension of text

Text is like a web of several propositions which constitute the semantic interpretations of single sentences. While reading, readers grasp the main "storyline" of a discourse and make inferences to fill up the parts untold by the discourse. The whole process is constrained by readers' limitation in short-term memory, the way arguments overlap across propositions, and the linguistic cues manifested in the text.

Ⅴ. Language and Thought

Generally speaking, there are two views concerning the relationship between language and thought. They are language determines thought, and thought determines language.

Ⅳ. 语言的理解

1. 发音的理解

发音的理解不是一个被动的过程。它通常依赖于听话者所处的语境。人们需要从整体上来理解意思，而不是孤立地将其分开，并不是单独地去听每一个词。对发音的成功理解要求人们具有区分细小的发音差别的内在能力，以及适应语言听觉种类的能力。

2. 词语的识别

词语的理解是一个非常复杂的心理过程，远比处理发音复杂得多。由于在传达意义过程中扮演极其重要的作用，词汇在语言理解中居于核心地位。单词辨识是指对口头词语和书面词语的识别。

3. 句子的理解

除了对发音、词汇意义的理解，语言的理解还包括对句子的理解。以下几个因素影响对句子的理解：第一，歧义词语的存在使得句子难以理解。词语含有的信息越复杂，句子也就越难理解。第二，句子的语言结构影响处理的时间。

4. 语篇的理解

文本是命题的网络，这些命题构成单个句子的语义解释。在阅读过程中，读者提炼出话语的主要线索和思路并推理出未出现在话语中的背景和关系。这样的提炼和推理过程受读者短时记忆时效的限制，也受制于论据在命题之间的互证方式以及文本所表明的语言组织形式。

Ⅴ. 思维和语言

关于思维和语言的关系，一般有两种观点：语言决定思维以及思维决定语言。

1. Language determines thought People holding that language determines thought believe that a particular language can shape human mind and influence culture. **Sapir-Wharf Hypothesis** is a representative example. **Sapir-Wharf Hypothesis**: our language can shape our thinking pattern and as a result people speaking different languages may have different of understanding the world. There are two parts in Sapir-Whorf Hypothesis. The first is **linguistic determinism**, which is to say that linguistic structure determines cognitive structure. In other words, can change how a person thinks. The second is **linguistic relativity**, which means that different languages lead to different cognitive systems. **2. Thought determines language** Proponents of that thought determines language believe that cognitive development comes before the language development in the early life of children and that cognitive categories shall determine the linguistic categories that they are about to acquire. In 1969, B. Berlin and P. Kay conducted a color experiment and the result suggests that Sapir-Whorf Hypothesis is implausible.	**1. 语言决定思维** 语言决定论者认为语言系统决定思维方式，某种语言决定某种自然观或文化。这种观点的代表是**萨丕尔—沃尔夫假说**。 **萨丕尔假说**认为，语言塑造了我们的思维模式，相应地，不同的语言表达决定了人们认识世界方式的不同。 萨丕尔假说有**两部分**： **语言绝对论**：语言结构决定认知结构，也就是，学习一门语言能改变一个人的思维方式。 **语言相对论**：不同的语言会导致认知系统的不同。 **2. 思维决定语言** 思维决定论者认为认知发展要早于语言发展，认知范畴决定学习者学习语言的范畴。 B. Berlin 和 P. Kay 1969 年的光谱实验有力地证明了萨丕尔假说的不合理性。

9.2 课后习题详解

1. Define the following terms briefly.

psycholinguistics	language production	language comprehension
Sapir-Whorf Hypothesis	linguistic determinism	linguistic relativity

2. How do psycholinguistic investigations of language differ from theoretical linguistic investigations?
3. Consider the following slips of the tongue. What does each reveal about the process of language production?
   (1) They *laked* across the *swim*.
   (2) The spy was *gound* and *bagged*.
   (3) I will *zee* you in the *bark*.
4. "I know what I want to say, but I can't find the word." What implication does this phenomenon have for the language and thought controversy?
5. Since 1949, great changes have taken place in China. Yet, the Chinese language has changed relatively little in terms of its basic syntax and phonology although some vocabulary changes, such as in forms of address, e. g. *tongzhi* (同志), *xiaojie* (小姐), and *xiansheng* (先生), have occurred. How does this fact (that the worldview of a people has changed radically but the

language has changed little) relate to the claim that knowing and using a particular language shapes one's world view?

参考答案

1. **Psycholinguistics**: Psycholinguistics, or the psychology of language, is the study of the mechanisms that process language. It explores the relationship between language and human mind. And it is a discipline that combines psychology and linguistics.

   Language production: Language production is the process where language creates and expresses meaning.

   Language comprehension: Language comprehension is the automatic and straightforward process of understanding language.

   Sapir-Whorf Hypothesis: Our language can shape our thinking pattern and as a result people speaking different languages may have different ways of understanding the world.

   Linguistic determinism: Linguistic structure determines cognitive structure. In other words, learning a language can change how a person thinks.

   Linguistic relativity: Linguistic relativity, as a part of Sapir-Whorf Hypothesis, says that Different languages lead to different cognitive systems.

2. Psycholinguistic investigations of language are different from theoretical linguistic ones in that there are two orientations. Firstly, we can use language to explain psycholinguistic processes and theories, such as accounting for the function of language when it is impacting attention, learning, memory and perception. Secondly, we can also investigate the effects that psychological constraints have on language use; for instance, we can investigate the way memory limitations impact speech comprehension and production. More often than not, psycholinguistic investigations are more concerned with the second orientation, because the subject is usually seen as the study of mental processes in which speech is planned, produced, perceived and comprehended.

3. (1) Exchange

   (2) Deletion (gound-ground)

   (3) Shift (zee, bark-see, park)

4. This phenomenon is suggesting that thought comes before speech, which is contradictory to Sapir-Whorf Hypothesis. Sapir-Whorf Hypothesis is that language shapes thought and is a necessity for thought.

5. This fact indicates that theoretically Sapir-Whorf hypothesis is problematic. Because if Sapir-Whorf hypothesis, or linguistic determinism, is totally true, then language changes should be synchronized with thought changes. Nevertheless, this fact suggests that thought changes can be independent of language ones. Thus, just like what Berlin and Kay have suggested, there should be some essential constraints limiting how thought is coded in language.

9.3 考研真题与典型题详解

Ⅰ. Fill in the blanks.

1. "Linguistic relativity" was proposed by __________ and __________. (清华 2001 研)

2. __________ is the study of psychological aspect of language.

Ⅱ. Explain the following terms

1. Linguistic determinism（上海交大 2007 研）
2. Sapir-Whorf hypothesis（武汉大学 2004 研）
3. Linguistic relativity（人大 2006 研）

Ⅲ. Short answer questions

1. What is the purpose of studying language and mind?（南开大学 2004 研）
2. What are the factors influencing sentence comprehension?
3. What are the four stages of language production and how do you understand them?

Ⅳ. Essay questions

1. Research has found that two-year-old English children produce negative sentences such as a) to d), but not e):

   a) He doesn't like cabbage.

   b) Doesn't like cabbage.

   c) Him no like cabbage.

   d) No like cabbage.

   e) * Him doesn't like cabbage.

   How can you account for this?（北外 2006 研）

2. In informal speech, people often omit sentence subjects because they are commonly understood. What are the omitted subjects in the following two sentences? Why do people know that these are the correct subjects?（南京大学 2008 研）

   a. *Hope you like everything here.*

   b. *Just imagine what has just happened here.*

3. Please briefly answer the following question IN ABOUT 500 WORDS:（四川大学 2010 研）
   Anthropological linguists E. Sapir and B. Whorf claim that the language people use shapes their perspective of perception, which in turn shapes their thought. The key notions of their famous "Sapir-Whorf Hypothesis" include "language determinism" and "language relativity". Do you know anything about the notions of theirs? If you do, what is your opinion on it? Please briefly express your ideas in a passage.

4. What is linguistic relativity and why is it so important in linguistic studies?（中山大学 2006 研）

5. Eskimos have many different words for different types of snow, Aborigines for different types of sand, and in Arabic one must choose from a whole range of words which are subsumed under the Western category CAMEL. Can you explain these phenomena with your linguistic knowledge?（北航 2008 研）

参考答案及解析

Ⅰ. Multiple Choice

1. Sapir, Whorf

（萨丕尔—沃尔夫假说认为，一方面，语言可以决定我们的思维方式；另一方面，语言之间的相似性是相对的，结构性差异越大，反映出对于世界认识的越不同。因此，这个假说也被称作“语言决定论”和“语言相对主义”。)

2. C （心理语言学(psycholinguistics)是研究语言活动中的心理过程的学科，它涉及人类如何掌握和运用语言系统，如何在实际交往中使语言系统发挥作用，以及为了掌握和运用这个系统应具有什么知识和能力。)

Ⅱ. Explain the following terms

1. As one of the two main points of Sapir-Whorf Hypothesis, linguistic determinism is the stronger version of this hypothesis. It could be summarized as follows:

   (1) One's thought is completely determined by his mother tongue, for that he can only perceive the world in ways of categorizing and distinguishing that are encoded in his native language.

   (2) One language system's categories and distinctions are unique to that system and distinctively different from those of other systems. The statement "If Aristotle had spoken Chinese, his logic would have been different" can well illustrate this point.

2. Sapir-Whorf hypothesis consists of two parts: linguistic determinism and linguistic relativity. Linguistic determinism refers to the notion that a language determines certain nonlinguistic cognitive processes. Different languages offer people different ways of expressions; they think and speak differently. Linguistic relativity refers to the claim that the cognitive processes that are determined are different for different languages. Thus, speakers of different languages are said to think in different ways. The hypothesis is now interpreted mainly in two different ways: a strong version and a weak one. The strong version believes that the language patterns determine people's thinking and behavior; the weak one holds that the former influences the later. So far, many researches and experiments are conducted to provide support for the weak version.

3. Linguistic relativity is one of two points in Sapir-Whorf hypothesis. It states that similarity between languages is relative, the greater their structural differentiation is, the more diverse their conceptualization of the world is. For example, not every language has the same set of words for the colors; in Spanish there is no word that corresponds to the English meaning of "blue".

Ⅲ. Short answer questions

1. The study of language and mind aims to model the workings of the mind in relation to language; for example, it helps explain how the language production and perception is achieved. Since structures and connections in the mind are inevitably unobservable, researchers put forward hypotheses based on fragmentary clues. The label most usually given to the study of "language and mind" is psycholinguistics, a term which is often perceived as being trendy. Psycholinguistics is concerned primarily with investigating the psychological reality of linguistic structures.

2. (1) Structural factors in comprehension. Comprehension of written and spoken language can be difficult because it is not always easy to identify the constituents (phrases) of a sentence and the ways in which they relate to one another. Psycholinguists have proposed principles interpreting sentence comprehension with respect to the grammatical constraints. The most popular principle is Minimal attachment which defines "structurally simpler", and it claims that structural simplicity guides all initial analyses in sentence comprehension. In this view, the sentence processor constructs a single analysis of a sentence and attempts to interpret it. The first analysis is the one that requires the fewest applications of grammatical rules to at-

tach each incoming word into the structure being built; it is the automatic consequence of an effort to get some analysis constructed as soon as possible. Consider the sentence *The second wife will claim the inheritance belongs to her.* When the inheritance first appears, it could be interpreted as either the direct object of claim or the subject of belongs. It was found that readers' eyes fixated for longer than usual on the verb belongs, which disambiguates the sentence. They interpreted this result to mean that readers first interpreted the inheritance as a direct object. Readers were disrupted when they had to revise this initial interpretation to the one in which the inheritance is subject of belongs. They described the readers as being led down a garden path because the direct object analysis is structurally simpler than the other possible analysis.

(2) Lexical factors in comprehension. Psycholinguists have proposed that the human sentence processor is primarily guided by information about specific words that is stored in the lexicon. In the sentences like *The salesman glanced at a/the customer with suspicion/ripped jeans*, the prepositional phrases with suspicion or with ripped jeans could modify either the verb glance or the noun customer. This is true only for action verbs, not for perception verbs like *glance at*. It has been noted that an actual preference for noun phrase modification only appeared when the noun had the indefinite article *a*.

3. (1) Conceptualization

Conceptualization refers to that before being translated into linguistic form thoughts exist in the form of mentalese.

(2) Formulation

As the second phase of speech production, formulation mainly analyzes the final output of the process. For example, analyzing choice of words or sentence structures and speech errors would facilitate the understanding of speech production.

The main types of slips of tongue include addition, deletion, shift, exchange, substitution, blend, anticipation and perseveration.

(3) Articulation

Articulation is the third and yet important phase of speech production. When we have translated our thoughts into a linguistic plan, our brains must convey the information to muscles in the speech system for them to perform the needed movements and vocalize the desired sounds.

(4) Self-regulation

The final phase of speech production is self-regulation. Since everyone can make mistakes, we would often conduct self-repairs while expressing.

Ⅳ. Essay questions

1. This founding firstly demonstrates one point that the acquisition of auxiliary verbs comes later than that of comparatively "simpler" morphemes such as pronouns. Therefore, it is unlikely for children to make mistakes as shown in e). The reason for this phenomenon could be explained by the fact that in the early stage of children's language acquisition, the speech at first only contains content words and lacks the function elements.

This founding also shows that children have a certain process of learning the negative form. There are generally three stages.

(1) At first, the negative element is not part of the structure of the sentences. It is simply attached to the beginning, as shown in d).

(2) The negative element is inserted into the sentence. The additional negative forms *don't* and *can't* are used, and with *no* and *not*, begin to be placed in front of the verb rather than at the beginning, as shown in c).

(3) Children begin to produce the appropriate part of *do*, *be* or the model verbs, to suit the person or tense, as shown in b) and a).

2. The omitted subject in sentence a is "I", and the omitted subject in sentence b is usually "You".

This is a matter of sentence comprehension in language comprehension. Psycholinguists have proposed principles interpreting sentence comprehension with respect to the grammatical constraints. The most popular principle is "Minimal attachment" which defines "structurally simpler", and it claims that structural simplicity guides all initial analyses in sentence comprehension. In this view, the sentence processor constructs a single analysis of a sentence and attempts to interpret it. The first analysis is the one that requires the fewest applications of grammatical rules to attach each incoming word into the structure being built; it is the automatic consequence of an effort to get some analysis constructed as soon as possible. In the first sentence, when "hope" as a verb is used to express the speaker's desire and expectation for something to happen, it conveys the will of the speaker. So, the subject of "hope" is usually the speaker her/himself and can be omitted when the two are talking to each other. When the speaker is making a statement and using "hope" to express other's will, the subject will not be omitted. Therefore, according to "minimal attachment" principle, when the hearer interprets this sentence, they automatically interpret "I"—the speaker, as the subject of "hope". Sentence b can be said to be an imperative sentence which is a sentence that gives advice or instructions or that expresses a request or a command. This instruction or request is always aimed to the hearer or the reader, so the subject of an imperative is always "you". When the hearer interpret this sentence, he/she will interpret the verb "imagine" as a request or advice through which the speaker tries to make he/she involved in this action, so it is easier for he/she to consider "you" as the subject.

Context is another important factor for people to understand the subjects. The subjects will be clearer in particular context although they are omitted.

(本题可从心理语言学中语言的理解的角度进行分析。根据心理语言学的一些理论，人们在理解句子的时候会遵循结构简单化的规则，因此，在此题中，人们最倾向于把“我”当作第一句的主语，而把“你”当作第二句的主语。)

3. Whorf attended some linguistic courses given by Sapir at Yale University and found particular resonance between his own ideas and those of Sapir. This experience and his study of Hopi, an American Indian language, helped him develop his unique understanding of linguistic relativity, which is widely known as the SAPIR-WHORF HYPOTHESES. What this hypothesis suggests is like this: our language helps mould our way of thinking and, consequently, different languages

may probably express our unique ways of understanding the world. Following this argument, two important points could be captured in this theory. On the one hand, language may determine our thinking patterns; on the other, similarity between languages is relative. For two different speech communities, the greater their structural differentiation is, the more diverse their conceptualization of the world will be. For this reason, this hypothesis has alternatively been referred to as "language determinism" and "language relativity".

Nowadays few people would possibly tend to accept the original form of this theory completely. Consequently, two versions of the Sapir-Whorf hypothesis have been developed, a strong version and a weak version. The strong version of the theory refers to the claim the original hypothesis suggests, emphasizing the decisive role of language as the shaper of our thinking patterns. The weak version of this hypothesis, however, is a modified type of its original theory, suggesting that there is a correlation between language, culture, and thought, but the cross-cultural differences thus produced in our ways of thinking are relative, rather than categorical.

If we go over the literature concerning the hypothesis, we'll soon discover that it has aroused a lively controversy. While some researchers claim to have found reliable evidence to justify its validity, others suggest to have obtained enough counter-evidence to jeopardize its feasibility. Facing a situation like this, we must be careful and do not rush to any hasty conclusion before we really obtain some reliable evidence to support or reject the hypothesis.

Here are two examples taken to show the complexity and controversy of the theory. One is quoted from Hopi, an American Native language spoken in Arizona; the other is taken from Dugum Dani, a Papuan language spoken in the central highlands of Irian Jaya. As far as the former is concerned, it serves as a good example to show how languages may differ from each other, possibly providing some positive evidence to support the hypothesis. On the other hand, by looking at the basic color word system in Dani language from an evolutionary perspective, we'll have an opportunity to get to know that linguistic relativity may equally meet some cross-cultural counter examples, a challenge to the theory hence formed.

Recent developments in linguistics predict that linguistic studies in the new century will become more fruitful if an evolutionary, cognitive, and interdisciplinary perspective is taken in its theoretic pursuit. Meanwhile, additional evidence has been collected to convincingly show the momentum and feasibility of the Sapir-Whorf hypothesis in dealing with linguistic differences from exotic cultures. These new changes not only bring more vitality to linguistic science but also call for more eclecticism in its theorizing. Following this line of argument, it seems still premature to completely reject the Sapir-Whorf hypothesis.

4. Linguistic relativity is one of the two points in Sapir-Whorf hypothesis, which states that distinctions encoded in one language are unique to that language alone, and "there is no limit to the structural diversity of language". Therefore, similarity between languages is relative, the greater their structural differentiation is, the more diverse their conceptualization of the world will be. For example, in English, the boundaries among the color spectrum are made in this way: red, orange, violet, blue, and yellow. In fact, these discriminations are arbitrary, and in other language the boundaries are indeed different. In neither Spanish, Italian nor Russian is there is a

word that corresponds to the English meaning of "blue".

Linguistic relativity is important in linguistic studies because it recognizes the fact of linguistic diversity, which stands as the base on which descriptive linguistics lies. Linguistic diversity also triggers out the study of the linguistic similarity.

The study of the linguistic relativity has shed light on two important insights: there is nowadays recognition that language, as a code, reflects cultural and preoccupations and constrains the way people think.

5. These phenomena can be explained from the following perspectives:

(1) These phenomena show a relationship between language and society. Language changes from region to region, from one social group to another and from individual to individual. The living environment makes great impact on the changes of language. As Eskimo are always living in an environment of a snowing world, they have made a good cognition to snow and classified it in different types. Humans use language to describe the world they have cognized.

(2) These phenomena can be explained from the Sapir-Whorf hypotheses. This hypothesis suggests that: our language can shape our thinking pattern and as a result people speaking different languages may have different of understanding the world. So Eskimos's different words for different types of snow reflect their different ways to understand snow.

(本题可从社会环境对语言的影响和萨丕尔－沃尔夫假说两方面说明。)

第 10 章　认知语言学

10.1　复习笔记

本章要点：

1. Cognitive linguistics
   认知语言学
2. Categorization and categories
   范畴化与范畴
3. Conceptual metaphor and metonymy
   概念隐喻与转喻
4. Iconicity and grammaticalization
   象似性与语法化

常考考点：

认知语言学定义；范畴化与范畴定义分类等；概念隐喻与转喻的定义，层次分类；象似性的分类以及语法化等。

本章内容索引：

Ⅰ. Definition of cognitive linguistics

Ⅱ. Categorization and categories

1. Definition of categorization
2. The classical theory
3. The prototype theory
4. Levels of categorization

Ⅲ. Conceptual metaphor and metonymy

1. Conceptual metaphor
2. Conceptual metonymy

Ⅳ. Iconicity

1. Iconicity of order
2. Iconicity of distance
3. Iconicity of complexity

Ⅴ. Grammaticalization

Ⅰ. Definition of cognitive linguistics 【考点：名词解释】 Cognitive linguistics is an interdisciplinary branch of linguistics, combining knowledge and research from cognitive psychology, neuropsychology and linguistics. Cognitive linguistics studies natural language and regards language as an instrument for arranging, interpreting, and conveying information.	**Ⅰ. 认知语言学定义** 认知语言学是语言学的一个跨学科分支，它结合了认知心理学、神经心理学和语言学的知识和研究。认知语言学研究自然语言，并将语言视为组织，处理与传达信息的工具。

Ⅱ. Categorization and categories

1. Definition of categorization and categories

Categorization is the action or mental process of placing into classes or groups.

Category is the products of categorization.

2. The classical theory

(1) Four assumptions

① The first assumption: A limited number of essential and sufficient conditions

② The second assumption: Features are binary.

③ The third assumption: Clear boundaries are set for categories.

④ The fourth assumption: A category's members all share the same status.

(2) Disadvantages

Certain items don't exactly fit into clear-cut categories. For examples, do ostriches and penguins belong to the BIRD category?

3. The prototype theory

(1) Definition of prototype

Prototype is what members of a certain group consider to be the finest example of a lexical category, e. g. in English "dog" (rather than, say, "whale") might be the prototypical animal.

(2) Advantages

① It can clarify how people cope with atypical examples in a category.

② It will clarify how people respond to damaged examples.

③ It can work for actions as well as objects.

4. Levels of categorization

(1) Three levels of categorization

① Superordinate level categories are categories placed at the top and thus display a low degree of class inclusion and a high degree of generality. E. g, plant and furniture are at the superordinate level.

② Basic-level categories are more precise, but not overly so. Tree and table are examples of basic-level categories.

③ Subordinate level categories display low degree of generality and a high degree of class inclusion. Pine is an example of subordinate categories.

Ⅱ. 范畴化与范畴

1. 定义

范畴化是人类对经验进行分类的心理过程或行为。

范畴是范畴化的产物。

2. 经典理论

(1) 四个假设

①假设1: 范畴由一套特定的且充分的条件而定义的。

②假设2: 特征是二元的。

③假设3: 范畴之间有清晰明确的界限。

④假设4: 范畴下的所有元素地位相同。

(2) 缺陷

有些事物并不属于界定明确的范畴中，比如鸵鸟或企鹅是否属于鸟类这个范畴。

3. 典型理论

(1) 定义

典型: 在词汇范畴中，最典型的元素且是最容易想到的例子。例如英语中，"狗"(而不是"鲸鱼")是最典型的一种动物。

(2) 优势

①解释了人们是怎样应对非典型例子的。

②揭示了人们怎样处理有损的例子。

③此理论同样适用于动词。

4. 范畴化的层次

(1) 范畴化的三个层次

①上一级范畴是指处于范畴的最上层，类包括度低，高概括性的范畴。植物与家具都是上位范畴的例子。

②基本层次范畴是比较具体的但又不是最具体的。比如树和椅子是基本层次范畴的例子。

③下属层次范畴处在最底层，是更加具体的，类包括度高的范畴。松树是下属层次范畴的例子。

(2) Three aspects in basic-level categories

① Perception

② Communication

③ Knowledge organization

Ⅲ. Conceptual metaphor and metonymy

1. Conceptual metaphor

【考点：名词解释】

(1) Definition of conceptual metaphor

In cognitive linguistics, conceptual metaphor, or cognitive metaphor, is the term that refers to the understanding of one idea, or conceptual domain, in terms of another. It is a powerful cognitive tool for our conceptualization of abstract categories.

(2) Components of conceptual metaphor

Source domain is the conceptual domain from which we draw metaphorical expressions. Target domain is the conceptual domain that we try to understand.

2. Conceptual metonymy

【考点：名词解释】

(1) Definition of conceptual metonymy

Metonymy is a cognitive process. Its main function is to provide mental access through one conceptual entity to another and it is based on idealized cognitive model (ICMs) with specific conceptual relationship among their elements.

(2) Types of conceptual metonymies

①The producer for the product (the author for the work)

I'm reading Ernest Hemingway.

②The place for the event

He resigned because of Watergate.

③The place for the institution

Wall Street responded quickly to the news.

④The controller for the controlled

Nixon bombed Hanoi.

⑤An object used for the user

The sax has the key right now.

Ⅳ. Iconicity

Iconicity is a property of language which indicates that the structure of language reflects the structure of experience, that is, the structure of the world, including the speaker's viewpoint on the world.

(2) 基本层次范畴的三方面

①感知

②交流

③知识系统

Ⅲ. 概念隐喻与转喻

1. 概念隐喻

(1) 定义

在认知语言学中，概念隐喻指用另一个概念或概念领域来理解一个概念。隐喻是概念化抽象范畴的有力的认知方法。

(2) 构成

源域是隐喻表达来源的概念域。目标域是我们试图理解的概念域。

2. 概念转喻

(1) 定义

转喻是一个认知过程。它的主要功能是通过一个概念实体向另一个概念实体提供认识渠道，它基于理想化的认知模型(ICMs)，各要素之间有特定的概念关系。

(2) 类型

①生产者代替产品(作者代替作品)

②地名代替事件

③地名代替组织机构

④掌控者代替受控者

⑤物体代替使用者

Ⅳ. 象似性

象似性是语言的一种属性，它表明语言结构在某种程度上反映了人们的经验结构，即世界的结构，包括说话者的世界观。

1. Iconicity of order Iconicity of order is the similarity of temporal occurrences and the sequential organization of components in a linguistic construction. The continuity of language with human cognition and the objective universe is reflected in iconicity of order.	**1. 顺序象似性** 顺序象似性是指语言在顺序上的安排对应于它所表达的事件的次序的安排。顺序象似性反映了人类认知语言与认知客观世界存在一致性。
2. Iconicity of distance Iconicity of distance is the term that explains why items that belong together conceptually appear to be grouped together linguistically, and items that do not belong together are separated.	**2. 距离象似性** 距离象似性是指概念间的距离对应于语言成分之间的距离，如果某实体在概念、功能以及认知方面靠得越近，其语言成分就靠得越近。
3. Iconicity of complexity Iconicity of complexity is the phenomenon of linguistic complexity reflecting intellectual complexity. Iconicity of complexity explains why we want to connect more structure with more meaning and less form with less meaning.	**3. 复杂象似性** 复杂象似性是指语言形式的复杂性反映概念上的复杂性。相对简单的概念用相对简单的语言表达形式，而相对复杂的概念则用相对复杂的语言结构表达。
V. Grammaticalization Grammaticalization is a process of language change by which words representing objects and actions (i. e. nouns and verbs) become grammatical markers (affixes, prepositions, etc.). Grammaticalization results in the usual shifts in meaning and form distribution. The restrictions on their grammatical uses appear to reflect their lexical histories, which is another feature of grammaticalized forms. Another common result of grammaticalization is nearly identical forms in different historical stages.	**V. 语法化** 语法化是代表对象和动作的词语成为语法标记的语言变化过程。语法化使词汇的意义与形式产生了典型性的变化。语法化形式的另一特征就是语法上的用法与限定反映了它们的词汇历史。语法化使词汇形式在不同历史阶段的变化发展中几乎保持不变。

10.2 课后习题详解

1. Define the following terms briefly.

cognitive	linguistics	categorization
category	prototype theory	metaphor
metonymy	iconicity	grammaticalization

2. The names of category prototypes tend to come to mind before those of peripheral examples. Check this hypothesis with two informal tests: Ask one group of friends to name as quickly as they can five types of dogs, birds, trees, and cars, and a second group to rate these examples according to their goodness-of-example status within the category. Compare the results and discuss reasons for discrepancies between the two tests.
3. Compile a list of English prepositions from a grammar book and discuss why some of them seem to be more basic than others.
4. According to Quinn (1987), the main metaphors with which Americans conceptualize MAR-

RIAGE are:

(1) MARRIAGE IS A MANUFACTURED PRODUCT

e. g. *We want to work hard at making our marriage strong.*

(2) MARRIAGE IS AN ONGOING JOURNEY

e. g. *We went in a common direction.*

(3) MARRIAGE IS A DURABLE BOND BETWEEN TWO PEOPLE

e. g. *They are tied to each other.*

Find other linguistic expressions which reflect these three metaphors.

5. Collect animal metaphors like "He is a real pig" or "She is a fox" from a dictionary and explain them with the notion of "source" and "target" domains. Find other linguistic expressions which reflect these three metaphors.
6. Look up definitions of emotion terms like "anger", "rage", "hate", "disgust", "fear", "panic", "love", "affection" in several dictionaries and decide whether they are helpful as descriptions of these emotions. Do these definitions make use of metonymies and metaphors?

参考答案

1. **Cognitive Linguistics**: Cognitive linguistics is an interdisciplinary branch of linguistics, combining knowledge and research from cognitive psychology, neuropsychology and linguistics. Cognitive linguistics studies natural language and regards language as an instrument for arranging, interpreting, and conveying information.

Categorization: Catergorization is the action or mental process of placing into classes or groups.

Prototype: Prototype is what members of a certain group consider to be the finest example of a lexical category, e. g. in English "dog" (rather than, say, "whale") might be the prototypical animal.

Category: Category is the term that stands for all the characteristics of the species it refers to. It is the products of categorization.

Prototype theory: Prototype is what members of a certain group consider to be the finest example of a lexical category, e. g. in English "dog" (rather than, say, "whale") might be the prototypical animal.

Metaphor: In cognitive linguistics, conceptual metaphor, or cognitive metaphor, refers to the understanding of one idea, or conceptual domain, in terms of another. It is a powerful cognitive tool for our conceptualization of abstract categories.

Metonymy: Metonymy is a cognitive process. Its main function is to provide mental access through one conceptual entity to another; it is based on idealized cognitive model (ICMs) with specific conceptual relationship among their elements.

Iconicity: Iconicity is a property of language which indicates that the structure of language reflects the structure of experience, that is, the structure of the world, including the speaker's viewpoint on the world.

Grammaticalization: Grammaticalization is a process of language change by which words representing objects and actions (i. e. nouns and verbs) become grammatical markers (affixes, prepositions, etc.). Grammaticalization results in the usual shifts in meaning and form distribution. The restrictions on their grammatical uses appear to reflect their lexical histories, which is another feature of grammaticalized forms. Another common result of grammaticalization is nearly identical forms in different historical stages.

2. Some tips for the tests: according to the prototype theory, prototype is what members of a certain group consider to be the finest example of a lexical category, e. g. in English "dog" (rather than, say, "whale") might be the prototypical animal. As a result, category prototype names appear to come to mind before those of peripheral instances, although several variables (such as culture, personal knowledge, and context) can influence the choice of category prototypes.

3. Because there are so many possible locations, there are quite a few prepositions. Below is the complete list of English prepositions:

   about/above/according to/across/after/against/along/
   along with/among/apart from/around/as/as for/at
   because of/before/behind/below/beneath/beside/between/beyond/but/by/by means of
   concerning/despite/down/during
   except/except for/excepting/for/from
   in/in addition to/in back of/in case of/in front of/in place of/inside/in spite of/
   instead of/into/like/near/next
   of/off/on/onto/on top of/out/out of/outside/over
   past/regarding/round/since/through/throughout/till/to/toward
   under/underneath/unlike/until/up/upon/up to
   with/within/without

   Some prepositions like "in", "on", "to", "of", "for" and so on are more basic than those like "by means of", "in addition to", "except for" because the former is a part of the latter, i. e. the prepositional phrases are composed of simple preposition and some English words; preposition like "under" is basic than "underneath" because the latter tends to be used in more formal conditions.

4. (1) It cost him three million to win his marriage back.
   (2) His early death indicates that they will not be able to come to the beautiful ending of their marriage together.
   (3) From now on, there is an undetachable connection between them.

5. (1) She is a beautiful snake.
   Source domain: a dangerous animal that kills other animals with poisonous secretion.
   Target domain: people who are cruel, cold-blooded, treacherous, untrustful
   (2) He is a horse!
   Source domain: a domesticated mammal used for riding and for drawing or carrying loads.
   Target domain: people who are diligent, loyal, conscious about personal hygiene.

6. Definitions of these words in dictionaries help us a lot to conceptualize them, most of which are descriptions of the causes, processes and properties of these emotions. We take "anger, love and fear" for example: (1) anger: the strong feeling you have when something happened you think is

bad and unfair (from Oxford Dictionary); a strong feeling of wanting to hurt or criticize someone because they have done something bad to you or been unkind to you (from Longman Dictionary). (2) love: to have a strong feeling of affection for someone, combined with sexual attraction (from Longman Dictionary); a strong feeling of deep affection for somebody/something, especially a member of your family or a friend, or for somebody you are sexually attracted to (from Oxford Dictionary). (3) fear: the bad feeling that you have when you are in danger, when something bad might happen, or a particular thing frightens you (from Oxford Dictionary); the feeling you get when you are afraid or worried that something bad is going to happen (from Longman Dictionary). In these definitions, a conceptual metonymy is extensively used, that is, THE BODILY SYMPTOMS OF AN EMOTION STAND FOR THE EMOTION (part for whole). Bodily symptoms are helpful for description of the concept of an emotion since generally they are peculiar to a particular emotion.

10.3 考研真题与典型题详解

Ⅰ. Fill in the blanks.

1. __________ is the mental process of classification, while __________ is the products of the preceding process.
2. __________ is an approach to the analysis of natural language that focuses on language as an instrument for organizing, processing, and conveying information.
3. There are three aspects in basic-level categories: __________, __________ and __________.

Ⅱ. Multiple Choice

1. In the following sentences, which is not a metonymy?
   A. The sax has the flu today.
   B. *Watergate* changed American politics.
   C. *Wall Street* is in a panic.
   D. She is the apple in her parents' eyes.
2. Which is not a type of iconicity?
   A. Iconicity of distance
   B. Iconicity of complexity
   C. Iconicity of intimacy
   D. Iconicity of order

Ⅲ. True or False

1. Metonymy involves using the familiar to stand for the unfamiliar. (对外经贸2005研)
2. As a new approach to the study of language and mind, popular linguistics began to appear in the 1970s and has been increasingly active since 1980s.

Ⅳ. Explain the following terms.

1. prototype
2. conceptual metonymy
3. iconicity
4. grammaticalization

Ⅴ. Short answer questions

1. What are the four assumptions of the classical theory of categorization?
2. What are the three levels of categorization?

参考答案及解析

Ⅰ. Fill in the blanks.

1. Categorization; Category

(范畴化是人类对经验进行分类的过程。范畴是范畴化的产物。)

2. Cognitive linguistics

(认知语言学是一种研究自然语言的方法，主要研究语言组织、处理与传达信息的作用。)

3. Perception; communication; knowledge organization

(基本层次范畴包括三方面：感知、交流和知识系统。)

Ⅱ. Multiple Choice

1. D (A、B、C 为转喻，D 为暗喻。)

2. C (象似性包括距离象似性，复杂象似性以及顺序象似性。)

Ⅲ. True or False

1. T (转喻是用一个实体去替代另一个实体的认知过程。)

2. F (作为研究语言和思维的一种方法，认知语言学在 20 世纪 70 年代开始出现，自 20 世纪 80 年代就变得日益活跃。)

Ⅳ. Explain the following terms.

1. Prototype is what members of a certain group consider to be the finest example of a lexical category, e.g. in English "dog" (rather than, say, "whale") might be the prototypical animal.

2. Metonymy is a cognitive process; its main function is to provide mental access through one conceptual entity to another; it is based on idealized cognitive model (ICMs) with specific conceptual relationship among their elements.

3. Iconicity is a property of language that indicates that the structure of language reflects the structure of experience, that is, the structure of the world, including the speaker's viewpoint on the world.

4. Grammaticalization is a process of language change by which words representing objects and actions (i. e. nouns and verbs) become grammatical markers (affixes, prepositions, etc.). Grammaticalization results in the usual shifts in meaning and form distribution. The restrictions on their grammatical uses appear to reflect their lexical histories, which is another feature of grammaticalized forms. Another common result of grammaticalization is nearly identical forms in different historical stages.

Ⅴ. Short answer questions

1. Four assumptions:

①The first assumption: A limited number of essential and sufficient conditions

②The second assumption: Features are binary.

③The third assumption: Clear boundaries are set for categories.

④The fourth assumption: A category's members all share the same status.

2. Three levels of categorization

①Superordinate level categories is categories placed at the top and thus display a low degree of class inclusion and a high degree of generality. E. g, plant and furniture are at the superordinate level.

②Basic-level categories are more precise, but not overly so. Tree and table are examples of basic-level categories.

③Subordinate level categories display low degree of generality and a high degree of class inclusion. Pine is an example of subordinate categories.

第11章 语言习得

11.1 复习笔记

本章要点：

1. First language acquisition
   第一语言习得
2. Two approaches of language acquisition
   语言习得的两种方式
3. Contrastive analysis
   对比分析
4. Error analysis
   错误分析
5. Individual Differences in Second Language Acquisition
   二语习得中的个体差异
6. Instruction and L2 Acquisition
   二语习得与教学

本章考点：

行为主义者的习得观；天生主义者的习得观；对比分析；错误分析；二语习得中的个体差异。

本章内容索引：

Ⅰ. First Language Acquisition

1. Definition of language acquisition
2. Distinction between acquisition and learning
3. Two approaches of language acquisition
   (1) The behaviorist approach
   (2) The innateness approach
4. Stages of acquiring the first language

Ⅱ. Second Language Acquisition

1. Definition of SLA
2. Contrastive analysis
3. Error analysis
   (1) Error vs. Mistake
   (2) Different types of errors
4. Interlanguage
   (1) Definition
   (2) Features

Ⅲ. Individual Differences in Second Language Acquisition

1. Language aptitude
2. Cognitive style
3. Personality traits
4. Learning strategies

Ⅳ. Instruction and L2 Acquisition

1. Form-focused instruction
2. Learner-instruction matching
3. Strategy training

<table>
<tr>
<td>

Ⅰ. First Language Acquisition

1. Definition of language acquisition

First language acquisition (L1 acquisition) is the child's acquisition of his mother language, i. e., how child comes to understand and speak the language of his community.

2. Distinction between acquisition and learning

Acquisition is a subconscious process without minute's learning of grammatical rules. Learners can hardly be aware of their leaning but they are using the language to communicate.

Learning is a conscious process of learning the grammatical rules and talking about the rules.

3. Two approaches of language acquisition

(1) **The behaviorist approach** believes that children learn language from other human role models through a process involving imitation, rewards, and practice. So learning is a process of imitation and habit formation. When a child attempts oral language or imitates the sounds or speech patterns, they are usually receiving rewards for their efforts.

(2) **The innateness approach** is proposed by Noam Chomsky. He hypothesizes that infants must be born with some special built-in ability to learn language. Language, among other biological functions like walking, develops in children.

4. Stages of acquiring the first language

The most well-known result of studies on children's language is the identification of stages of acquisition. Several stages have been identified: **pre-language stages, the one-word or holophrastic stage, the two-word stage and telegraphic speech.**

</td>
<td>

Ⅰ. 第一语言习得

1. 定义

第一语言习得是指孩子对母语的习得，即孩子如何理解和说其社区语言。

2. 语言习得和语言学习的区别

习得是一个无意识的过程，它没有对语法规则的正式学习。学习者几乎无法意识到自己在学习，但他们正在使用该语言进行交流。

学习是学习语法规则和谈论规则的自觉过程。

3. 语言习得的两种研究

（1）**行为主义观点**认为，儿童通过模仿、获得反馈和练习等过程从其他人类角色学习语言。学习实际上就是模仿与习惯形成的过程。当一个孩子尝试口头语言或模仿声音或语音模式时，他们通常会因为他们的努力而收到反馈。

（2）**天生主义观点**由乔姆斯基首次提出。语法天生主义观点认为婴儿天生具有某种特殊的内在语言学习能力。而且语言的发展和儿童的其他生物功能的发展一样，如行走。

4. 母语习得的阶段

对儿童语言的研究最著名的是儿童语言习得阶段的明确。有几个被认可的阶段：**前语言阶段、单词句阶段、双词句阶段和电报语阶段。**

</td>
</tr>
</table>

Ⅱ. Second Language Acquisition

1. Definition of SLA

【考点：名词解释】

Second language acquisition (SLA) is the process by which people learn a second language. In the 1970s, SLA was formally established as a discipline.

2. Contrastive analysis

Contrastive analysis is the systematic study of target language and native language with a view to identify their structural differences and similarities. Contrastive analysis was used as a method of explaining why some features of a target language were more difficult to acquire than others.

3. Error analysis

Error analysis is a method used to document the errors that appear in learner language, determining whether those errors are systematic, and (if possible) explain what caused them.

(1) Error vs. Mistake

Errors are typically the product of a learner's lack of knowledge; they reflect a lack of competence, i. e., learners are unable to use language properly because they do not know the proper form. When learners struggle to perform their competence, they often make mistakes. In other words, the learner has already mastered the knowledge or skill but is unable to apply it due to some reasons.

(2) Different types of errors

① interlingual errors and intralingual errors

Errors may be divided into two types based on their source: interlingual errors and intralingual errors. Interlingual errors (or transfer errors) are caused by the interference of the native language, whereby the learner tends to use their linguistic knowledge of native language on some linguistic features in the target language. Intralingual errors (or developmental errors) are caused by incorrect or incomplete leaning of the target language, regardless of the native language.

② omissions, additions, double markings, misformations and misorderings

Errors are often classified into five types based on their nature: omissions, additions, double markings, misformations and misorderings.

Ⅱ. 第二语言习得

1. 定义

第二语言习得(SLA)指人们学习第二语言的过程。第二语言习得研究于二十世纪七十年代左右被正式确立为一门学科。

2. 对比分析

对比分析是对目的语和母语进行系统研究，以确定其结构上异同的研究方法。对比分析被用来解释为什么目的语的某些特征比其他特征更难习得。

3. 错误分析

错误分析是一种用来记录学习者语言中出现的错误，确定这些错误是否是系统的，并(如果可能的话)解释造成这些错误的原因的研究方法。

(1) 错误与失误

错误(error)通常是由于学习者知识不足所致。换言之，由于学习者不知道正确的形式所以不能正确地使用语言而出现的错误。失误(mistake)则是由于学习者没能发挥出自己的能力而出现差错。也就是说，学习者学会了某种知识或技能，但是由于一些因素的影响而没能正确地使用语言。

(2) 不同类型的错误

① 语际错误与语内错误

根据错误来源，错误经常分为语际错误和语内错误。语际错误(或迁移错误)指由于母语的干扰造成的，学习者倾向于将母语的语言知识运用到目的语的一些语言特征上的错误。语内错误(或发展性错误)指由于对目的语的错误或不完全的学习造成的错误，它与本族语无关。

② 省略、添加、双重标记、形式错误和顺序错误

根据错误性质，错误经常可以被划分为五种类型：省略、添加、双重标记、形式错误和顺序错误。

4. Interlanguage

【考点：名词解释】

(1) Definition

Proposed by S. Pit Corder and Larry Selinker, an interlanguage is an idiolect that has been developed by a learner of a second language which preserves some features of their first language, and can also overgeneralizes some writing and speaking rules of the target language. This makes the interlanguage **a continuum or approximation** from his native language to the target language.

(2) Features

①**systematicity**: When acquiring L2, there is some in-between structure that incorporates elements of both L1 and L2. It is an entirely variable system with its own set of rules.

②**permeability**: The rules that make up the learner's knowledge of the L2 at any given time are not set and can be updated at any time.

③**fossilization**: A phenomenon in which incorrect linguistic features become permanent in a person's spoken or written language over time. When learning a second or foreign language, certain aspects of pronunciation, vocabulary usage, and grammar may become fossilized.

Ⅲ. Individual Differences in Second Language Acquisition

1. language aptitudes

Language aptitude is the potential that a person has for learning second languages. It is thought to be linked to a learner's general intelligence. John Carroll proposed some components of language aptitude: phonemic coding ability, grammatical sensitivity, inductive language learning ability, and rote learning ability.

2. Cognitive style

Cognitive style refers to the individual manner in which a learner attempts to learn a language. Two different cognitive styles are field dependence and field independence.

① Field dependence

【考点：名词解释】

Field dependence is a concept in the field of cognitive styles. In general, people who exhibit field dependence tend to rely on information provided by the outer world, the field or frame of a situation. They are very dependent on the opinions of others and rely heavily on constructive feedback in their L2 learning. They are seen as outgoing and concerned about others, and have good interpersonal communication skills in the L2.

4. 中介语

1. 定义

中介语由 S. P. 科德和莱瑞·塞林克提出，中介语是第二语言学习者在保留了母语的一些特点的情况下形成的一种个人语型，它也有目的语的一些写作和口语规则。中介语是一个处于本族语和目的语之间的**连续体或临界体**。

2. 特征

①**系统性**：二语习得中有一个中间系统，它既涉及母语也涉及二语的一些方面，但这个系统是一个有规则的可变系统。

②**渗透性**：渗透性指每一个阶段学习者所获得的语言经验不是固定的，而是可以修正和增加的。

③**语言石化现象**：语言石化现象指外语学习者的一些不正确的语言运用趋向于固定下来的状态。发音、词汇和语法在第二语言或外语学习中可能会变得固定或石化。

Ⅲ. 二语习得中的个体差异

1. 语言学能

语言学能是指**学习第二语言的天生潜能**。人们认为它与学习者的总体智力有关。约翰·卡罗尔认为语言学能包括如下几个组成部分：音素代码能力、语法感知能力、语言学习归纳能力和机械记忆能力。

2. 认知风格

认知风格指学习者学习一种语言的方式，它包括场依存和场独立两种风格。

①场依存

场依存是认知风格领域的一个概念。一般来说，场依存的人倾向于依赖外部世界、语场或情境框架提供的信息。场依存者对物体的认知倾向于把外部参照作为信息加工的依据。他们的态度和自我认知更易受周围人的影响和干扰，善于吸纳二语学习中的积极反馈。场依存者大都外向，对周围事物饶有兴趣，因此被认为具有良好的人际沟通技巧。

②**Field independence**

【考点：名词解释】

Field independence is a learning style in which learners tend to separate details from the surrounding context. They are less reliant on being provided with a structure to the language learning and are more self-motivated. They are willing to analyze and evaluate on their own in order to decide if it is right or not. They have a clear sense of self-identity and often seem indifferent to and detached from others. As a result, they could be predicted to be less skilled in developing interpersonal skills in the L2.

②**场独立**

场独立指将细节从周围的环境中分离出来的认知风格，场独立者较少依赖于别人所提供的学科结构，更倾向于自我激励。场独立者有着强烈的自我意识，似乎总是疏远他人，对周围人显得漠不关心，因此被认为缺乏良好的人际沟通技巧。

3. Personality traits

Many language teachers believe that certain personalities tend to aid in language learning activities. Traditionally, it was commonly assumed that extroverts would have better performance in L2 learning than introverts.

3. 人格特征

多数语言教师认为某些人格特有助于语言学习活动。人们通常认为外向的人比内向的人学语言学得更好。

4. Learning strategies

Learning strategies are learners' conscious, goal-oriented and problem-solving based efforts to maximize learning productivity.

①**Cognitive strategies** are the specific methods that people use to solve problems and/or exploit opportunities, including all sorts of reasoning, planning, arithmetic, etc.

②**Metacognitive strategies** are methods used to help students understand the way they learn; in other words, it means processes designed for students to "think" about their "thinking".

③**Social/affective strategies** is the way in which learners communicate with other L2 speakers.

4. 学习策略

学习策略是指学习者有意识地、以目的为导向的、以解决问题为基础的、为提高学习效率而作出的努力。

①**认知策略**指人们用来解决问题或利用机会的特定方法，包括各种推理、计划、算术等。

②**元认知策略**指帮助学生理解他们学习方式的方法；换句话说，它是指为学生"思考"他们的"思考"而设计的过程。

③**社交/情感策略**指学习者与其他二语使用者进行交流的方式。

Ⅳ. Instruction and L2 Acquisition

1. Form-focused instruction

Form-focused instruction is an approach in language education that emphasizes the acquisition of linguistic forms such as lexical features, phonological features, grammatical forms, etc.

Studies have shown that form-focused instruction do influence second language acquisition, but it remains unknown that what kind of form-focused instruction works best.

Ⅳ. 二语习得与教学

1. 以形式为焦点的教学

形式为焦点的教学是一种强调词汇特征、语音特征、语法形式等语言形式习得的语言教学方法。

研究表明，**以形式为焦点的教学**对二语习得有一定影响，但哪种形式更有效至今还无定论。

2. Learner-instruction matching Learner-instruction matching attempts to guarantee that the instructional style is appropriate for the learner. It is grounded on the assumption that learners have diverse learning styles and that if the instruction is adjusted to their own learning styles, they can achieve better learning efficiency. **3. Strategy training** Strategy training is an attempt to engage directly in interlanguage development by teaching learners specific grammatical structures. Another alternative is to engage more indirectly by recognizing techniques that are likely to encourage acquisition and providing instruction.	**2. 学习者与课堂教学法的匹配** 学习者与课堂教学法的匹配是指教师的教学风格符合学生自身。它基于这样一种设想：学生有着不同的学习风格，如果老师的教学风格符合学生的学习风格，那么学生会学得更有效率。 **3. 学习策略的训练** 教授学生具体的语法结构无疑是干预中介语发展的最直接的方法；另一种方式是教给学生有助于提高学习的方法策略，这种干预方法就不那么直接了。

11.2 课后习题详解

1. Define the following terms briefly.

first language acquisition	behaviorist approach	innateness approach
second language acquisition	contrastive analysis	error analysis
language aptitude	field dependence	field independence
learning strategies		

2. Find a child between two and four years old and play with him/her for about thirty minutes. Keep a list of all his/her Words and/or "sentences" that are used inappropriately. Describe what are the possible meanings of these words. Describe the syntactic or morphological errors (including omissions). If the child is producing multi-word sentences, write a grammar that could account for the data you have collected.
3. "Baby talk" is a term used to label the word forms that many adults use when speaking to children. Examples in English are *choo-choo* for "train" and *bow-wow* for "dog". Baby talk seems to exist in every language and culture. At least two things seem to be universal about baby talk: the words that have baby talk forms fall into certain semantic categories (for example, food and animals) and the words are "phonetically simpler" than the adult forms (for example, tummy [ˈtʌmɪ] for "stomach" [ˈstʌmək]). List all the baby talk words you can think of in Chinese; then (1) separate them into semantic categories, and (2) try to state general rules for the kinds of phonological simplifications that occur.
4. Discuss why second language learners, regardless of their first language, might produce forms such as *goed*, *sheeps*, and *coulds* given that they never hear these forms in input from native speakers of English. Give some other forms analogous to the above that might be generated.
5. In what way does Mandarin Chinese interfere with your English studies? Give examples to illustrate your point.
6. Identify the errors in the following sentences and explain the possible cause for each error:

(1) Please do not hinder my work.

(2) – Would you mind lending me your dictionary?

– Yes, certainly.

(3) During the meeting we discussed about the research project.

(4) Alice is in poor health. She is easy to catch cold.

(5) The light can impress the film and in this way to fix the image of the film.

(6) The scenery is too beautiful to describe it.

7. What happens when an interlanguage fossilizes? Have you ever experienced any fossilization in your language learning?
8. What factors can you think of that might influence fossilization? In other words, do you think that some people are more likely to fossilize than others? Do you think it can be reversed? How?

参考答案

1. **First language acquisition:** First language acquisition (L1 acquisition) refers to the child's acquisition of his mother language, i. e., how child comes to understand and speak the language of his community.

Behaviorist approach: The behaviorist approach believes that children learn language from other human role models through a process involving imitation, rewards, and practice. So learning is a process of imitation and habit formation. When a child attempts oral language or imitates the sounds or speech patterns, they are usually receiving rewards for their efforts.

Innateness approach: The innateness approach is proposed by Noam Chomsky. He hypothesizes that infants must be born with some special built-in ability to learn language. Language, among other biological functions like walking, develops in children.

Second language acquisition: Second language acquisition (SLA) is the process by which people learn a second language. In the 1970s, SLA was formally established as a discipline.

Contrastive analysis: Contrastive analysis is the systematic study of target language and native language with a view to identify their structural differences and similarities. Contrastive analysis was used as a method of explaining why some features of a target language were more difficult to acquire than others.

Error analysis: Error analysis is a method used to document the errors that appear in learner language, determining whether those errors are systematic, and (if possible) explain what caused them.

Language aptitude: Language aptitude is the potential that a person has for learning second languages. It is thought to be linked to a learner's general intelligence. John Carroll proposed some components of language aptitude: phonemic coding ability, grammatical sensitivity, inductive language learning ability, and rote learning ability.

Field dependence: Field dependence is a concept in the field of cognitive styles. In general, people who exhibit field dependence tend to rely on information provided by the outer world, the field or frame of a situation. They are very dependent on the opinions of others and rely heavily on constructive feedback in their L2 learning. They are seen as outgoing and concerned about others, and have good interpersonal communication skills in the L2.

Field independence: Field independence is a learning style in which learners tend to separate details from the surrounding context. They are less reliant on being provided with a structure to the language learning and are more self-motivated. They are willing to analyze and evaluate on their own in order to decide if it is right or not. They have a clear sense of self-identity and often seem indifferent to and detached from others. As a result, they could be predicted to be less skilled in developing interpersonal skills in the L2.

Learning strategies: Learning strategies are learners' conscious, goal-oriented and problem-solving based efforts to maximize learning productivity.

2. The sentences and words are like this: 饭要我，我要，光光。

   In these examples, "饭要我" is a syntactically wrong sentence, which means that "我要饭". "我要"is a sentence with omissions. Sometimes the child does not know how to name what he wants, so he just says"我要". If he does not point at or look at what he wants, the other party will not know what he really wants. A child says "光光"which may mean lamp bulb. He uses the light the lamp bulb gives out to mean the lamp bulb.

3. **Category**: **Food**: "饭饭", "果果", "豆豆", "糖糖"

   Animal: "咪咪"(猫), "汪汪"(狗), "哞哞"(牛)

   Toy: "球球", "咚咚"(鼓)

   General rules for Chinese baby talk: the repetition of the main characters and use the sound of animal calls or the toy produces to indicate the animal or the toy.

4. Forms like "goed", "sheeps", and "coulds" result from analogous creation of second language learners. It is a kind of interlanguage produced in the process of second language acquisition. Having acquired some basic English grammars, for example, the common past form for English verbs is to add a suffix "-ed" to the end of the verb, those English-learners easily assume that all the English verb should change their form like that in past tense. However, there are exceptions as "go-went", "sing-sang" and so on. Those English-learners fail to see those exceptions and create all the past forms analogously, thus produce the wrong forms like "goed".

   Other examples:

   run-runned(ran), child-childs(children), must-musts.

5. First language exerts a great influence in the process of second language acquisition. The interference of mother tongue is usually called "negative transfer". Chinese, as my mother tongue, has a great influence in my L2 acquisition procedure, too. It is explicitly represented in the occurrence of Chinglish, which is a kind of interlanguage produced by Chinese English-learners in general.

   For example, I produce sentence like this:

   The government abolished the policy <u>totally</u>.

   Here, "totally" is an unnecessary and redundant word if viewed by native speakers because "abolish" already contains the meaning of "totally", since one can not "abolish sth. partially". It is duplicating in English but perfect right in Chinese. Therefore, when acquiring a second language, we are unconsciously influenced by our Chinese way of speaking.

6. (1) **Error** caused by incomplete knowledge of the rules of the target language or mother tongue

interference.

The corresponding Chinese sentence is "请勿妨碍我的工作", the using of "hinder" to replace "妨碍" is caused by mother tongue interference because the proper word here should be "disturb".

(2) **Error** caused by incomplete knowledge of the rules of the target language or mother tongue interference.

The answer in Chinese is "是，当然可以。". In English, however, we should answer "No, go ahead." because the previous question is "Would you mind...?" If we answer "Yes", that means we do not want this man to do the thing he proposed.

(3) **Error** caused by incomplete knowledge of the rules of the target language or mother tongue interference.

Preposition "about" should be deleted since "discuss" is a transitive verb. We Chinese people always say "讨论关于……", however it is Chinglish to say "discuss about sth".

(4) **Mistake** caused by lack of attention, carelessness, fatigue.

The correct form of "catch cold" should be "catch a cold". It doesn't mean that the speaker does not know the grammar but he fails to perform it in real speech.

(5) **Error** caused by mother tongue interference.

"Impress" is an action of animate creatures, the light cannot impress sth. The correct sentence should be: The film can be impressed by the light.

(6) **Error** caused by mother tongue interference.

"Describe" is an action of animate creatures, the scenery cannot describe sth. and the correct relationship between "describe" and "scenery" should be: the scenery is the object of the action-describe. Therefore, the correct sentence should be: The scenery is too beautiful to be described.

7. It is extremely rare for the learner of an L2 to achieve full native-like competence. Selinker coined the term "Fossilization" to refer to this phenomenon—non-target forms become fixed in the interlanguage. Many examples can be found—continually making errors such as the use of simple past instead of simple present—no amount of grammatical explanation or of error correction had any effect.

8. We have also seen that learners of a second language tend to fossilize. They may be partially fossilized, retaining certain errors while progressing in other ways, or they may get stuck upon a plateau. The sociological situation of the learner and of the learner's community in relation to the community that speaks the L2 can have a significant effect on language learning. There are also other factors which intervene in the process, and which may either induce fossilization or prevent it. Among the most important variables are:

- affective factors
- amount of exposure-input
- opportunities for expression
- negative feedback (note: not correction, but signaling incomprehension)
- absence or presence of pressure on communication

11.3 考研真题及真题详解

Ⅰ. Fill in the blanks.

1. The type of language constructed by second or foreign language learners who are still in the process of learning a language is often referred to as ________. (中山大学 2008 研)
2. Error is the grammatically incorrect form; ________ appears when the language is correct grammatically but improper in a communicational context. (中山大学 2008 研)
3. In learning a second language, a learner will subconsciously use his L1 knowledge. This process is called language ________.
4. Such errors as "teached" and "womans" are caused by ________.

Ⅱ. Multiple Choice

1. ________ is defined as a conscious process of accumulating knowledge of a second language usually obtained in school settings.

   A. Competence B. Performance C. Learning D. Acquisition

2. A child acquires his/her mother tongue invariably through these phases: ________, one-word, two-word and multiword.

   A. no-word B. babbling C. talking D. uttering

3. In Krashen's monitor theory, "i" in "i + 1" hypothesis of second language acquisition refers to ________. (对外经贸 2006 研)

   A. interaction B. interference C. input D. intake

4. Negative transfer in learning a second language is known as ________.

   A. interference B. interlanguage C. fossilization D. acculturation

5. ________ sees errors as the result of the intrusion of L1 habits over which the learner had no control.

   A. error analysis B. performance analysis
   C. contrastive analysis D. discourse analysis

Ⅲ. True or False

1. Universal Grammar refers to the principles and properties that pertain to the grammars of all human languages. (对外经贸 2005 研)
2. All normal children have equal ability in learning their first language.
3. It is easy for parents to teach their children grammar.
4. The ability to learn a second language as an adult may vary considerably between individuals.

Ⅳ. Explain the following terms.

1. Interlanguage (上海交大 2005 研)
2. Universal Grammar (西安交大 2008 研)
3. contrastive analysis (浙江大学 2004 研)
4. Error Analysis (中山大学 2011 研)
5. Language transfer (山东科技大学 2018 研)

Ⅴ. Short answer questions

1. How do you understand interlanguage? (西安交大 2008 研)

2. What are the four obvious barriers to adult L2 acquisition?（浙江大学 2003 研）
3. Please state the factors that cause errors and mistakes in foreign language learning.（厦门大学 2006 研）
4. To what extent is second language learning similar to first language learning? Can you list some proof from your own learning experiences?
5. Identify personality factors that may contribute to the SUCCESS of learning a second/ foreign language.
6. What is communicative competence? How should we develop it in our foreign lauguage learning?（四川大学 2010 研）

Ⅵ. Essay questions

1. Comment on the following statement based on your own experience.
   "Knowing words is the key, to understanding and being understood. The bulk of learning a new language consists of learning new words. Grammatical knowledge does not make for great proficiency in a language."（Vermeer1992）（武汉大学 2005 研）
2. What do you think are the similarities and dissimilarities between learning a first and a second language?（北外 2003 研）
3. Analyze the following speech errors, by commenting on how they might have arisen:
   a. He rode his bike to school tomorrow.（←yesterday）
   b. gone mild.（←wild/mad）
   c. He misfumbled the ball.（←mishandled/fumbled）
   d. That's torrible.（←terrible/horrible）（北外 2006 研）
5. Use contrastive or non-contrastive strategies to analyze the underlined errors and mistakes committed by Chinese learners of English.（浙江大学 2007 研）
   a. As for meal, we Chinese like <u>to eat chopsticks</u>, and you spoons.
   b. You have helped me a lot. <u>Really troubled you</u>.
   c. They are happy but we are <u>far more happier</u>.
6. Read the following paragraphs and then answer four questions.（北外 2011 研）
   The idea behind the experiential vision of learning is that the use of the target language for communicative purposes is not only the goal of learning, but also a means of learning in its own right. This may clearly involve students using language which they may not have fully mastered, and contrasts with other more 'traditional' approaches which emphasize part practice (i. e. , isolating parts of the whole for explicit study and learning) leading up in a more or less controlled manner to integrated language use for communicative purposes. An experiential approach to learning may therefore involve a degree of what Johnson (1982) refers to as an 'in at the deep end strategy'. Simply throwing learners into wholly uncontrolled and undirected language use is, of course, as dubious a strategy with respect to language learning as doing the same with someone who is learning to swim. For this reason, considerable effort has been devoted by methodologists, material writers, and teachers in recent decades to the way in which two sets of factors can be combined. One is the basic insight that language use can serve a significant role in promoting learning, and the other is the acknowledgement that use of the language needs to be structured in

a coherent and pedagogically manageable way. The experiential vision of learning has evolved in a variety of ways since the 1960s and is now encountered in a number of differing forms. Nevertheless, most experiential approaches to learning rest on five main principles which were developed in the earlier days of the communicative movement, even if certain receive more attention in one variant than in another. These principles are the following: message focus, holistic practice, the use of authentic materials, the use of communication strategies, and the use of collaborative modes of learning. (Tudor 2001: 79)

An analytical view of learning posits that according explicit attention to the regularities of language and language use can play a positive role in learning. Each language manifests a number of structural regularities in areas such as grammar, lexis and phonology, and also with respect to the ways in which these elements are combined to communicate messages. The question, therefore, is not whether languages have structural regularities or not, but whether and in which way explicit attention to such regularities can facilitate the learning of the language. An analytical approach to learning rests on a more or less marked degree of part practice, i. e., isolating parts of the whole for explicit study and learning, even if its ultimate goal remains the development of learners' ability to put these parts together for integrated, holistic use. At least, two main considerations lend support to an analytical approach to learning. First, in terms of learning in general, the isolation and practice of sub-parts of a target skill is a fairly common phenomenon... Second, explicit identification of regularities in a language has advantages which Johnson (1996: 83) refers to as 'generativity' and 'economy'. Mastering a regularity in a language gives learners access to the generative potential of this regularity in new circumstances... Explicit presentation or discovery of the structural regularities of a language can therefore represent a short-cut to mastery of this language and support learners' ability to manipulate these regularities for communicative purposes. (Tudor 2001: 86-7)

(1) What are the differences between experiential and analytical modes of language learning?

(2) What serves as the theoretical foundation for the experiential mode of language learning and what are its advantages and disadvantages?

(3) What serves as the theoretical foundation for the analytical mode of language learning and what are its advantages and disadvantages?

(4) How would you balance the two modes of learning in your teaching or learning of a foreign language?

9. What are the major external factors that affect the process of L2 learning? (厦门大学 2010 研)

参考答案及解析

Ⅰ. Fill in the blanks.

1. interlanguage

(中介语是在外语或第二语言学习中形成的。)

2. mistake

(失误是指在语法上正确但在交流语境中不恰当运用语言的现象。)

3. transfer

（学习第二语言时不自觉地使用第一语言的过程叫语言迁移。）

4. second language learners

（这些错误一般是第二语言学习者犯的。）

Ⅱ. Multiple Choice

1. C （在学校里我们会学到第二语言，对第二语言知识的这种有意识的积累，叫做“学习”。）
2. B （婴儿学习母语的过程分为四个阶段：牙牙学语阶段，单语词阶段，双语词阶段和多语词阶段。）
3. C （克拉申在“监控理论”中提到二语习得输入假说（i + 1），i 表示学习者的现有水平，1 表示略高于现在的水平。）
4. A （语言学习者在学习第二语言时，难免受到母语的影响。正面的影响称作正迁移，负面的影响称作负迁移或者干扰。）
5. C （对比分析是通过对比不同的语言来确定潜在错误的方法，它将错误看作是受母语作用的结果，并认为这是学习者无法控制的。）

Ⅲ. True or False

1. T （普遍语法指符合所有人类语言特征的语法。）
2. T （乔姆斯基的语言习得机制（LAD）认为儿童均有习得其母语的同等能力。）
3. F （语法的获得一方面是语言掌握能力的提升，另一方面是语言表达能力的提高。孩子在十岁之前很难掌握一些语法之间的细微差异。）
4. T （不同的个体有不同的学习环境，并且他们的学习能力也会受到学习动机和个人爱好的影响。）

Ⅳ. Explain the following terms.

1. Interlanguage. refers to the type of language constructed by second or foreign language learners who are still in the process of learning a language. It's a language system between the target language and the learner's native language, and imperfect compared with the target language, but not mere translation from the learner's native language. For example, when a Chinese student is learning English, he may make errors like “to touch the society”.
2. Universal grammar is a theory of linguistics postulating principles of grammar shared by all languages, thought to be innate to humans (linguistic nativism). It attempts to explain language acquisition in general, not describe specific languages. Universal grammar proposes a set of rules intended to explain language acquisition in child development.
3. Contrastive analysis is the systematic study of target language and native language with a view to identify their structural differences and similarities. Contrastive analysis was used as a method of explaining why some features of a target language were more difficult to acquire than others.
4. Errors are significant in telling the teacher what needs to be taught, in telling the researchers how learning proceeds and those errors are a means whereby learners test their hypotheses about the language to be learnt. They are worth further probing what Error Analysis involves, first independently or objectively, describing the learners' interlanguage (that is, their version of the target language and the target language itself), and then a comparison of the two is followed to locate mismatches. Different from contrastive analysis, Error Analysis, EA for short, gives less

consideration to learners' native language. The procedure of Error Analysis consists of the following steps:

(1) Recognition

(2) Description

(3) Explanation

For example, explanation—the absence of an item that must appear in a well-formed utterance. e. g. She sleeping. Type of error: Omissions.

5. In learning a second language, learners will subconsciously use their mother tongue knowledge. This is known as language transfer. Two types of transfer, namely negative transfer and positive transfer may occur. Positive transfer is learning in one situation which helps or facilitates learning in another later situation. Negative transfer is learning in one situation which interferes with learning in another later situation.

V. Short answer questions

1. The type of language constructed by second or foreign language learners who are still in the process of learning a language is often referred to as interlanguage. nterlanguage is often understood as a language system between the target language and the learner's native language. It is imperfect compared with the target language, but it is not mere translation from the learner's native language. However, interlanguage should not really be seen as a bridging language between the target language and native language. Interlanguage is a dynamic language system, which is constantly moving from the departure level to the native-like level. Therefore, "inter" actually means between the beginning stage and the final stage. There are many examples of interlanguage, such as *I no have a book* and *I like read books*.

(本题考查中介语的含义。)

2. A variety of explanations have been put forward for the apparent decline in adults:

(1) physical factors such as the loss of "plasticity" in the brain and "lateralization" of the brain;

(2) social factors such as the different situations and relationships that children encounter compared to adults;

(3) cognitive factors such as the interference with natural language learning by the adult's more abstract mode of thinking;

(4) input factors that adults spend only a few hours each week of school time, rather than via the constant interaction experienced by a child, with a lot of other occupations.

3. There are generally two types of factors that cause errors and mistakes in foreign language learning, one is inter-lingual, traced to the influence of the mother tongue, the other is intra-lingual, committed by language learners regardless of their L1.

In second language learning, the learners attempt to transfer the features of their mother tongue to the second language. When the structures of the two languages are similar, we can get positive transfer; when the two languages are different in structures, negative transfer or interference occurs and results in errors.

Not all errors are caused by the interference of the mother tongue. There are cases that the learner knows some rules of the target language but applies them in the wrong place. Errors of overgeneralization and hypercorrection belong to this type.

4. Theoretically the new findings and advances in first language acquisition especially in learning theories and learning process are illuminating in understanding second language acquisition. The techniques used to collect and analyze data in first language acquisition also provide insights and perspectives in the study of second language acquisition. For example, we started to learn our native language from listening, then speaking.
5. In terms of communicative ability rather than grammatical accuracy or knowledge of grammatical roles, the personality traits such as extroversion, talkative, self-esteem, self-confidence can be found in successful second language learners. Certain personality traits appear helpful in completing certain tasks in learning a second language.
6. Communicative competence is what a learner knows about how a language is used in particular situations for effective and appropriate communication. Communicative competence includes knowledge of the grammar and vocabulary, knowledge of rules of speaking, knowledge of how to use and respond to different types of speech acts and social conventions, and knowledge of how to use language appropriately.

   In order to develop communicative competence in our foreign lauguage learning, language learners are encouraged to deal with accomplishing actions, which are believed to help them acquire the target language. Two types of tasks are usually required to be performed by the learners: real-world tasks and pedagogical tasks. For example, students may be asked to work or discuss in groups.

   Besides, teachers can adopt the communicative syllabus which aims at the learner's communicative competence. It teaches the language needed to express and understand different kinds of functions, and emphasizes the process of communication.

Ⅵ. Essay questions

1. The nature of a word implies an association with something in the real world and a sequence of sounds that convey that something to other people. It is words which, expressed as sounds, convey the thought of a thing, of a concept, from the mind of one person to the mind of another person, providing that these two people speak the same language. Therefore, whether knowing the words of a language will affect whether one can speak that particular language even the understanding of it.

   As we all know, what grammar is about is the linguistic form. The grammatical hierarchy could be roughly described as: sentences, word groups, words, morphemes. Therefore, without knowledge of the words, one in fact could not assert to have really grasped the grammatical knowledge. Having grammatical knowledge without knowledge of the words is like having an empty frame without any content.

   Knowing the vocabulary of a new language, on the other hand, does not merely mean recognizing the words; it also includes knowing how the words are used. For example, as to the two words, "chat" and "conversation", one will be supposed to know what different situations these two expressions are used.

2. Similarities between first and second language acquisition:

(1) Both L1 and L2 are constructed from prior conceptual knowledge. Language emerges as a procedural acquisition to deal with events that the child already understands conceptually and to achieve communicative objectives that the child can realize by the other means.

(2) Second language learners seem to use similar strategies to those learning their first language.

(3) Overgeneralization and transfer are used by both L1 and L2 learners as the result of a necessity to reduce language to the simplest possible system, as an effort to lessen the cognitive burden involved in trying to master something as complex as language.

(4) The L2 learner, like the first, attempts to "regularize, analogize, and simplify" in an effort to communicate.

(5) Speech addressed to children (motherese) and speech addressed to foreigners (foreign talk) present similarities: shorter sentences, high-frequency vocabulary, "here and now" times, indirect correction, frequent gesture, lake of overt attention to form.

(6) A reasonable hypothesis is that the brain and nervous system are biologically programmed to acquire language (L1 and L2) in a particular sequence and in a particular mode (silent period).

(7) Both groups are probably using the same learning process. For example, the L2 sequence for English grammatical morphemes was similar, though not identical, to that found in L1 acquisition. Other similar sequences of syntactic acquisition have been found in L1 and L2 learning. L2 learners , like L1 children, at first put negative elements at the beginning of the sentence "No the sun shining" and then progress to negation within the sentence "That's no ready."

Differences between L1 and L2 acquisition:

(1) L2 learners are usually older when learning their L2. Therefore, they are more developed cognitively. They have a greater knowledge of the world in general; they have more control over the input they receive; they are able to learn and apply rules that may aid in facilitating the acquisition process; they have one or more cultures that give them advanced information about expectations, discourse in general, and how to get things done with language.

(2) Older learners may have increased inhibition and anxiety and may find themselves afraid to make errors (poor attitudes and lack of motivation); there might be interference from the L1, particularly from items that are similar, either structurally or semantically.

(3) L1 acquisition is completely successful, but L2 learning is not. The evidence for this deficiency is held to be the lack of completeness of L2 grammars or the fossilization in L2 learning where the learner cannot progress beyond some particular stage, both familiar 'facts' in some sense.

(4) The variation in situation and other factors also produces many differences between L1 acquisition and L2 learning. L1 children mostly acquire language in different settings with different exposure to language than L2 learners and they are at different stages of mental and social maturity.

In all, the differences exist in levels of cognitive development and the similarities exist in the process of acquisition itself.

3. The speech errors arise above can be grouped into two: instance a as one group, and b, c, d as another.

   Producing a speech may involve the following 5 steps:

   (1) the message-level representation;

   (2) the functional-level representation;

   (3) the positional-level representation;

   (4) the phonetic-level representation;

   (5) the articulatory-level representation.

   The error occurring in *a* is possibly related to the Semantic Association Network. Therefore, it probably arises in step 3, in which the words of the sentence that is to be produced are incorporated. And Semantic Association Network is such a network that it represents the relationships between various semantically related words. Thus, it may happen like this: when the speaker wants to express the meaning of "yesterday", some other members of the association network referring to the time is activated, such as "tomorrow". Then the later probably replace the original one "yesterday", and through the proceeding steps of 4 and 5, the meaning of "tomorrow" is produced, although what the speaker originally wanted to mean is "yesterday".

   The errors that arise in *b*, *c*, *d*, may be related to steps 3 and 4. We can see obviously from *b* to *d* that after step 2, what the speaker wants to express is already clear. And for a same meaning, the speaker obviously has two different words in his mind. However, he may go into the step 3 before make a definite selection between the two different expressions. Therefore, going into step 4, which indicates some the necessary information about the ways in which words in the intended sentence are pronounced, he has two phonetic representation emerged altogether. As a consequence, in the last step, the articulating of the words, with two different expressions at a time, the speaker presents an expression involving the two words.

4. Contrastive analysis and non-contrastive analysis are two major approaches to error analysis. It has been found a large percentage of the errors are directly related to the learner's mother tongue. The systematic study of evidence of the influence of the mother tongue is called contrastive analysis. Therefore, contrastive analysis has to take the source and the target language into consideration. However, not all errors are caused by the interference of the mother tongue, such as overgeneralizations and hypercorrections. The analysis based on such intra-language factors is called non-contrastive analysis.

   As for sentence *a*, the correct expression should probably be "eat *with* chopsticks". When recalling the corresponding expression in Chinese, we might get "我们中国人喜欢用筷子吃", and therefore it could be seen that in Chinese a preposition is also required. In this sense, the mistake occurring in this sentence is probably not caused by the interference of Chinese. Therefore, it might be more proper to be regarded as an inter-lingual error which might be caused by the unfamiliarity of the preposition "with".

   The mistake in sentence *b*, however, could be attributed to the negative transfer of Chinese, since in Chinese, there exists a corresponding expression "真是麻烦你了。". This transfer has in some way shown the differences between Chinese and English, such as the difference in syntactic structure. The Chinese language does not obligatorily require the occurrence of the Subject in a sentence, while in English it is obligatory to have a Subject in a sentence.

The mistake in sentence *c* is one obviously not caused by the interference of Chinese. This mistake is also an inter-lingual one, as it concerns about the use of the comparative form of adjectives in English. In Chinese, there is no corresponding structure as in English. And this could be seen as a misuse of the comparative form of adjectives.

5. (1) The experiential mode is totally different from the analytical mode of learning. An experiential approach to learning may involve a degree of what Johnson (1982) refers to as an "in at the deep end strategy". Simply throwing learners into wholly uncontrolled and undirected language use is, of course, as dubious a strategy with respect to language learning as doing the same with someone who is learning to swim. For this reason, considerable effort has been devoted by methodologists, material writers, and teachers.

An analytical approach to learning rests on a more or less marked degree of part practice, i. e. , isolating parts of the whole for explicit study and learning, even if its ultimate goal remains the development of learners' ability to put these parts together for integrated, holistic use.

(2) The experiential mode provides a holistic model of the learning process and a multilinear model of adult development, both of which are consistent with what we know about how people learn, grow, and develop. The theory is to emphasize the central role that experience plays in the learning process, an emphasis that distinguishes experiential mode of language learning from other learning theories. The term "experiential" is used therefore to differentiate experiential mode of language learning both from cognitive learning theories, which tend to emphasize cognition over affect, and behavioral learning theories that deny any role for subjective experience in the learning process.

However, simply throwing learners into wholly uncontrolled and undirected language use is, of course, as dubious a strategy with respect to language learning as doing the same with someone who is learning to swim. Therefore, this mode of language learning requires the methodologists, material writers, and teachers to combine two sets of factors. One is the basic insight that language use can serve a significant role in promoting learning, and the other is the acknowledgement that use of the language needs to be structured in a coherent and pedagogically manageable way.

(3) An analytical approach to learning emphasizes the explicit study of the language learning a linguistic and communicative system. It is characteristic of the grammar-translation method found in the cognitive code approach, in various CALL exercises, and in form-focus learning activities. It is also present in certain types of learner training or awareness-raising activities involving the explicit analysis by learners of aspects of the languages teaching and learning or of their own language production.

Each language manifests a number of structural regularities in areas such as grammar, lexis and phonology, and also with respect to the ways in which these elements are combined to communicate messages. The question, therefore, is not whether languages have structural regularities or not, but whether and in which way explicit attention to such regularities can facilitate the learning of the language.

The main criticism of analytical learning is that declarative knowledge does not necessarily feed through to the ability to use a language for communicative purposes. In other words, someone may have a good knowledge of structural regularities of a language without being able to make use of the language with the spontaneity and fluency which are required in normal communicative situations.

(4) I would combine the two approaches together to learn a foreign language. First, following the analytical mode of language learning, the basic grammatical knowledge could be captured. Second, with the basic knowledge of structural regularities of a language, the experiential mode of language learning should be followed.

For example, when I learn how to greet in English, the first thing I should know about is how to pronounce "Hello!" or "How are you?" and the meaning of the expression. Then the next, I should learn in the relevant situations. Native speakers may respond to the phatic greeting in a variety of ways depending on the context and on how well they know about the interlocutor; e. g. "Fine. And you?", "Can't complain.", "You know me!" are just a few instances from the wide repertoire of native speakers of English.

Through that process, the knowledge of the language which is gained by the analytical approach could improve the ability to use the language in reality, which can be developed by the experiential approach.

(此题为开放性题目，从如何运用两种语言学习方法来学外语的角度谈即可。)

6. The study of learner-external factors in SLA is primarily concerned with the question: How do learners get information about the target language? Study has focused on the effects of different kinds of input, and on the impact of the social context.

Social effects. The process of language learning can be very stressful, and the impact of positive or negative attitudes from the surrounding society can be critical. Community attitudes toward the language being learned can also have a profound impact on SLA. Where the community has a broadly negative view of the target language and its speakers, or a negative view of its relation to them, learning is typically much more difficult. Other common social factors include the attitude of parents toward language study, and the nature of group dynamics in the language classroom.

Input and intake. Generally speaking, the amount of input learners take in is one of the most important factors affecting their learning. However, it must be at a level that is comprehensible to them.

Interaction. Long's interaction hypothesis proposes that language acquisition is strongly facilitated by the use of the target language in interaction.

Pedagogical effects. Efforts have been made to systematically measure or evaluate the effectiveness of language teaching practices in promoting second language acquisition.

What's more, during L2 acquisition, there exists the influence of L1, or the transfer of expressions or structures from the L1. The positive transfer of L1 knowledge results from the similarity of L1 and L2, while the difference between them results in the negative transfer.

第12章 应用语言学

12.1 复习笔记

本章要点:

1. Language teaching method
   英语教学法的种类
2. Language tests
   语言测试的种类
3. The principles of language tests
   语言测试的原则

常考考点:

各个语言教学法的特点、理论基础、优缺点；语言测试主要的种类；语言测试的原则。

本章内容索引:

Ⅰ. Definition of Applied Linguistics

Ⅱ. Language Teaching Method

1. The Grammar-translation Method
   (1) Definition
   (2) Main features
2. The Direct Method
   (1) Definition
   (2) Main features
3. The Audiolingual Method
   (1) Definition
   (2) Main features
   (3) Theoretical base
4. Situational Language Teaching
   (1) Definition
   (2) Main features
   (3) Theoretical base
5. Functional Language Teaching
   (1) Definition
   (2) Main features
   (3) Theoretical base
6. Communicative Language Teaching
   (1) Definition
   (2) Main features

(3) Theoretical base

7. Other Approaches

Ⅲ. Main Types of Language Tests

1. Achievement and proficiency tests
2. Subjective and objective tests
3. Discrete-point and integrative tests
4. Criterion-referenced and norm-referenced tests
5. Language aptitude tests
6. Diagnostic tests

Ⅳ. Principles of language Testing

1. Validity
2. Reliability
3. Practicality

Ⅰ. Definition of Applied Linguistics

【考点：名词解释】

Broadly speaking, applied linguistics is the study of the applications of findings in linguistics to the solution of practical problems such as the recovery of speech ability.

Narrowly speaking, applied linguistics is the study of the application of linguistic principles and theories to language teaching, especially the teaching of foreign and second language.

Ⅱ. Language Teaching Method

【考点：语言教学方法的种类】

1. The Grammar-translation Method

(1) Definition: It is a method of foreign language teaching by which students translate sentences between the target language and the native language to learn grammatical rules and then apply those rules.

(2) Main features: The impart of grammar rules, as well as the subsequent translation of sentences and passages into the new language making use of those rules.

2. The Direct Method

(1) Definition: It is a method of foreign language teaching by directly using the target language and associating language with action, motion, objects, and situations. The direct method of teaching refrains from using the learners' native language and uses only the target language, and the students are supposed to learn the second language in the same manner they learned their first.

Ⅰ. 应用语言学的定义

从广义上讲，应用语言学是指研究如何将语言学的研究成果应用于解决实际问题的学科，例如恢复语言能力。

从狭义上讲，应用语言学是研究将语言学原理和理论应用于语言教学，特别是外语和第二语言的教学的学科。

Ⅱ. 语言教学法

1. 语法翻译法

(1) 定义：语法翻译法是一种教学外语的方法，学生通过在目的语和母语之间翻译句子来学习语法规则，然后应用这些规则。

(2) 主要特点：外语教学以教授语法和句子翻译为主要教学手段。

2. 直接教学法

(1) 定义：在外语教学中直接用目标语教学，并使月动作、手势、物体和情境等手段。直接教学法不使用学习者的母语，只使用目的语，学生应该像学习第一语言一样学习第二语言。

（2）**Main features**: It only uses the language to be learned in the classroom, and the students memorize the language patterns presented orally. The learning is based on speaking and listening, with an emphasis on language at the sentence level.	（2）**主要特点**：在课堂中只能说目标语，语言形式的记忆对学生来说非常重要。教学过程注重听说训练，强调句子层面。
3. The Audiolingual Method	**3. 听说法**
（1）**Definition**: It is a method of foreign language teaching which emphasizes the teaching of listening and speaking before reading and writing. It uses dialogues as the main form of language presentation and drills as the main training techniques. Mother tongue is discouraged in the classroom.	（1）**定义**：这是一种通过模仿、反复和强化强调来学习外语的教学方法。它强调语言的听说先于读写。母语不允许在课堂上使用。
（2）**Main features**: The main characteristics of audiolingual method are an emphasis on language structures that can be acquired as normal patterns of verbal activity and the assumption that learning is a habit-forming mechanism. The pattern drill is one of the most common methods used. Speaking and listening are considered to be the most important aspects of the learning process.	（2）**主要特点**：以句型为中心，通过句型操练能来使学习者掌握每一个句型，从而使其养成学习习惯。听说被认为是学习过程中最主要的。
（3）**Theoretical base**: American structuralist linguistics and behaviorist psychology.	（3）**理论基础**：美国结构主义语言学和行为主义心理学。
4. Situational Language Teaching	**4. 情景语言教学法**
（1）**Definition**: It is a grammar-based language teaching method focusing on the practice of language in meaningful situation-based activities.	（1）**定义**：这是一种基于语法的教学方法，强调在有意义的情景活动中进行语言实践。
（2）**Main features**: Its key feature is the assumption that language is tied up with the social context within which it occurs.	（2）**主要特点**：认为语言与应用语言的社会情境密切相关。
（3）**Theoretical base**: The psychological base is the linguistic theory of London School and the constructivism.	（3）**理论基础**：伦敦学派的语言学理论和心理学的建构主义。
5. Functional Language Teaching	**5. 功能语言教学法**
（1）**Definition**: It is a teaching method that emphasizes the functions of language. We should teach students what role that language plays in communications.	（1）**定义**：这是一种强调语言功能的教学法，它认为我们应该教学生语言在交流中扮演什么角色。
（2）**Main features**: Its key feature is that we should teach people about what purposes different linguistic forms fulfill.	（2）**基本特点**：教师要教给学生各种语言形式所要实现的功能。
（3）**Theoretical base**: the study of speech acts and the Systemic Functional Linguistics of Halliday.	（3）**理论基础**：言语行为理论及韩礼德的系统功能语言学。
6. Communicative Language Teaching	**6. 交际语言教学法**
（1）**Definition** : It is an approach to language teaching that emphasizes interaction as both the means and the ultimate goal of study.	（1）**定义**：它是一种强调互动作为学习手段和最终目的的语言教学方法。

(2) **Main features**: It aims at carrying out language teaching and learning in communication. (3) **Theoretical base**: Linguistic semantics, speech act theory, sociolinguistics and psycholinguistics. **7. Other Approaches** Total physical response, The silent way, The natural approach, etc. **Ⅲ. Main Types of Language Tests** 【考点：主要的语言测试类型】 **1. Achievement and proficiency tests** **Achievement tests** are tests of developed skill or knowledge. The most common type of achievement test is a standardized test developed to measure skills and knowledge learned in a given grade level, usually through planned instruction, such as training or classroom instruction. They examines how well learners have learned, such as the Chinese MET test. **Proficiency tests** do not appear to be dependent on any specific textbook or syllabus. They, like TOEFL and IELTS, tend to examine a learner's skill at any given time. **2. Subjective and objective tests** From the marking point of view, tests fall into one of the two categories: subjective test and objective test. **A subjective test** is the evaluation of the learners' personal opinion, as in an essay examination. **An objective test** is the test which has right or wrong answers and so can be marked objectively. **3. Discrete-point and integrative tests** **A discrete point test** is the testing of one element at a time, item by item, such as a grammar test which test on tenses, adverbs, and prepositions separately. **An integrative test** refers to the assessment of a learner's capacity using many skills all at the same time, such as a dictation test or oral interview, because it entails the usage of vocabulary, syntax, and listening comprehension skills spontaneously. **4. Criterion-referenced and norm-referenced tests** **Criterion-referenced tests** are evaluation of a student's performance against a set of agreed-upon standards or criterion.	（2）**主要特点**：教与学在交际活动中进行。 （3）**理论基础**：语义学、言语行为理论、社会语言学、心理语言学。 **7. 其他教学法** 全身反应法、沉默教学法、自然法等。 **Ⅲ. 主要的语言测试类型** **1. 学业成绩测试和水平测试** **学业成绩测试**是对成熟技能或知识的测试。最常见的成绩测试类型是一种标准化测试，用于衡量在给定年级水平上学习到的技能和知识，通常通过有计划的指导，如培训或课堂指导。学业成绩用以检查学习者对所学内容的掌握情况，如大学入学英语考试。 **水平测试**不以教学大纲及教材为依托，目的在于检查受试者现有的整体语言实际运用能力，如托福与雅思。 **2. 主观性测试和客观性测试** 按照评分方式的不同，语言测试可分为主观性测试和客观性测试。 **主观性测试**是按照通过个人意见来评分的，如写作考试。 **客观性测试**是有正确或错误答案的测试，因此可以客观打分。 **3. 分离式测试和综合式测试** **分离式测试**是把语言分成不同的语言点进行的测试，如语法测试可以分不同的部分对时态、动词和介词进行测试。 **综合式测试**是对学习者同时使用多种技巧能力的测试，如听写测试或口语测试，因为它们要求考生要综合运用词汇、语法和听力理解等知识。 **4. 标准参照测试和常模参照测试** **标准参照测试**是指通过制定一定的标准来测试学生的表现。

Norm-referenced tests are used to compare a student's or a group of students' performance to the performance of another student or group of students whose scores are regarded as the norm.	**常模参照测试**是指比较一个学生或一组学生的表现与另一个学生或一组学生的表现，其分数被视为标准。
5. Language aptitude tests	**5. 语言学能测试**
Language aptitude test is designed to predict a student's likelihood of success and ease in learning a foreign language.	**语言学能测试**语言能力倾向测试旨在预测学生学习外语成功的可能性和容易程度。
6. Diagnostic tests	**6. 诊断性测试**
Diagnostic test is usually carried out at the start of a new topic to identify what students already know and can do, enabling the teaching content of the new topic to be planned.	**诊断性测试**通常在新课题开始时进行，以确定学生已经知道什么，能够做什么，以便对新课题的教学内容进行规划。
Ⅳ. Principles of language Testing	**Ⅳ. 语言测试的原则**
1. Validity	**1. 效度**
Validity is the extent to which an assessment accurately measures what it is intended to measure. And the two most important aspects of validity are content and construct validity.	**效度**是指测试是否准确考察想考察的内容的程度。效度最重要的两个方面：内容效度和结构效度。
2. Reliability	**2. 信度**
Reliability is the degree to which scores from a particular test are consistent from one use of the test to the next. There are two aspects to reliability: test reliability and scorer reliability.	**信度**指的是一个特定测试，从一次测试到另一次测试的一致性程度。信度包括两个方面：测试信度和评分者信度。
3. Practicality	**3. 实用性**
Practicality is a term which means to what extent the test is easy to design, easy to administer and easy to score.	评估的实用性意味着测试易于设计，易于管理，易于评分。

12.2 课后习题详解

1. Define the following terms briefly.

   applied linguistics　grammar-translation method　audiolingual method
   communicative language teaching　testing　achievement test　validity
   reliability　proficiency test　subjective test　objective test
   language aptitude test　diagnostic test　backwash effect

2. What advantages and disadvantages does the grammar-translation method have?
3. If the communicative language teaching method is used in foreign language teaching, what changes are required from more traditional approaches?
4. What are achievement tests?
5. Explain the qualities of validity.
6. Explain the qualities of reliability.

参考答案

1. **Applied linguistics**: Broadly speaking, applied linguistics refers to the study of the applications of findings in linguistics to the solution of practical problems such as the recovery of speech ability. Narrowly speaking, applied linguistics studies the application of linguistic principles and theories to language teaching, especially the teaching of foreign and second language.

Grammar-translation method: It is a method of foreign language teaching by which students translate sentences between the target language and the native language to learn grammatical rules and then apply those rules.

Audiolingual method: It is a method of foreign language teaching which emphasizes the teaching of listening and speaking before reading and writing. It uses dialogues as the main form of language presentation and drills as the main training techniques. Mother tongue is discouraged in the classroom.

Communicative language teaching: It is an approach to language teaching that emphasizes interaction as both the means and the ultimate goal of study.

Testing: It refers to the use of test, or the study of the theory and the practice of their use, development, evaluation, etc.

Achievement test: Achievement tests are tests of developed skill or knowledge. The most common type of achievement test is a standardized test developed to measure skills and knowledge learned in a given grade level, usually through planned instruction, such as training or classroom instruction. They examine how well learners have learned, such as the Chinese MET test.

Validity: Validity is defined as the extent to which an assessment accurately measures what it is intended to measure. And the two most important aspects of validity are content and construct validity.

Reliability: Reliability refers to the degree to which scores from a particular test are consistent from one use of the test to the next. There are two aspects to reliability: test reliability and scorer reliability.

Proficiency test: Proficiency tests do not appear to be dependent on any specific textbook or syllabus. They, like TOEFL and IELTS, tend to examine a learner's skill at any given time.

Subjective test: A subjective test refers to the evaluation of the learners' personal opinion, as in an essay examination.

Objective test: An objective test is the test which has right or wrong answers and so can be marked objectively.

Language aptitude test: Language aptitude test is designed to predict a student's likelihood of success and ease in learning a foreign language.

Diagnostic test: Diagnostic test is usually carried out at the start of a new topic to identify what students already know and can do, enabling the teaching content of the new topic to be planned.

Backwash effect: The backwash effect (also known as the washback effect) is the influence that a test has on the way students are taught (e. g. the teaching mirrors the test because teachers want their students to pass).

2. The advantages of grammar-translation method:

(1) Since the grammars mentioned in this method provide very detailed examples of the proper construction of phrases and sentences in a language, accuracy is emphasized and enhanced.

(2) Because the technique emphasizes written work, students' ability to read and write is encouraged and enhanced.

(3) For an instructor whose oral proficiency is lacking, this technique is less demanding than others.

(4) This method is popular among people who want to study English independently, especially adult learners who want to learn grammar rules and apply them to new materials on their own.

The disadvantages of grammar-translation method:

(1) It stresses language at the sentence level independent of context, hence language organization above the sentence level is not as well examined.

(2) Because the emphasis is on written work, oral fluency and spontaneity are not as effectively developed, and common everyday language is not well taught.

(3) The basic methods in this approach are rote learning of the laws and vocabulary, and grammar rules are learned deductively as general statements to be used in specific translation experiments, which can be tedious for the learners to understand.

(4) Because of the focus on grammar, students typically know a lot about the language but are reluctant to use it. As a result, they frequently employ the new language in a literal or inappropriate manner.

3. Changes are required from traditional approach if the communicative language teaching method is used in foreign language teaching.

(1) Change in teacher role. The teacher will no longer be where the language knowledge comes from. The teacher's job is mostly one of introducing activities.

(2) Change in learner role. Passivity is no longer an option for the learner. The student must take an active role in the activities.

(3) Change of materials. These can, as far as possible, retain the characteristics of authentic language use.

(4) Change of techniques. These should highlight the tasks to be completed (rather than drills) and identify the skills being practiced.

(5) Change in attitude. If the above goals are to be met, we must change people's views toward teaching and learning in general.

4. Achievement tests are tests of developed skill or knowledge. The most common type of achievement test is a standardized test developed to measure skills and knowledge learned in a given grade level, usually through planned instruction, such as training or classroom instruction. They examine how well learners have learned, such as the Chinese MET test.

5. Validity is the degree to which a test measures what is meant to. If the candidates know some items before the exam the validity will be reduced. There are four kinds of validity. (1) Content validity refers to the extent to which the test adequately covers the syllabus area to be tested.

(2) Construct validity requires the test to prove the theoretical construct whereupon it is based.

(3) Empirical validity demands the results of the test to correlate with some external criteria.

(4) Face validity is based on the subjective judgment of an observer, unlike the other forms of validity. If the test appears to be measuring what it intends to measure, the test is considered to have face validity.

6. Reliability refers to the extent to which an assessment method or instrument measures consistently the performance of the student. Assessments are usually expected to produce comparable outcomes, with consistent standards over time and between different learners and examiners.

For example, if a person takes a personality assessment today and scores high in a trait like dominance, and we retest that same person six weeks from now, we would expect the score to still be high in dominance. If the individual scored low in dominance, we would have to conclude that the measure was inaccurate and unreliable. The measure would be of little value to us.

12.3 考研真题与典型题详解

Ⅰ. Fill in the blanks.

1. ___________ is a method of foreign or second language teaching which makes use of translation and grammar study as the main teaching and learning activities.
2. ___________ is a grammar-based language teaching method in which principles of grammatical and lexical gradation are used and new teaching points presented and practiced through situations.
3. There are three principles of language testing: ___________, ___________ and ___________.

Ⅱ. Explain the following terms.

1. applied linguistics(武汉大学 2006 研)
2. the audiolingual method of language teaching
3. the direct method of language teaching
4. Validity (华南理工大学 2018 研)

Ⅲ. Short answer questions

1. What are the main features and theoretical base of the audiolingual method?
2. Describe the three main types of language tests.

Ⅳ. Essay questions

1. Explain one of the teaching approaches that you're familiar with and discuss its advantages and disadvantages. (浙江大学 2004 研)
2. Explain the term "Communicative competence" and discuss its usefulness in language teaching. (浙江大学 2005 研)
3. Put yourself into the position of an English teacher in China. What are your goals and the goals of the students and the educational system in the teaching and learning of English? When the goals do not converge, how can you reconcile the differences between them? (北外 2002 研)
4. It has been noticed that Chinese learners of English tend to make mistakes in the marking of past tense, even at the advanced level of proficiency. What do you think are the possible causes of this problem? How call language teachers help solve this problem and why? (北外 2005 研)

5. The relation of linguistics to language teaching and learning.（武汉大学 2006 研）
6. What can linguistics do for language learning and teaching?（北京师范大学 2004 研）
7. Read the following passage and answer three questions.

Teachers employ different types of conceptual organization and meaning. One level of meaning relates to subject matter knowledge and how curricular and content aspects of teaching are conceptualized (Shulman l987). Woods (1996) describes teachers' conceptions of lessons as made up of conceptual units at different levels of abstraction. He distinguishes between the following: *overall conceptual goals*—the overall purposes teachers identify for a course; *global conceptual units*—the individual subcomponents of the curriculum (e. g. , the grammar, reading, writing, and listening components of an integrated skills course); *intermediate conceptual units*-activities or clusters of activities framed in terms of accomplishing one of the higher-level conceptual goals; and *local conceptual units*—the specific things teachers do to achieve particular instructional effects. Other constructs that have been proposed to account for how teachers realize the curricular agendas they set for lessons and the kinds of cognitive processes they employ include *lesson formats* (Wong-Fillmore 1985), *tasks* (Doyle 1983), *scripts*, and *routines* (Shavelson and Stem 1981). Constructs such as these seek to describe how teachers approach the subject matter of teaching and how they transform content into learning. Much of this research draws on a framework of cognitive psychology and has provided evidence of the kinds of pedagogical content knowledge, reasoning, and problem solving teachers make use of as they teach (Cliff 1991).

In addition to the curricular goals and content, teachers have other more personal views of teaching (Johnston 1990). Zeichner, Tabachnick, and Densmore (1987) try to capture this with the notion of perspective, which they define as the ways in which teachers understand, interpret, and define their environment and use such interpretation to guide their actions. They followed teachers through their year-long professional training and their first year in the classroom, and found that their personal perspectives served as powerful influences on how they taught. In describing the basis for teachers' conceptualizations of good practice, Clandinin (1985, 1986) introduced the concept of *image*, which she describes as "a central construct for understanding teachers' knowledge" (1985: 362). An image is a metaphor, such as "the classroom as home," "setting up a relationship with children", or "meeting the needs of students," that teachers may have in mind when they teach. Johnston (1992) suggests that images such as these are not always conscious, that they reflect how teachers view themselves in their teaching contexts, and that they form the subconscious assumptions on which their teaching practices are based. In a study of what second language teachers perceive to be good classes, Senior (1995) found that experienced ESL teachers in an Australian educational setting attempting to implement a communicative methodology appeared to have arrived at the tacit assumption that, to promote successful language learning, it is necessary to develop a bonded class—that is, one in which there is a positive, mutually supportive group atmosphere. The teachers appeared to employ a range of both conscious and unconscious strategies in order to develop a spirit of cohesion within theft class groups.

Halkes and Deijkers (1984) refer to teachers' teaching criteria, which are defined as "personal subjective values a person tries to pursue or keep constant while teaching." Teachers hold personal views of themselves, their learners, their goals, and their role in the classroom and they presumably try to reflect these in practice. Marland (1987) examined the principles used to guide and interpret teaching, and identified five such working principles that were derived from stimulated recall interviews with teachers. For example, the "principle of progressive checking" involved checking students' progress periodically, identifying problems, and providing individual encouragement for low-ability students. Conners (1978) studied elementary teachers and found that all of those in her study used three overarching principles of practice to guide and explain their interactive teaching behavior: "suppressing emotions," "teacher authenticity," and "self-monitoring." The principle of "teacher authenticity" involved the teacher presenting herself in such a way that good personal relationships with students and a socially supportive classroom atmosphere would be achieved. This principle required the teacher to attempt to be open, sincere, and honest, as well as fallible.

(1) What could be the title of this passage?

(2) What are the functions of those conceptual units as described by Woods (1996) in language teaching?

(3) Discuss the relationship between "perspective" and "image" and between "image" and "teaching criteria" as mentioned in this passage?

参考答案及解析

Ⅰ. Fill in the blanks.

1. Grammar-translation Method
(语法翻译法即在外语教学中主要运用翻译和语法学习为教学活动的方法。)
2. Situational language teaching
(情景语言教学法是一种基于语法的教学方法，强调在情境中呈现语法规则和词汇级别等教学要点。)
3. Validity; reliability; practicality
(语言测试有三个原则：效度原则、信度原则及实用性原则。)

Ⅱ. Explain the following terms.

1. It is a branch of linguistics which studies the application of linguistics in reality. For example, there are studies on multilingualism, language acquisition, first and second language teaching and learning.
2. It is the teaching of a second language through imitation, repetition, and reinforcement. It emphasizes the teaching of speaking and listening before reading and writing and the use of mother tongue in the classroom is not allowed.
3. The learning of a second language by using the target language directly and associating speech form with action, gesture, objects and situations. Mother tongue is never or rarely used in the classroom, and the students supposedly acquire the second language in a way similar to the way they acquired their first language.
4. Validity is the degree to which a test measures what is meant to. If the candidates know some

items before the exam the validity will be reduced. There are four kinds of validity. (1) Content validity refers to the extent to which the test adequately covers the syllabus area to be tested. (2) Construct validity requires the test to prove the theoretical construct whereupon it is based. (3) Empirical validity demands the results of the test to correlate with some external criteria. (4) Face validity is based on the subjective judgment of an observer, unlike the other forms of validity. If the test appears to be measuring what it intends to measure, the test is considered to have face validity.

Ⅲ. Short answer questions

1. The main characteristics of audiolingual method are an emphasis on language structures that can be acquired as normal patterns of verbal activity and the assumption that learning is a habit-forming mechanism. The pattern drill is one of the most common methods used. Speaking and listening are considered to be the most important aspects of the learning process. It took the ides of American structuralist linguistics and behaviorist psychology as its theoretical basis.
2. Three main types of language tests:
   (1) Subjective and objective tests: A subjective test refers to the evaluation of the learners' personal opinion, as in an essay examination. An objective test is the test which has right or wrong answers and so can be marked objectively.
   (2) Language aptitude tests: Language aptitude test is designed to predict a student's likelihood of success and ease in learning a foreign language.
   (3) Diagnostic tests: Diagnostic test is usually carried out at the start of a new topic to identify what students already know and can do, enabling the teaching content of the new topic to be planned.

Ⅳ. Essay questions

1. Functional language teaching is a teaching method that emphasizes the functions of language. We should teach students what role that language plays in communications. Its key feature is that we should teach people about what purposes different linguistic forms fulfill. Linguistic forms can never be viewed as abstract structures, but rather as performing a specific language role. If the basic present tense is to be learned, for example, it should not only be a matter of learning to correctly repeat the form, but also of remembering what the structure is used for. Functional language teaching takes the study of speech acts and the Systemic Functional Linguistics of Halliday as the theoretical ground.

   Language for organizing Functional teaching discusses what we can do with words. Linguistic forms are introduced and learned in relation to their function. Such instruction promotes language appropriateness in terms of the respective roles of speaker and hearer, as well as the subject of discussion. Fluency is stressed and developed.

   The teaching of language functions also poses some problems. For example, what is a language function? How many different functions are there? What kind of order should they be taught in?

   Though functions are an important aspect of language usage, placing too much focus on them can lead to a neglect of other aspects of language, not least its structure. Since there is no rigid correspondence between function and form, some argue that if the syllabus is completely constructed on the basis of functions, we would lose too much control over grammatical complexity. Furthermore, others claim that while fluency and acceptable language usage should be promoted, standardized consistency should not be sacrificed.

2. Communicative competence was proposed by D. H. Hymes, with four components: possibility, the ability to produce grammatical sentences; feasibility, the ability to produce sentences which can be decoded by the human brain; appropriateness, the ability to use correct forms of language in a specific socio-cultural context; performance, the fact that the utterance is completed.

   In Hymes' view, the learner acquires knowledge of sentences not only as grammatical but also as appropriate. The aim of language learning is the ability to perform a repertoire of speech acts so as to take part in speech events. This is another way of saying that learning language is learning to perform certain functions. Hymes' theory leads to notion/function-based syllabuses, and a step further, communicative syllabuses.

   The theory of communicative competence stresses the context in which an utterance occurs. In its application, the teacher may teach how in different situations the same sentence can perform the function of statement, command, or request. On the other hand, while introducing different linguistic forms with the same semantic structure, for example the two forms of "you" in Chinese; he may draw special attention to different contexts in which they are used. The conceptual approach also leads to a concentration on discourse, in Hymes' term linguistic routines—the sequential organization beyond sentences. Thus in the teaching of literature, the teacher can focus on features of different genres. In the teaching of conversation, he can introduce such strategies as opening, continuing, turn-taking and closing. To present teaching contents of this kind, a learner-centered teaching methodology is necessary.

3. Whenever we talk about the goal or objectives of TEFL, we might think of the so-called "language skills" including listening, speaking, reading and writing. This is the basic object for both students and teachers in learning English. The curricula in the school are mainly centered on these four aspects. Students usually spend much time on improving their language ability by doing grammatical exercises, listening to the types, etc. Certainly, the learning-well of English depends on the four good foundations; however, we think that this aim is too general. The goal of language teaching is shifting from linguistic competence to communicative competence and the mode of teaching from single skill development to integrated skills training. For it is widely agreed that in learning a language, it is necessary to develop one's ability to use the language in addition to learning the formal rules of the language and the thought of teaching a language for communication is accepted by most, if not all, people in the TEFL circles. In the syllabus, the ultimate goal of TEFL has been set at "developing students' communicative competence", and cultural aspect of TEFL has been taken into account. The teaching objective of English is to help students develop a relatively strong reading ability and general skills of listening, speaking, writing and translating, and by so doing makes students able to use English for communications. "English teaching is intended to help students lay a solid foundation for language skills, acquire good language learning strategies, nourish their liberal accomplishment, and adapt themselves to

the requirements of social development and economic construction."

If I were the English teacher, I would focus on the combination of linguistic competence (mainly the grammar, vocabulary, etc,) and the communicative competence. Because each language is composed of the basic grammar and vocabulary, the learning of a second language is necessary beginning with these language elements. The formal rules should not be neglected even the communicative competence is emphasized. On the base of teaching linguistic elements, TEFL should also be aimed at developing students' communicative competence. That language teaching recognizes a social, interpersonal and cultural dimension and attributes to it just as much importance as to the grammatical and phonological aspect. Then in the same logical sense, the goal of FLT should also be to develop the learner's communicative competence, or the competence of using the foreign language in communication. Goal of foreign language instruction is to help the learners to develop a competence to use the foreign language for communication with people of different cultural backgrounds.

Because the students are under much test pressure, their motivation for learning English is to obtain a high exam score. They prefer the traditional grammar-translation teaching methods. Sometimes there are contradictory between students' goal of learning English and teacher's goal of teaching English. In this case, I will try to minimize the goal's difference and make the consistent goal executed maximally. I will pay much attention improving the students' communicative competence in the process of learning linguistic elements. Still, I will give the students sufficient cultural knowledge for them to better understand and master the real communicative manner.

4. Tenses are one of the most difficult aspects for Chinese to master because of the non-inflected nature of the Chinese language In English, the different forms of the verb can tell us whether something is or was happening at the present or in the past. This information is technically termed as tense. The tense is shown by adding related morphemes at the end of the verb. So the learners can judge the tense easily by looking at the different verb forms. However, the Chinese verb does not have a well-defined past, present or future tense. In writing or in speaking, the Chinese verb in the sentence does not necessarily inform the reader or listener as to whether they are referring to the past, present or future. Therefore, Chinese often places prepositional, phrases, as well as conjunctive adverbs (e. g. Mandarin Chinese le, guo) that indicate time in the sentence so as to inform the speaker or the reader of the appropriate tense. The different ways of expressing the tense let Chinese learners of English tend to make mistakes in the marking of tense. When translating into English, Chinese writers sometimes forget that English has a well-defined past/ present/ future verb tense. Therefore, the unconscious tendency of placing several prepositional or other phrases that indicate time in the sentence or lacking different tense forms of verb is frequently found. Another factor which contributes to the difficulties is the difference in the concept of time of Chinese as compared to native speakers of English. In other words, different concepts of time of non-native speakers with those of native speakers make it difficult to learn the English tenses.

As the learning of tenses, Chinese learners are faced with a totally new set of classification of temporal situations that have no counterparts in their mother tongue. So in teaching English tenses teachers have to explain English time attributes thoroughly. In fact, L2 learners will understand them as long as they have acquired the rules. For example, the past tense is used for situations which are less probable, or more remote. Instead of spending time clarifying this to learners, teachers may allow learners to understand the meanings of English and Chinese tenses as well as their differences on their own. Through the comparison of different ways of expressing tense, the teacher can provide the students with a clear framework and students are hoped to have a good mastery of verbs associated with tenses.

5. There is a branch of linguistics called applied linguistics, which studies the application of linguistics in the reality, such as in language teaching and learning. Applied Linguistics serves as a mediating area which interprets the results of linguistic theories and makes them user-friendly to the language teacher and learner. It is conducive to foreign language teaching in two major aspects:

   Firstly, applied linguistics extends theoretical linguistics in the direction of language learning and teaching, so that the teacher is enabled to make better decisions on the goal and content of the teaching. Applied linguistics provides the teacher with a formal knowledge of the nature of language and language system, and thus increases his understanding of the nature of language teaching. As a result, the teacher can make more informed decisions on what approach to take, hence what to teach.

   Secondly, applied linguistics states the insights and implications that linguistic theories have on the language teaching methodology. Once the goal and content of the teaching are settled, the teacher has to consider questions of how to teach. Should the teaching learning process be teacher-centered, textbook-centered, or learner-centered? How should the learner's errors be treated? What techniques should be adopted in the classroom? Since applied linguistics defines the nature of language learning in connection with various linguistic theories, it helps the teacher to choose teaching methods and techniques.

6. Since linguistics is defined as the scientific study of language, it seems obvious that such a study would help a lot in language teaching and learning. Applied linguistics serves as a mediating area that interprets the results of linguistic theories and makes them user-friendly to the language teacher and leaner. Applied linguistics is conductive to foreign language teaching in two major aspects. Firstly, applied linguistics extends theoretical linguistics in the direction of language learning and teaching, so that the teacher is enabled to make better decisions on the goal and content of the teaching. The teacher can make more informed decisions on what approach to take, hence what to teach. Secondly, applied linguistics states that the insights and implications that linguistics theories have on the language teaching methodology. Once the goal and content of the teaching are settled, the teacher has to consider questions of how to teach. Since applied linguistics defines the nature of language learning in connection with various linguistic theories, it helps the teacher to choose teaching methods and techniques.

7. (1) The title of this passage could be "Two Dimensions of Teacher Knowledge".

   This passage mainly introduces two different kinds of knowledge that influence teachers' understanding and practice of teaching. One is subject matter and curricular issues, and how the content of a lesson can be presented in an effective and coherent way. This is the aspect of teaching that has to do with curricular goals, lesson plans, instructional activities, materials, tasks, and teaching techniques. The other is the knowledge about teachers' implicit theories of teaching—that is, their personal and subjective philosophy and their understanding of what constitutes good teaching. It is this dimension that forms the focus of this passage.

(根据文章内容自拟题目，并分析拟此题目的根据。)

(2) Woods (1996) describes teachers' conceptions of lessons as made up of conceptual units at different levels of abstraction. He distinguishes between the following: *overall conceptual goals*—the overall purposes teachers identify for a course; *global conceptual units*—the individual subcomponents of the curriculum (e. g., the grammar, reading, writing, and listening components of an integrated skills course); *intermediate conceptual units*—activities or clusters of activities framed in terms of accomplishing one of the higher-level conceptual goals; and *local conceptual units*—the specific things teachers do to achieve particular instructional effects.

The function of these conceptual units is to clear the theme of the class, to design the content and each sector of the lesson, to adopt the form of teaching such as presentation, activity and group discussion, to plan the details of the process of a lesson. By those concepts, the teaching of a class could be better evaluated and those concepts give teachers a clear guideline of the preparation of a class.

(3) Perspective, which they define as the ways in which teachers understand, interpret, and define their environment and use such interpretation to guide their actions.

Image is described as "a central construct for understanding teachers' knowledge." An image is a metaphor, such as "the classroom as home," "setting up a relationship with children," or "meeting the needs of students," that teachers may have in mind when they teach.

Teachers' teaching criteria, which are defined as "personal subjective values a person tries to pursue or keep constant while teaching." Teachers hold personal views of themselves, their learners, their goals, and their role in the classroom and they presumably try to reflect these in their practice.

From the above, we can see clearly the "perspective" is knowledge about teachers' implicit theories of teaching—that is, their personal and subjective philosophy and their understanding of what constitutes good teaching. It is teacher-oriented. While the image is the context that the teacher shows for the students, the perspective and the image may be the same or not.

Image is what the teachers think and they feel necessary to do while teaching. Teachers' teaching criteria is the evaluation made by teachers themselves. And the important part is the image may also be the part of their teaching criteria.